MW01245066

Homelessness in America

HOMELESSNESS IN AMERICA

Volume 3

Solutions to Homelessness

Edited by Robert Hartmann McNamara

Praeger Perspectives

Westport, Connecticut
London

Library of Congress Cataloging-in-Publication Data

Homelessness in America / edited by Robert Hartmann McNamara.
p. cm.
Includes bibliographical references and index.
ISBN-13: 978-0-275-99555-3 ((set) : alk. paper)
ISBN-13: 978-0-275-99557-7 ((vol.1) : alk. paper)
ISBN-13: 978-0-275-99559-1 ((vol.2) : alk. paper)
ISBN-13: 978-0-275-99561-4 ((vol.3) : alk. paper)
1. Homelessness—United States. 2. Homeless persons—United States. I. McNamara, Robert Hartmann.
HV4505.H65114 2008
362.50973—dc22 2008012487

British Library Cataloguing in Publication Data is available.

Library of Congress Catalog Card Number: 2008012487
ISBN-13: 978-0-275-99555-3 (set)
978-0-275-99557-7 (Vol. 1)
978-0-275-99559-1 (Vol. 2)
978-0-275-99561-4 (Vol. 3)

First published in 2008

Praeger Publishers, 88 Post Road West, Westport, CT 06881
An imprint of Greenwood Publishing Group, Inc.
www.praeger.com

Printed in the United States of America

The paper used in this book complies with the Permanent Paper Standard issued by the National Information Standards Organization (Z39.48-1984).

10 9 8 7 6 5 4 3 2 1

To Doug: Wherever you might be. I wish your circumstances were different but I am grateful for all that your life has taught me about homelessness.

CONTENTS

PREFACE

My interest in homelessness has been a lifelong one. While today it includes an intellectual fascination with the many dimensions of homelessness, there was a time when homelessness was a very personal experience. In fact, even now I invariably find myself thinking about people on the street whenever the weather is poor. During downpours, a common feature in the southeastern part of the country where hurricanes are common, I find myself thinking about those individuals who search for a dry place to sleep. This perspective gives me a grasp of the issues that my academic training does not.

This collection of articles has been a dream of mine for some time. I have talked for years about a comprehensive book that draws from the country's leading experts who share their insight and knowledge about the problems and solutions to homelessness. This type of book would give researchers, students, and anyone interested in homelessness a place to begin their understanding of the many issues surrounding this topic. Thanks to a long-standing relationship with the Greenwood Publishing Group, an editor approached me two years ago about a research guide on the topic. Seizing the opportunity, my editor and I quickly began to see the possibilities of my dream book becoming a reality.

Hopefully the insight gained from this collection of exceptionally talented people will be a constructive starting point for a dialogue about the actual nature of homelessness, the realities experienced by members of the population, and the viability of solutions proposed to impact the problem.

ACKNOWLEDGMENTS

A project such as this one cannot be undertaken without a significant amount of assistance. Many thanks go to The Citadel Foundation for their financial support during the course of this project. Similarly, I would like to thank my Department Chair, Gardel Feurtado, for his support and understanding in allowing me time to work on this book. Additionally, I am grateful for the assistance of Ms. Lucy Clark Sanders for her invaluable help in bringing this project to completion. Lucy's attention to detail and commitment to excellence are clearly seen in the final product—I am so grateful for her help and her friendship.

Similarly, Hilary Claggett earns my thanks for supporting the project and was instrumental in navigating the institutional landscape in moving the process forward. In taking the reins as my current editor, Shana Jones has been a wonderful source of insight, support, and encouragement. A book like this presents numerous administrative challenges and Shana has been a wonderful resource during the entire process. Finally, I would like to thank all of the contributors who submitted chapters for each of the volumes—this book is a far better version with your input than anything I might have done on my own. Thank you for your commitment to the population and for being willing to share your expertise so that others might learn more about the homeless.

INTRODUCTION

Robert Hartmann McNamara

In this volume, the final of three, the solutions to homelessness as well as an assessment of its future will be offered. As was mentioned, the proposed programs or solutions are often based on what the public believes causes the problem. As we have seen in the last volume, this is a difficult task given the complexity and diversity of the homeless population and the reasons they became homeless. Moreover, there remain several structural and cultural barriers that will likely preclude a solution to homelessness. For instance, as long as housing is not perceived as a right in this country, as opposed to seeing it as a privilege, little will be done to ensure that all Americans have access to basic and affordable housing.

Another problem relates to the durational quality of homelessness. As we have seen, the problems of homelessness are often chronic and are not likely to be eradicated in the near future. This is true despite time, money, and energy dedicated to solving the problem. A consequence of this is that many Americans grow weary of their efforts, particularly if few tangible results are achieved. Instead of redoubling the commitment to finding a solution, many Americans have begun to swing their emotions in the other direction. That is, instead of sympathy toward the plight of a group of people who are down on their luck, communities across the country are growing apathetic to the presence of the homeless. In some ways this is understandable. After all, many Americans may feel as though they have dedicated a great deal of effort to solving the problem, only to find that little headway has been achieved. Despite the benefit concerts by rock stars, other celebrity benefits such as Comic Relief, or programs designed to reintegrate people back into society as productive members, the problems for the homeless remain or grow more severe.

In an effort to shed light on what actually works, in the first chapter of this volume, Mary Cunningham, Sharon McDonald, and Norm Suchar offer several promising strategies that hold the most hope for success. Related to this is a subsequent chapter by Ralph da Costa Nunez, who examines one example of the possible future for the homeless and how a sense of community can generate hope and success for its members.

Chapter 3 examines the role of social control and homelessness. As Chip (Ronald) Burns contends, given the potential problems members of the homeless can present to a community, the law enforcement response plays a key role in determining the success of community-based programs.

Charles Crawford then explores the apathy that has been generated by the presence of the homeless population in America. Although many attempts have been made to solve the problem, its continued presence has led to a series of efforts to make the behavior of homeless individuals less visible.

In Chapter 5, an assessment of life as a service provider is offered. This chapter, written by an agency director, offers insight into the day-to-day struggles service providers and agencies encounter in trying to help minimize the impact of homelessness.

Chapter 6 follows up on Crawford's work on the criminalization of homelessness and offers examples and insight into the nature of how many communities are demonstrating their frustration toward the homeless problem.

In the next three chapters of this volume, the future of homelessness is forecasted. In Chapter 7, James Petrovich and Emily Spence-Almaguer offer insight into the nature of what homelessness will look like in the future as well as how agencies and researchers might better meet the needs of their clients. Similarly, in Chapter 8, Maria Foscarinis explores the implications of the criminalization movement and what is likely to occur in the future with regard to the legal standing of the homeless.

Amy Presley Hauser then considers some of the legal responses that have been created because of the criminalization movement toward the homeless. Several court cases have determined the status of the homeless and their constitutional rights to use public space.

Finally, in Chapter 10, Stephen Poulin, Stephen Metraux, and Dennis Culhane discuss what is perhaps the most promising way to determine the size and shape of the homeless population in the future.

In summary, the future of homelessness presents several challenges and a variety of issues. Hopefully these three volumes have shed light on the problems facing the homeless as well as prompted discussion and contemplation of the issues surrounding a common feature of the social landscape.

Chapter One

PROMISING STRATEGIES TO END HOMELESSNESS

Mary Cunningham, Sharon McDonald, and Norm Suchar

The problem of homelessness, many say, is an unsolvable problem. Communities across the country struggle with getting homeless people off the street by building shelters, transitional housing, and soup kitchens. Although these much-needed programs help address the immediate needs of our nation's homeless people by providing food and temporary shelter, they do not provide permanent solutions and thus have not been successful in decreasing homelessness, leaving communities frustrated and hopeless. In 2000, the National Alliance to End Homelessness announced *A Plan, Not a Dream: How to End Homelessness in Ten Years*.[1] Drawing on research and innovative programs from around the country, the plan outlined a new vision to address the problem of homelessness.

Today, how communities respond to homelessness is changing dramatically. In the last decade a handful of communities began to test new approaches that focus on minimizing the time homeless people spend in shelter and on helping people access permanent housing more rapidly. Hundreds of communities have undertaken planning efforts to end homelessness.[2] These plans outline new, promising strategies—permanent supportive housing for people with disabilities, systems prevention, designing local housing subsidy programs, targeting housing and services based on need, new approaches to emergency prevention, and collecting data for planning and managing for results. As a result, several of these communities are showing reductions in homelessness.

This chapter begins by providing a brief history of the movement to end homelessness in the United States. Next, it reviews what we know from research and program outcome data about new responses to homelessness.

Finally, it discusses the how the broader landscape of affordable housing and social supports affect the success of the community effort to end homelessness.

ENDING HOMELESSNESS IN THE UNITED STATES

There is an extensive homeless assistance system—including hundreds of thousands of temporary beds—currently available to individuals and families who experience homeless. This system is funded by the federal government (approximately $1.3 billion in 2006)[3] and is made up of emergency shelters (short term, sometimes congregate living arrangements, sometimes only open in the evening, and usually providing minimal services); transitional housing (longer term, often with single family units or smaller shared units, usually offering more intensive services, but often with time limits on how long a family may stay, ranging from six months to two years); and some permanent supportive housing (permanent housing linked with services, available to individuals and families with multiple barriers to housing or disabled households members). For the most part, nonprofit organizations and faith-based organizations operate these programs, which are funded by the federal government, state and local governments, and private donations. Most of the organizations that provide housing and services to homeless populations participate in Continuums of Care, local or regional bodies that coordinate services and funding for homeless people and families; there are approximately 500 Continuums of Care across the country.

This system, set up in the early 1990s, is undergoing a dramatic transformation. During the past five years, hundreds of communities have committed to ending homelessness by radically transforming their homeless assistance systems. Each commitment starts with a plan that outlines a framework to guide community-wide efforts. These plans have become a critical component of efforts to prevent, reduce, and end homelessness nationwide.

The development of local ten-year plans began in 2000 when the National Alliance to End Homelessness announced *A Plan, Not a Dream: How to End Homelessness in Ten Years.*[4] The Ten-Year Plan focuses on using data to plan for outcomes, closing the front door to homelessness through prevention programs, and opening the back door out of homelessness by rapidly rehousing individuals and families. Finally, it calls for building an infrastructure by increasing incomes, expanding affordable housing, and helping individuals and families access needed services.

Since that time, the concept of local planning to end homelessness has taken root, and local ten-year plans have proliferated across the country. In 2000, Indianapolis Mayor Bart Peterson was the first mayor to endorse the creation of a plan to end homelessness.[5] In 2002, Chicago, Memphis, and Indianapolis became among the first cities to complete ten-year plans.[6] At the same time that a local effort to end homelessness started to develop, U.S. Department of Housing and Urban Development (HUD) Secretary Mel Martinez endorsed ending chronic homelessness in ten years.[7] President Bush echoed this endorsement, making ending chronic homeless an administration-side goal. Congress committed to creating 150,000 units of permanent supportive housing for chronically homeless people. The administration also reinvigorated the once dormant U.S. Interagency Council on Homelessness (USICH), an agency dedicated to coordinating federal efforts to end homelessness.

The movement to end homelessness continued to grow when, in 2003, the USICH Director Philip Mangano challenged 100 cities to create plans to end homelessness. Spurred by the federal goal of ending chronic homelessness in ten years, resolutions by the U.S. Conference of Mayors, the National League of Cities, and the National Associates of Counties, and encouragement and technical assistance from the National Alliance to End Homelessness, a parade of plans followed. As of this writing, over 300 cities, counties, and states have initiated a planning process to end homelessness, and 160 jurisdictions have completed plans.[8]

A NEW APPROACH

Homelessness in the United States is widely misunderstood. Misperceptions and stereotypes of homelessness exist partly because of what we see every day. Walk down the street in any city and you will see a homeless person—and mostly likely the person you will see is a single male; many will have a serious mental illness or substance abuse problems. This image has become the "brand identity" of American homelessness. However, people who are chronically homeless—living on the street for long periods or repeatedly and having a disability—make up only twenty-three percent of the 744,313 people who experience homelessness on any given night.[9] About two-thirds of homeless persons are individuals and there are more men than single women who experience homelessness. However, most Americans underestimate the number of families who experience homelessness.[10] At last count, they made up about forty-one percent of the homeless population on any given night.[11]

More importantly, although many think that homelessness is an unsolvable problem, recent research shows that housing linked with the appropriate services can help even the hardest to house individual or family back into permanent housing.[12] During the past few years, communities have adopted a major paradigm shift in responding to homelessness. Although emergency shelters are necessary to ensure that individuals and families are not literally sleeping on the street, it is not an ideal environment for families, children, and adults and many may spend months, even years, living in temporary living conditions. Recognizing this, many communities are reorganizing their response to homelessness to minimize the time people spend homeless and in shelter. This response, called "Housing First" is an approach that puts an immediate and primary focus on helping individuals and families quickly access and then sustain housing. It is designed to help individuals and families transition more rapidly out of the shelter system and includes crisis intervention, rapid rehousing, follow-up case management, and housing support services to prevent the reoccurrence of homelessness.

The following sections describe what works for minimizing the time individuals and families spend in shelter and how to help get them back into permanent housing. Although these strategies have demonstrated success in some communities, policy-makers and program administrators should look to these models as a menu of options that will have varying degrees of success in different contexts rather than "cookie cutter" solutions. Furthermore, although many of the terms—such as permanent supportive housing, Housing First, and other model names—have become a part of the homeless services lexicon, the terms do not always mean the same thing to different people. In addition, some of these strategies have undergone the scrutiny of rigorous research and others are only beginning to emerge and although they show promise illustrated through successful program outcomes, they need further testing and evaluation to serve as models that should be replicated nationwide. These cautions are noted because as programs move to replicate model programs, they must take their community need, capacity, and challenges into consideration.

Permanent Supportive Housing for Chronically Homeless Single Adults

Ending chronic homeless requires permanent housing with supportive services, and implementing policies to prevent people who are at high risk from becoming chronically homeless. The most successful model for housing people who experience chronic homelessness is permanent supportive housing using a Housing First approach.[13] Permanent supportive housing combines affordable rental housing with supportive services such as case management, mental health and substance abuse services, health care, and employment. The Housing First approach is a client-driven strategy that provides immediate access to an apartment without requiring initial participation in psychiatric treatment or treatment for sobriety. After settling into new apartments, clients are offered a wide range of supportive services that focus primarily on helping them maintain their housing and improve their lives.

A landmark study of homeless people with serious mental illness in New York City found that on average, each homeless person utilized over $40,000 annually in publicly funded shelter, hospital (including U.S. Department of Veterans Affairs hospitals), emergency room, prison, jail, and outpatient health care resources. Much of the cost was for psychiatric hospitalization, which accounted for an average of over fifty-seven days and nearly $13,000.[14] When people were placed in permanent supportive housing, the public cost to these systems declined dramatically

The documented cost reductions—$16,282 per unit of permanent supportive housing—were nearly enough to pay for the permanent supportive housing. If other costs, such as the costs of police, court, and homeless services were included, the cost savings of providing people with permanent housing and services would likely have been higher. In other words, the study found that it cost the public the same amount to house a person with serious mental illness as it did to keep that person homeless. But although the costs were the same, the outcomes were much different. Permanent supportive housing results in better mental and physical health, greater income (including income from employment), fewer arrests, better progress toward recovery and self-sufficiency, and less homelessness.

In 2007, HUD reported that there were 208,000 units[15] of permanent supportive housing available to homeless individuals moving through the homeless assistance system and there is a commitment from Congress and the Bush administration to complete a total of 150,000 additional units (approximately 50,000 of which are already completed) by 2012. There is also a movement to change national policies so that families who meet the definition of chronically homeless are eligible for permanent supportive housing. Although there is no national estimate of the number of chronically homeless families, in a select number of communities research indicates that between two and eight percent of families may need permanent supportive housing.[16] It is important to note that although permanent supportive housing is successful at helping the highest need households getting back into housing, many individuals and families may not need such an intensive intervention. Permanent supportive housing has higher costs associated with it than mainstream housing subsidies. As the reliance on permanent supportive housing as intervention for ending homelessness increases, policy-makers should proceed with caution and ensure that it is targeted to those who need it the most.

Systems Prevention for Individuals and Families

The vast majority of people who become chronically homeless interact with multiple service systems, providing a multitude of opportunities to break the cycle by preventing a recurrence of homelessness. Promising strategies focus on people who are leaving hospitals, psychiatric facilities, substance abuse treatment programs, prisons, and jails. Public systems or institutions, such as jails and prisons, hospitals, the child welfare system, and mental health facilities too often "graduate" people directly into the homeless system. One aspect of prevention is to stop these discharges into homelessness through basic transition planning so that people leaving these institutions have stable housing and some means for maintaining it.

Almost all of the plans to end homelessness (ninety-one percent) outline systems prevention activities; eighty-six percent include strategies to improve discharge planning for correction facilities; sixty-two percent include transitional services from foster care; and sixty-one and sixty-seven percent of the plans outline efforts to improve discharge plans from mental health facilities and hospitals, respectively.[17]

Quincy, Massachusetts' plan to end chronic homelessness serves as a model example of a plan that addresses systems prevention. According to the plan, an average of twenty-five to thirty youth, individuals with mental health needs, or former prisoners who are discharged from systems of care—including discharges from the Department of Youth Services, Department of Corrections, Department of Mental Health, regional hospitals, and regional courthouses—are ending up in emergency shelters. Local city officials plan to work with state agencies to create a "zero-tolerance policy" toward discharges into homelessness. Quincy's goal is to reduce inappropriate discharges by ten percent each year until they reach zero.

Discharge planning is a process that begins before the person leaves the institution and assesses the person's needs in arranging housing, employment, health care providers, and reconnecting with family or friends. Often it involves starting benefits such as Supplemental Security Income (SSI) and arranging for post-release employment and housing. The level of services needed depends on the person—some may need more intensive supports when leaving an institution, particularly those with serious mental illness or health conditions, whereas others may only require help reconnecting.

Arranging housing is important pre-release, particularly for ex-offenders coming out of jail or prison who face limited housing options because of criminal records and lack of employment history. Because of the limited supply of affordable housing, several communities are developing housing specifically for re-entering prisoners. Alabama created a short-term residential housing program that is targeted to re-entering women with children and shared housing for those without children. Maine's re-entry housing program provides rental assistance vouchers and support services for re-entering prisoners for up to two years. The initiative targets youthful offenders (ages sixteen to twenty-five).

Designing Local Housing Subsidy Programs for Individuals and Families

Often homeless individuals and families need help paying for housing, particularly in Housing First programs. Some can move out of a homeless shelter with minimal financial assistance, for example, a security deposit and first month's rent. Others need slightly more assistance—perhaps a short-term subsidy that helps households pay for housing for several months or a shallow subsidy of $100–$300 that lasts for a year or more. Short-term assistance is often coupled with intensive services designed to help the household increase their income so they will be able to continue to pay for housing after the subsidy ends. Many other individuals and families experiencing homelessness will simply be unable to transition out of shelter without ongoing assistance to pay for housing.

Communities have used various federal, state, and local funding streams to help homeless people pay for housing. The extent and source of the funding typically determines how communities design the subsidies that help pay for housing. Federal housing assistance, including housing vouchers that can be used to subsidize the cost of private rental housing and subsidized or public housing, allows low-income households to pay thirty percent of their income for rent and the subsidy is typically not time-limited. There is strong evidence that indicates that the vast majority of homeless families who are offered a federal housing subsidy will exit homelessness and not re-enter shelter.[18] Unfortunately, federal housing assistance is in critically short supply and waiting lists extend for years. In some jurisdictions, including Seattle, Washington, and Massachusetts, federal housing resources are set aside to help homeless families exit homelessness more rapidly. But there are simply not enough federal housing resources available to communities to end homelessness. With limited federal housing resources, some states and localities have dedicated other resources to help families pay for housing. This includes using other federal funding resources to subsidize the cost of housing for homeless families such as the Temporary Assistance to Needy Families (TANF) block grant program. It has also included raising revenues and fees to develop housing trusts to fund local and state housing subsidies that help low-income households transition out of homelessness.

Communities and programs showing progress adopt different housing assistance strategies, ranging from one-time financial assistance to short-term or long-term housing subsidies—but all offer some type of rental housing assistance. They have also used various sources to fund this assistance. In Columbus, Ohio; Hennepin County, Minnesota; and Portland, Oregon, resources are dedicated to providing households with short-term rental assistance, usually the equivalent of four months rent. Such short-term assistance, where appropriate, can significantly reduce the time people spend in emergency shelter, and are a fraction of the cost of continuing to shelter households while they try to save enough money to afford rent. New York's Westchester County relies on TANF resources to supplement homeless families' welfare benefits to provide housing subsidies. In New York City, the supplement gradually declines for five years, whereas Westchester's housing subsidy has no time limits and remains level over time. Chicago is in the process of designing a housing subsidy program to help households transition out of homelessness, relying on resources from the state's housing trust fund.

Short-term and shallow subsidies are showing positive results in communities across the country; however, these interventions need further testing and evaluation to ensure that individuals and families who receive such subsidies are not coming back into the system. The question of how much is enough housing subsidy and level of services still remains.

Targeting Housing and Services for Families

Families experiencing homelessness need and benefit from services. Services can help families access and maintain stable housing as well as increase economic self-sufficiency and improve family and child well-being. Because families who experience homelessness have different needs, there is no cookie-cutter service delivery model that works for all families. Although some families are able to transition out of homelessness with minimal supportive services, others require more intensive supportive services to exit the homeless assistance system and remain stably housed. Once back in housing, links to mainstream services—for example, mental health counseling, child development services, or employment training—are important for building strong families that are no longer at risk of homelessness. With these considerations in mind, communities and programs that show promise are targeting services to meet the unique needs of each family. Some communities, like Los Angeles, are using classifications systems that place families into low-, moderate-, and high-intensity service needs. One of the primary tasks in working with a homeless family is helping them get back into housing—this means services to help the family overcome barriers to accessing housing, which helps families prepare for a successful transition into housing by resolving issues that might threaten housing stability. Services include helping families successfully manage conflicts with landlords, manage unanticipated expenses and their budget, and providing assistance to help families access and sustain employment. For example, a Housing First program in state-funded shelters in Massachusetts assigns caseworkers to help each family develop a service plan to move back into housing; this plan outlines the family's services needs along different outcomes. In Hennepin County, providers conduct landlord outreach, help families fill out apartment applications, and work with families on rebuilding their credit history—all obstacles to finding housing. Some families need ongoing services after they move into housing. For example, in Hennepin County most families placed rapidly into housing receive up to six months of case management services before the services phase out. Families with more intensive service needs, such as families that include a parent with a major mental illness or a substance abuse disorder, will receive ongoing services. Families with high service needs in San Francisco, such as families in which the parent has a substance abuse disorder, are referred to permanent supportive housing that provides ongoing, wraparound services to all family members. Although these types of service interventions are more expensive, they have important long-term benefits for families. Furthermore, research indicates that helping families maintain housing could save thousands of dollars in shelter costs or costs to other public systems—such as foster care.

Many homeless assistance providers rely on the expertise of traditional community-based service organizations to provide services to families.

Portland, Oregon, New York City, and Washington, D.C., rely on neighborhood-based agencies to provide prevention, housing placement, and stabilization services to families. These agencies typically have long histories of providing social services to low-income families within the community—services that link families to income support programs, employment services, child care and recreation, and support services for children. Using neighborhood-based programs to provide these services solidifies a relationship between the family who is vulnerable to homelessness and a neighborhood-based organization that has the capacity to provide ongoing support services. Most families who experience homelessness are extremely poor and have service needs that go beyond the homeless assistance system, which does not have the capacity to fulfill all service needs. Linking to mainstream public services, such as child care, employment, TANF benefits, and Medicaid, is often critical to promoting housing stability and is important for ensuring child and family well-being. Furthermore, although housing is critical to ensuring family well-being, it is not the panacea. If policy-makers and program administrators want to help families move up the economic ladder, services should focus specifically on job-skill enhancing programs, employment, and job retention programs.

Emergency Prevention Programs for Individuals and Families

Every day in the United States people lose their housing and find themselves homeless and seeking help at shelters or on the steps of friends and family. Even with the most effective strategies for helping people leave homelessness, as a nation we will never end homelessness if we do not prevent it from occurring in the first place. Prevention strategies are the cornerstone efforts of communities making progress in ending homelessness. Prevention efforts include a wide range of activities.

Mediation services that help households negotiate with their landlord; financial assistance to help pay for back rent or utilities; and emergency assistance in food, clothing, transportation vouchers, and other basic necessities are a few examples. It can also involve, as it does in Washington, D.C., efforts to help homeless families move directly from a doubled-up situation or a finalized eviction into housing on their own, without ever having to subject their children to homelessness. Some programs offer budgeting and credit counseling immediately following a housing crisis with the intention of helping the household stabilize and avoid homelessness in the future.

The challenge facing program administrators is how to target families and individuals at the highest risk of becoming homeless. It is not easy to identify which households will become homeless and which households will remain housed. Who programs target is important because program resources are scarce and inadequate to meet all levels of need. Communities and program administrators are utilizing data and research to identify those at the greatest risk of entering shelter, including those living in doubled-up housing, facing an eviction, and families with a young woman who is pregnant or has recently given birth. By applying what they know about people that are most likely to experience homelessness, programs are able to target outreach and assistance to at-risk families in subsidized housing developments, housing courts, and through community-based agencies. In Louisville, Kentucky, for example, Volunteers of America of Kentucky and Tennessee (VOA) partners with the local public housing authority to provide services to families residing in public housing that are at risk of eviction. Families are referred to VOA for financial assistance and services to help the family address the issues that are threatening their housing. The housing authority pays for the prevention services because it is often less expensive to help a family through a hard time than to go through the process of eviction and re-leasing the housing unit. Eviction has obvious costs to families, too. When a family faces eviction, VOA case managers help identify what the family needs to do to avert losing their housing. This may mean getting on a payment plan for utilities or a onetime infusion of rental assistance.

Other communities are experimenting with neighborhood-based prevention programs. New York City, for example, uses its client data systems and geographic information systems (GIS) to match prevention resources to the neighborhoods from which the largest numbers of families enter the city's shelter system. Each day, the city's homeless department provides community-based organizations with information about who is seeking shelter assistance in their community. These data help refine outreach efforts—targeting specific streets or buildings, for example—to ensure organizations are reaching the highest risk households. In these "high-risk" neighborhoods, organizations provide financial assistance and supportive services to families at risk of losing their housing. The city evaluates service organizations using outcomes—that is, by the reduction in the number of families entering the shelter system—instead of by the amount or type of services provided.

DATA AND PLANNING: MANAGING FOR RESULTS

Shifts in how communities respond to family homelessness have largely been a result of careful examination of data. Data are essential in formulating plans to end homelessness, evaluating programs, assessing cost-effectiveness, and efficiently targeting scarce resources. It is often data that lead communities to adopt new strategies or plans to end homelessness. Washington, D.C., for example, used the annual point-in-time estimate in their ten-year plan to end homelessness. These data helped D.C. identify how many housing units are needed to end homelessness. Conversely, each of the communities and programs we highlight can demonstrate progress because they have established data systems. Communities usually collect data on homelessness using two different but complementary methods: point-in-time data collected annually at a specific time, and administrative data that are continually collected by organizations that operate homeless assistance programs then aggregated into a community-wide system called homelessness management information systems (HMIS). HMIS are, for the most part, new developments. In 2002, HUD required Continuums of Care in each community to develop HMIS. According to HUD, about 284 Continuums (about sixty percent of all continuums) have implemented HMIS. The use of data goes well beyond bureaucratic reporting requirements.[19] Communities are using data from point-in-time estimates and HMIS to develop plans to end homelessness.

Currently about 300 communities across the country have plans to end homelessness. Nearly all of the plans rely on data to set a baseline count of how many homeless people are living in their community and to illustrate how different housing interventions can be cost-effective. The plans also rely on data to measure performance and to ensure the appropriate tools are in place or under development. Outcomes and results generated by data systems can help build broad support and leadership around the plan—both are critical to the success of plans to end homelessness. Leadership from the executive level—for example, the mayor or city council member—can make or break a plan. Communities are also using data to set a goal and form broad coalitions to come together behind that goal. In Chicago, for example, nearly 100 different agencies serving homeless individuals and families will have to modify their programs to conform to the city's ten-year plan to end homelessness. This transformation from a shelter-based model to a Housing First model requires education for program staff and board members, modification of program and public policies, and assistance undergoing the system change required. The broad coalition, led by the Continuum of Care, uses data to monitor progress regularly.

Promising communities are able to demonstrate progress because they identify performance measures, collect data, and continually monitor progress. The ability to track outcomes of interventions allows leaders to make informed decisions regarding whether to continue the investment in new strategies or explore other interventions. In many instances success attracts greater public investment in strategies demonstrating effectiveness. In communities such as Seattle, Salt Lake City, and Philadelphia, public housing agencies and housing departments—agencies with budgets independent of the homeless assistance system—are allocating housing resources towards ending homelessness among families. In Norfolk, Virginia, and Atlantic City, New Jersey, welfare agencies are dedicating funds to help transition families out of shelter and motels and into their own housing.

At the program level, data help communities identify cost-effective solutions. Examining the cost of various interventions has been a large impetus for creating change in response to family homelessness. Hennepin County and Massachusetts both have a "right to shelter policy" so when shelters are at capacity, these localities must find alternatives for sheltering families. In the past, these communities have relied on motels to compensate for lack of available shelter beds. The cost of motel stays is exorbitant, surpassing the cost of rental apartments (in Massachusetts, the cost of staying in a motel for two months is about $6,000). Data on the public costs of sheltering families in motels led to greater investment in strategies to reduce the demand for shelter—including expanding homelessness prevention programs and Housing First initiatives.

Finally, data can help administrators evaluate service contractors and implement performance-based contracting. Columbus, Ohio; Hennepin County; and New York City are assessing performance using indicators based on family outcomes rather than services expended. For example, are shelters and Housing First providers successfully helping families access housing? Are families re-experiencing homelessness? In some cases, how an agency performs will determine whether they continue to receive a contract to perform those services or whether the agency needs technical assistance to improve performance. In other cases, it may lead to re-evaluating the goals of specific programs and types of services provided.

COMMUNITIES MAKING PROGRESS

To date, hundreds of communities have adopted ten-year plans and are beginning to implement some of the strategies highlighted above. The adoption of these models in communities across the country is beginning to show results.

- Homelessness decreased eight percent in Montgomery, Alabama, from 521 in 2004 to 479 in 2006.[20]
- Portland, Oregon, has reduced homelessness thirteen percent and chronic street homelessness by seventy percent since 2005.[21]
- Westchester County, New York, reduced homelessness among families by fifty-seven percent.[22]
- Hennepin County, Minnesota, reduced family homelessness forty-two percent between 2002 and 2004.[23]
- In the District of Columbia, it was just reported that homelessness was reduced by 6.5 percent and chronic homelessness by six percent in the past year.[24]
- Homelessness decreased twenty-seven percent in Nashua, New Hampshire, from 606 in 2004 to 444 in 2007.[25]
- In Denver, homelessness decreased eleven percent from 4,444 in 2005 to 3,954 in 2007.[26]

What can we learn from communities and programs that are showing results in ending homelessness? At a minimum, these communities, and other success stories like them from around the country, offer us insight into promising strategies to end homelessness. At best, they hold the key to solving the problem. With further testing, evaluation, and expansion of these strategies to other communities there is hope for national declines in homelessness.

THE BROADER AFFORDABLE HOUSING LANDSCAPE

The communities highlighted above are reforming their homeless assistance systems, making them work more efficiently and effectively. There, is however, the broader context to consider. The existing and most conclusive research identifies the lack of affordable housing as the primary driver of homelessness in the United States.[27] This is both because there is an inadequate supply of affordable housing and because incomes are so low that households cannot pay for the housing that is available. The rising cost of housing accompanied by declining wages creates conditions that put people at risk of losing their housing and make it even more difficult to find housing once they become homeless. The picture is not getting better—it is getting worse. Housing is considered "affordable" when a household pays no more than thirty percent of its income for housing. Currently, as a nation we have a severe affordable housing shortage, with about 5.9 million households reporting "worst-case" housing needs.[28] These households are severely rent burdened (pay more than fifty percent of their income for rent) are living in overcrowded situations, or are living in substandard housing.[29] The affordable housing shortage is likely to get worse over the next ten years because of the growing gap between income and housing, the tightening of rental markets, and the permanent removal of older rental units from the stock of affordable housing. A recent study conducted by the Joint Center for Housing Studies at Harvard University estimates that approximately 200,000 affordable housing units will be lost over the next ten years.[30]

Some government programs, such as Section 8 vouchers and public housing, help low-income people pay for housing. However, at current funding levels federal programs cannot close the gap between those who can afford housing and those who cannot. Only one in four households who are eligible for housing assistance currently receive a subsidy.[31] Most cities have long waiting lists—from two to five years—for housing units or rent subsidies. Without a housing subsidy a family has to make $15.78 an hour ($32,822 annually) to afford housing at the national fair market rent; the hourly rate is much higher in higher cost rental markets like Washington, D.C.; Boston, Massachusetts; and Alameda County, California.[32] Although the cost of housing continues to rise, the minimum wage, unchanged in the past ten years, is worth only three-fourths of what it was worth ten years ago. Today, a full-time minimum wage worker earns only one-third of what they would need to rent a modest apartment. As a result, many poor households pay more than fifty percent of their income for rent, leaving very little for other expenses such as food, clothing, and health care. As the demand for affordable housing grows, our nation's most vulnerable households—the ones that need the most help—will find themselves priced out of housing or living in unstable housing, leaving them at high risk of homelessness.

ENDING HOMELESSNESS: THE PATH AHEAD

Because housing is the key to ending homelessness, federal programs—both mainstream housing programs and homeless assistance programs—should follow the lead of the communities showing promise and focus on getting people housed as quickly as possible. To help communities do this, the federal government needs to significantly expand affordable housing programs, particularly programs like the Section 8 Housing Choice Voucher program, and target federal housing programs to the families who need them the most. These programs help households afford housing and avoid the devastating consequences of homelessness.

Although housing solves the problem of homelessness, it is not a cure-all for the myriad needs of poor people. To give families and individuals the opportunity to move up the economic ladder, much more can be done. The federal government and state and local governments have a role in building and supporting strong families and adults. This means helping increase incomes and supporting households while they work. Child-care subsidies, child support enforcement, Head Start, TANF assistance, Medicaid, and Earned Income Tax Credit, job training, and support are all necessary for ending homelessness. State and local governments should expand these programs as well and work to align their child and family welfare policies with the goals of ending homelessness. These programs and policies help people increase their incomes and move closer to self-sufficiency; they are the supports that ensure they are not left vulnerable, at risk of homelessness in lean or hard times.

Will these promising strategies end homelessness? It is still too early to tell. The number of homeless people is going down in a handful of communities, but in many more the numbers are increasing. What is clear is that homelessness is a solvable problem, but it will take all hands on deck. State and local governments will need to continue to adopt innovative, public policy interventions that demonstrate successful outcomes. Nonprofit and faith-based organizations must continue to test solutions and overcome the hurdle of implementing a new way of approaching homelessness—one that focuses on permanent solutions. Communities cannot end homelessness on their own. The federal government needs to significantly increase the supply of affordable housing and recast a safety net. Finally, the private sector (hospitals, businesses, banks, foundations, etc.) should contribute financial support and know-how. It will take all of these stakeholders, working together, to end homelessness in America.

NOTES

1. National Alliance to End Homelessness, *Toolkit for Ending Homelessness* (Washington, DC: National Alliance to End Homelessness, 2003).

2. M. Cunningham, M. Lear, E. Schmitt, and M. Henry, *A New Vision: What is in Community Plans to End Homelessness?* (Washington, DC: National Alliance to End Homelessness, 2006).

3. National Alliance to End Homelessness, *How Much Does the Federal Government Spend on Homelessness?* (Washington, DC: National Alliance to End Homelessness, 2006).

4. National Alliance to End Homelessness, *A Plan, Not a Dream: How to End Homelessness in Ten Years* (Washington, DC: National Alliance to End Homelessness, 2000).

5. City of Indianapolis, *Blueprint to End Homelessness* (Indianapolis, IN: City of Indianapolis, 2002).

6. For a complete list of community plans, please visit http://www.endhomelessness.org.

7. "Taking on a Problem that 'Cannot Be Solved,'" Remarks prepared for delivery by Secretary Mel Martinez, Friday, July 20, 2001.

8. Cunningham et al., *New Vision*, 2006.

9. M. Cunningham and M. Henry, *Homelessness Counts* (Washington, DC: Homelessness Research Institute, National Alliance to End Homelessness, 2007).

10. The National Alliance to End Homelessness and Freddie Mac commissioned the Winston Group to conduct a poll on homelessness. This poll asked 1,000 registered voters a series of questions on homelessness. The poll was conducted on March 4–5, 2006.

11. Cunningham and Henry, *Homelessness Counts,* 2007.

12. D. Culhane, S. Metraux, and H. Trevor, "Public Services Reductions Associated with Places of Homeless Persons with Severe Mental Illness in Supportive Housing," *Housing Policy Debate* 13, no. 1 (2002).

13. S. Tsemberis, L. Gulcur, and M. Nakae, "Housing First, Consumer Choice, and Harm Reduction for Homeless Individuals with a Dual Diagnosis," *American Journal of Public Health* 94, no. 4 (2004): 651–6.

14. Culhane, Metraux, and Trevor, "Public Services Reductions," 2002.

15. Office of Community Planning and Development, *The Annual Homeless Assessment Report to Congress* (Washington, DC: Office of Community Planning and Development, U.S. Department of Housing and Urban Development, 2007).

16. D. Culhane, S. Metraux, J.M. Park, M. Schretzman, and J. Valente, "Testing a Typology of Family Homelessness Based on Patterns of Public Shelter Utilization in Four U.S. Jurisdictions: Implications for Policy and Program Planning," *Housing Policy Debate* 18, no. 1 (2007).

17. Cunningham et al., *New Vision,* 2006.

18. M. B. Shinn, B. Witzman, D. Sojannovic, D. Kickerman. J. R. Jimenz, L. Duchon, L. James, and D. H. Krantz, "Predictors of Homelessness among Families in New York City: From Shelter Request to Housing Stability," *American Journal of Public Health* 88, no. 11 (1998): 1561–1657.

19. U.S. Department of Housing and Urban Development, *Report to Congress: Fifth Progress Report on HUD's Strategy for Improving Homeless Data Collection, Reporting and Analysis* (Washington, DC: U.S. Department of Housing and Urban Development, 2006).

20. City of Montgomery, *Progress Report* (Montgomery, AL: City of Montgomery, 2006).

21. National Alliance to End Homelessness, *Community Snapshot: Portland* (Washington, DC: National Alliance to End Homelessness, 2007).

22. National Alliance to End Homelessness, *Community Snapshot: Westchester County* (Washington, DC: National Alliance to End Homelessness, 2007).

23. National Alliance to End Homelessness, *Community Snapshot: Hennepin County* (Washington, DC: National Alliance to End Homelessness, 2007).

24. Community Partnership for the Prevention of Homelessness, *Progress Report to the Community* (Washington, DC: Community Partnership for the Prevention of Homelessness, 2007).

25. National Alliance to End Homelessness, *Community Snapshot: Nashua, New Hampshire* (Washington, DC: National Alliance to End Homelessness, in press).

26. National Alliance to End Homelessness, *Community Snapshot: Denver* (Washington, DC: National Alliance to End Homelessness, in press).

27. M. Burt, *What Will It Take to End Homelessness?* (Washington, DC: Urban Institute Press, 2001).

28. U.S. Department of Housing and Urban Development, *Affordable Housing Needs: A Report to Congress on the Significant Need for Housing* (Washington, DC: U.S. Department of Housing and Urban Development, 2006).

29. Ibid.

30. Harvard University Joint Center for Housing Studies, *America's Rental Housing* (Cambridge, MA: Harvard University Joint Center for Housing Studies, 2006).

31. D. Rice and B. Sard, *The Effects of the Federal Budget Squeeze on Low Income Housing Assistance* (Washington, DC: Center on Budget and Policy Priorities, 2007).

32. D. Pelletiere, K. Wardrip, and S. Crowley, *Out of Reach* (Washington, DC: National Low Income Housing Coalition, 2006).

Chapter Two

A SHELTER IS NOT A HOME ... OR IS IT? NEW COMMUNITIES OF OPPORTUNITY

Ralph da Costa Nunez

New York City is the homeless capital of the world. Each evening 32,000 individuals (16,000 adults and 16,000 children) reside in city shelters. But New York's homeless problem is not unique; the characteristics of its homeless are the same as everywhere—the magnitude of the problem is simply greater. This chapter focuses on a powerful tool for ending homelessness—the shelter—and how it can and should be put to work anywhere that homelessness exists. Case studies illustrate how such programs can dramatically impact the lives of children and their parents.

Twenty years ago, city shelters were no place for any family to call home. Their basic mission was simply emergency housing and little more. As a result, families remained entrenched in poverty, and many became homeless a second, third, or even fourth time. New York City's recidivism rate was a full fifty percent, and many of today's shelter residents themselves came of age within the emergency shelters that defined the period.[1]

Two decades later, shelters are still there, but many have evolved into very different places—dynamic, multiservice centers addressing the comprehensive needs of homeless families. With very little affordable housing being built, shelters have become one of the only housing options low-income families have. In fact, they may be the twenty-first century's version of affordable housing.

As we attempt to end the cycle of family homelessness, the answer may lie in these facilities of the new millennium, shelters turned into "communities of opportunity." Shelters have become powerful places where enormous changes in people's lives and habits are taking place. They either are, or can be, residential educational training centers where families live and participate in programs that address the root causes of poverty. In fact, today these facilities are at the forefront of the war on poverty—fighting domestic violence, teen pregnancy, illiteracy, illness, and foster care placements, while simultaneously providing job readiness, employment training, and education, all on-site.

Indeed, by meeting community needs in a residential setting under one roof, shelters have become the new "main streets" of poor communities, serving as an alternative approach to scattered service delivery. And why not? If shelters have become more permanent than ever before, and in many ways have replaced old, newly gentrified neighborhoods, then their power should be harnessed and their potential to transform people's lives recognized.

Some argue that this view of a shelter is misguided, acting as a barrier to the construction of permanent housing, but we must ask the fundamental question: when will this housing be built? Whether intentional or not, government has essentially abandoned its commitment to low-income housing. Today when government speaks of affordable housing, the question remains—affordable for whom? New York City's new initiative to develop 300 units of affordable housing in downtown Manhattan is a perfect example. Qualifying applicants must earn between $50,000 and $85,000 annually. No low-income families meet that criteria, and homeless families never will. For the time being, shelters are all that is left. They have become temporary low-income housing where poor families presently reside and will probably continue to do so for the foreseeable future. And, if, as we have seen, homelessness is more complex than just housing, shelter communities can play a highly significant role in reducing poverty and homelessness itself.

SHELTERS AND LEARNING

A lack of education lies at the heart of today's poverty problems. Nearly one-half of homeless parents have not completed high school, limiting not only their own potential, but also rendering them less able to promote their children's educational development.

An investment in homeless parents is also an investment in homeless children, and shelter communities are places where parents have a chance to connect with their children in ways they never may have before. Parenting classes, parent-child activities, and on-site child care are amongst the programs giving parents insight into their children's emotional, physical, and intellectual development and helping them become more active and engaged mothers and fathers. Parent-child literacy programs, like the "Together In Learning" model piloted in several New York City shelters and shelters in fifteen other cities nationwide enable parents to further their own literacy level while engaging in games, stories, and literacy projects with their children.[2] For the first time, young homeless parents are gaining the skills to become their children's first teachers and, later, to become advocates in their classrooms. With nearly half of the nation lacking the basic reading skills necessary to function in our society, shelters can become important frontline vehicles for supporting literacy efforts.[3]

At the same time as parents are making these crucial educational strides, we can ensure that their children do not develop similar educational deficits. If we are to prevent yet another generation of children from becoming homeless parents themselves, we must recognize the issues they face and address them early and comprehensively. As we have seen, homeless children have profound educational, health, and emotional needs that must be met through early intervention and ongoing educational support. With shelter stays getting longer for families, homeless children have come to know a shelter as their "home," and it is in this home that they receive support, encouragement, and guidance as they embark on their educational paths.

In New York City, over half of homeless children change schools at least once a year, resulting in months of academic setbacks. They miss weeks of classes because of homelessness and are held back and wrongfully placed in remedial programs. Moreover, many of them spend over an hour traveling to and from school, and many are regularly taunted by their classmates for being homeless. These are hardly the ingredients for a child's success.

However, there is proof that focusing on the needs of these children results in remarkable academic, social, and emotional gains. A recent study of a New York City shelter-based after-school program found that children made significant academic gains in as little as six months, with fifty-nine percent improving their overall grade point average and sixty and fifty-six percent showing increases in their reading and math scores, respectively.[4] Not only do children's grades improve, their self-esteem and behavior positively change as well; over three-quarters of these children report increased confidence in their own abilities since attending the program and eighty-three percent are demonstratively more cooperative.[5]

Furthermore, shelter-based educational enrichment activities have a positive impact on school attendance and parental involvement. One study found that ninety-two percent of homeless children in after-school programs have a high rate of daily school attendance, compared to only sixty-three percent of those not attending such programs. In addition, these programs have proven beneficial in helping homeless parents form partnerships with their children's schools—almost all of those with children enrolled in these programs visit their children's schools frequently, whereas only one-quarter of those with children not attending do the same.[6]

For younger children, preschool programs in shelter communities have had an enormous impact on their social, emotional, and developmental growth. In as little as eight weeks, homeless children attending preschool have demonstrated dramatically improved language skills, longer attention spans, more cooperative behavior, and greater self-confidence.[7] Although it is widely acknowledged that preschool programs are an important precursor for academic success, for many of these children, this is the first time they have had access to it, because it is more readily available to them in a shelter community than in their former neighborhoods.

An Example: Shelly

Shelly saw the inside of New York City's Emergency Assistance Unit (EAU), the gateway to the city's shelter system, before she saw the inside of a school. A childhood marked by transience, homelessness, and time in foster care perpetuated an intergenerational cycle of poverty and dependence. Because of the circumstances of Shelly's upbringing, she was unable to complete high school. After having children as a teenager, it wasn't until she entered the shelter system that she had the opportunity to resume her education. Once she entered a transitional housing facility, Shelly was able to put her two young children in daycare and after-school programs and attend classes at the shelter's alternative high school. At the high school, Shelly successfully achieved high school equivalency, learned how to use computers, and was referred to the shelter's job training program, all while her children acquired their own skills in the facilities downstairs.

Today, Shelly works six days a week as an office manager for a local construction company, takes evening classes at a community college, volunteers with the local police force, and lives in a comfortable two-bedroom apartment in Harlem. Perhaps most remarkably, Shelly says, "the shelter system made me a stronger person."

SHELTERS AND EMPLOYMENT

With few homeless parents having ever held a job, and fewer still having graduated from high school, we must initiate educational programs within shelters and teach the writing and math skills necessary for success in the workplace.[8]

Shelters should include education and GED preparation, mentoring and skill building, and job internships and actual employment, both on-site and in the community. For underemployed parents, who usually have held only brief, part-time positions, the emphasis is on gaining the skills to embark on a more stable career path. For those with work experience, the emphasis is on job retention and advancement. Shelters can become the equivalent of a school campus, where some parents "major" in computers, whereas others prepare to become home daycare providers, some are trained as security officers, and others become teacher's aides or maintenance workers. The possibilities are endless.

If the goal is to move people from public assistance to work and to end homelessness, then we must provide the tools to make it happen. And in a shelter-turned-community we can begin this process. It is time to take seriously the opportunity to deal with the poverty problems homeless families currently face and to do so where they currently live, in the shelter communities that exist within larger communities.

"My past is my past. I'm just blessed I've had a chance to feel like I'm making it up. I'm giving something back. That's how I look at it. I'm giving it back. I'm giving it back." Sitting hunched over his workspace, with textbooks and notes piled up around him, it's difficult to imagine that this hardworking young college student has a criminal record and a history of homelessness. Although never a drug user, in his late teens and twenties Andre was involved in dealing crack cocaine. Like an astonishing percentage of African-American men, he spent years in the criminal justice system, was branded early as a "drug dealer," and was never able to shake the stigma and blame that accompanies such a label.[9]

An Example: Andre

To this day, Andre feels tremendous regret and anxiety over his past involvement with drugs. He is also one of the few men who entered the shelter system along with his partner and their children. In 2001, he, his longtime girlfriend Monica, and their three young children entered the New York City shelter system. The shelter proved pivotal for the family—and eventually Andre started working in the very same recreation department his children played in while they were living there. He explains,

> I had people out there that helped me out a whole lot. We had a case manager; she was great. I benefited a lot. And then, actually it was her that spoke to my supervisor about me getting the position that I got now. I'll be honest with you, I don't know where I'd be if it weren't for someone like her, you know. I can't speak for all of the case managers, but you know, she cared, she cared a whole lot. That's what happens when people care.

In 2005, Andre started taking college-level classes in human services at a local community college. He's planning to major in Human Services Administration, but his ultimate goal is simply to have a positive impact in his community. He explains,

> I just want to be one of the decision-makers in what happens. Because a lot of things that's going on, say with the kids, for instance, decisions could be a whole lot different. They could make the situation better for them, but [they're] not. I think there's not enough outlets for young kids nowadays, that's why they turn to the gangs and the drugs. Especially like in the areas [where] I grew up, it's not enough. I hope I could try to change something.

SHELTERS AND FOSTER CARE

With one-third of today's shelter residents having spent some part of their childhood in foster care and many moving directly from the foster care system into the shelter system, there is an immediate need to prevent their children from doing the same.[10]

One approach is shelter crisis nurseries, which provide twenty-four-hour, seven-day-a-week temporary placements for children at risk of abuse or neglect. Parents deal with emergencies and sort out stressful situations that put their children at risk, and a whole new way of handling crises is learned. Through aftercare and support services, crisis nursery staff work with each family to ensure their long-term stability, keeping families together in a safe and nurturing environment. In the end, it is not just the children and their families who benefit, but the public, too: a foster care placement can cost up to $40,000 per child annually, whereas the annual cost of the shelters' crisis services are approximately $750 per child.[11] Shelter crisis nurseries can offer powerful alternatives, and within the larger network of services available in the shelter-turned-community, they can prevent a lifetime of dependency within the foster care system.

An Example: Anita

Anita endured severe physical abuse from her grandmother as well as sexual abuse from her cocaine-addicted aunt and uncle when she lived with them. Anita was then placed with foster families. Already eleven years old, Anita was unable to adapt to life in foster care. For the next nine years, Anita would live in fourteen different foster homes, five psychiatric hospitals, two group homes, and three residential centers before ending up in the New York City shelter system.

Once she entered the shelter system, Anita believed she became calmer and more patient. "I've learned to not let too many things get to me now. Everything is a process. Everything is a process, and I'm just one of those little notches waiting to get moved on." Her priorities while living in shelter were regaining custody of her children—who had themselves entered the foster care system—and finding an apartment suitable for a family of four, something the shelter's social work staff would help her achieve.

Anita had been without a home for most of her life. As an adult she was upset that she was not living independently; however, her experience at the shelter was a positive one. "A lot of people think that the shelter system is a bad experience or is not the best place to be, but you have to do what you have to do. If it's something that needs to be done in *your* life, you just need to do it." Anita was approved for a Section 8 housing subsidy and moved into a Brooklyn apartment. Shortly thereafter, she received full custody of her daughters.

SHELTERS AND TEEN PREGNANCY

Many homeless heads-of-household had their first child while still teenagers and more than half are themselves the products of adolescent childbearing.[12]

Most of these young mothers may lack the maturity and skills to make good parenting decisions and manage their own lives. For members of this group, most of whom dropped out of high school, educational programs can help establish goals and direction, while allowing them to gain a sense of their own potential—natural incentives to family planning and the postponement of future childbearing. They can attend GED classes to complete their schooling as well as job readiness, employment training, and parenting skills workshops. They can learn that education and work are important precursors to having children, successfully raising a family, and ensuring that their children have a solid foundation for the future. And they can begin to do this all within the residential educational environment of a shelter-turned-community.

An Example: Monique

When Monique was just fifteen, she became sexually active. Within one year, she gave birth to her first son. Fleeing her mother's physical abuse, Monique quit school and, with her son, entered a group home for teen mothers. Only a year after entering the group home, she became pregnant a second time. Unfortunately, her decision to keep the baby meant that she had to leave the group home since pregnant women were not permitted there. With little job experience and no high school diploma, Monique had little choice but to enter the New York City shelter system. Five months pregnant and with one child, nineteen-year-old Monique was placed in a family shelter. The family shelter would prove to be pivotal in Monique's life, as she explains:

> Going into the shelter was like the best thing that happened to me. Yeah, that I believe. They had a daycare for my baby. They had daycare for my three-year-old. I took my GED, they had computers in the afternoon that I did. And I did a job-training program. I did my internship—reception and the mail. So I got a lot of experience.

One of her favorite programs was one aimed at encouraging literacy for parents and children together. Monique describes the program's effect:

> [It] was really helpful to me because I had to read to my son, which was something I always did anyway, but even more so. We learned together—mother and son. It was so much fun, doing things together. I teach my children to stand up for what you believe in, be proud of who you are and where you came from. And the things that happened to me, I think pretty much made me stronger. I'm more eager to do this. I really want to prove to people that I can do this. And I refuse to settle for anything less. That's what makes life grand. Life is a learning process. And it's a game. My game ain't over yet. Not even close.

SHELTERS AND DOMESTIC VIOLENCE

Almost half of all homeless parents have a history of domestic violence, and nearly one-third of homeless children have witnessed it. Boys who do so have a 1,000 percent greater chance of becoming abusers themselves.[13] In fact, many homeless families cite domestic violence as their primary reason for becoming homeless.

With these victims entering the shelter system at increasing rates, there is an immediate opportunity to tackle this problem in a safe and nurturing environment. A mother can access supportive services to address both her physical and emotional health within the stable, safe shelter environment. Her children can have the opportunity to address the emotional ramifications of living in an abusive household; educational, social programs provide the support they need to fully recover.

An Example: Belle

"I had a pretty good life, I just went astray. I just basically needed structure. That's where the shelters came in." On the surface, Belle's story seems typical: her homelessness was precipitated by a violently abusive marriage and heroin addiction. But viewing it simplistically glosses over the uniqueness of her story. She grew up in a happy, stable home, and her parents' marriage is so solid that in 2004, they happily celebrated their fiftieth wedding anniversary. She was raised with all the trappings of a middle-class childhood, including horseback-riding camp, vacations abroad, and dedicated, supportive parents. Today, looking back on her life experiences, Belle repeats what so many women who have been through similar experiences say: that self-sufficiency was the most important lesson she learned. Were it not for her dependencies, everything might have been different.

Belle was able to seek help for her drug addiction because she found a facility that would accommodate her rehabilitation while she maintained custody of her infant daughter. The basic assurance that a child will be safe and protected while a parent receives the help that he/she needs often proves pivotal for parents who need assistance.

Shortly after leaving the shelter, Belle was hired by its recreation department and has been working there ever since. "I enjoy my job here, the people I've met. You know, it's like, I don't know any other way to put it, but ever since I came here, my whole life has changed. And it's changed for the better."

SHELTERS AND CHILDREN'S HEALTH

Homeless children are sick more frequently and have significantly higher rates of hunger than their non-homeless counterparts. In New York City, almost three-quarters of all homeless families have no primary care physician, and instead utilize emergency rooms and walk-in clinics for their medical care.[14]

Shelters should, and many do, have on-site medical services, nutrition classes, and exercise programs. They connect parents and children to the services of area hospitals. For care not available on-site, shelters partner with local health providers and other community organizations. For the first time, these families have access to the primary care services that are critical for staying healthy, and they gain resources that promote a healthy lifestyle.

An Example: Brittany

Brittany suffered from chronic asthma, which had gotten so severe she was often unable to leave the family's apartment. Her mother explained that,

> Her asthma was so bad, she was allergic to trees; she was allergic to air; she was allergic to roaches. She was allergic to basically everything. Brittany couldn't go to school every day. Brittany would get a block away; she would catch an asthma attack. My mother would have to bring her back, put her on the machine. My mother asked for home schooling. They never sent it, so she basically was neglected of an education.

Brittany spent hours waiting to be treated at the emergency room because she lacked a primary care physician. By the tender age of eight, her escalating Medicaid bills likely totaled more than the annual cost of providing health insurance to her entire family, with an average three-day stay for a serious attack averaging more than $9,000.[15]

Brittany's fortunes changed when her family arrived at a service-enriched transitional shelter. Her new home has equipped with an on-site clinic and a local physician attuned to the unique health needs of homeless children. Brittany had access to stable, affordable care that had the added public benefit of not draining taxpayer-supported funds. Brittany's health vastly improved to the point where she was able to attend school regularly; she even enrolled at the shelter's sleep-away camp and spent two weeks playing in the country, which was excellent medicine for her lungs.

SHELTERS AND COMMUNITY

Part of the power of a shelter-turned-community is the potential for positive collaborations with the wider community. Local libraries, community colleges, museums, and cultural institutions can help enhance a shelter's services and provide extracurricular activities. Children can be connected to mentors at a high school, receive one-on-one academic assistance at a library, and find a place in the spotlight in a local theater troupe. Adults can be linked to employment opportunities with community businesses and take their first steps on the road to independent living. In fact, New York City is rich with access to such opportunities; and with a shelter recognized as a new community within the larger community, all kinds of needs can be met.

Shelters are much more than just temporary housing for the poor. Many have become visionary residential community centers handling frontline poverty and dealing it a powerful blow. These new communities, partnering with the broader community, offer enormous benefits to those in need, and they do so at a reasonable cost. In New York City, the estimated cost of a shelter-turned-community is roughly twenty-five dollars per person per day, including housing, education, child care, and a full spectrum of programs and activities.[16]

In addition to cost, these communities offer families a safer, more respectable living environment than the congregate emergency shelters that preceded them. With private living suites, indoor and outdoor play areas, computer labs, and classrooms, the atmosphere is one of a community center rather than a stark city shelter. These residences are essentially "one-stop shops," where all the programs and services a family needs to move forward are found under one roof.

Furthermore, this on-site approach, coupled with positive peer pressure from shelter residents and counselors, removes many of the traditional obstacles to program participation. The logistical nightmares of attempting to participate in educational and social programs, historically spread throughout the community, are gone. The search for transportation and child care no longer stands in the way. Parents and children simply have to walk down the hall or go up the stairs to participate in services that will change their lives. Such is the power of a shelter community.

This is an approach already proven successful. In New York City, many transitional shelter facilities are working to address poverty and homelessness in new and dynamic ways. Shelters have transformed into communities of opportunity, where shelter directors advocate for resources for their residents just as elected officials do for their constituents, and staff members link families to a variety of education and employment options just like guidance counselors do for their students. Furthermore, residents often advocate for each other. Theresa is an example of this. Within a few months, Theresa had become her shelter's de facto cheerleader.

> I did all the little groups. Finished it. Got other people to sign up for them. Yeah, we got women's group—we have so much fun! We watch movies. Parenting is good, it lets you know how to talk to your kids. Yeah, so I was bringing in other people. So the groups were getting kind of full. They was looking nice and healthy. We loved it.

SHELTERS AS COMMUNITIES

Simply put, turning shelters into communities of opportunity is an approach that works. It is truly the first step to ending family homelessness as we have known it. Families who partake in the power of a shelter are able to overcome their homelessness, move into new homes, and stay housed. Studies have shown that after two years, ninety percent of program participants in such communities have maintained their permanent housing.[17]

Already, thousands of families who have come through these new communities have found housing and secure jobs while furthering their education and strengthening their families. They have emerged from homelessness largely because of a common sense approach that takes a negative circumstance and transforms it into a unique opportunity for success.

A city government, which for so long has tried to curtail and deal with the growth of family homelessness, has unexpectedly laid the groundwork to effectively reduce it permanently. The family shelter system in New York City is a national model for effectively managing homelessness. The only drawback is that few people readily recognize it for what it truly is—one of the most ambitious and comprehensive anti-poverty programs ever launched in America. These facilities have harnessed all of the previously dispersed community-based services and redeployed them in new, innovative, cost-effective ways, within new temporary communities. But they are temporary in that they are only the first step. The steps in this transition are similar to those all young people take after graduating from school. They move away from home, become independent, get their first jobs, and rent their first apartments. At the beginning, their living arrangements and their jobs may not be ideal; however, as they develop more skills and obtain more education, they are better equipped to move up and out of one community into another.

In the early 1980s, the Reagan administration set all this in motion when they began eliminating funding for low-income housing. The dissipation of this funding ensured that court-mandated integrated housing for the poor would be kept away from urban and suburban middle-class neighborhoods. If you don't have the money, you can't build the housing. From that day forward it was clear that it was only a matter of time before the poor were living in places other than low-cost housing; the family shelter system was born. Shelters became the supposed temporary alternative, springing up in dilapidated industrial or residential areas. But twenty years later, they are both more permanent and more numerous than ever. Still, it would not be until the Clinton presidency and the tenure of HUD Secretary Andrew Cuomo that the federal government would play an active role in enhancing shelters and their services by supporting transitional housing and the funding of a complete Continuum of Care. More services were added to make shelters more humane, and the whole nature of a shelter began to change.

The Ten-Year Plan

Today, there is a new response to homelessness—a Ten-Year Plan coming out of Washington, D.C. It purports to end homelessness by closing the so-called "front door." By closing shelters and dismantling programs, the plan expects the homeless to be absorbed into other existing service systems. It is in fact, reminiscent of the 1980s "Just Say No" anti-drug and teen pregnancy campaigns—illogical approaches that do nothing about a problem except expect it to disappear. The Ten-Year Plan is already several years old and little has changed; the homeless keep coming, and only lip service is paid to the development of new low-income housing. Truthfully, without a massive, immediate infusion of affordable housing for the poor, no plan, regardless of its timetable, can succeed. And with the national government functioning in a quasi-war economy, and national and local deficits estimated to be in the trillions of dollars, it is inconceivable that any such initiative will be taken anytime soon. In reality, the Ten-Year Plan is already dated, and represents an abdication of responsibility rather than a viable solution to the multifaceted problem of homelessness.

Instead, those truly concerned with ending family homelessness are at a crossroads. They could, and should, continue to advocate for new housing, understanding that it still remains a long-term goal. They could also abandon viable solutions and buy into the national ten-year plan, discovering several years from now that they have helped to usher in a new generation of the homeless. Or they could recognize the true breadth and depth of the problem, work within the environment and infrastructure already in place, and deal a powerful blow against family homelessness and severe poverty.

This chapter has described the history and reality of family homelessness in New York City, but the problems and solutions are similar everywhere, only the magnitude of the problem differs. New York has inadvertently developed a viable framework for ending family homelessness; it is now up to government officials and the public to recognize it and put it to work. Simply put, if we are ever going to end family homelessness as we have known it, we have to realize that it will take a community to do so—a new community of opportunity, which begins in shelters themselves. If we don't, we will be faced with yet another generation of homeless families and children, idling in shelters across this country, waiting for the housing that may never come. For the time being at least, a shelter has indeed become a home.

NOTES

1. New York City Commission on the Homeless, *The Way Home: A New Direction in Social Policy* (New York: New York City Commission on the Homeless, 1992), 75.

2. Institute for Children and Poverty, *Together in Learning Family Literacy Curriculum* (New York: Institute for Children and Poverty, 1996).

3. National Institute for Literacy, "Frequently Asked Questions," 2007, http://www.nifl.gov/nifl/faqs.html#literacy%20rates.

4. Institute for Children and Poverty, *Back to the Future: The Brownstone and Future-Link After-School Programs for Homeless Children* (New York: The Institute for Children and Poverty, 2001).

5. Ibid.

6. Ibid.

7. R. Nunez, "Access to Success: Meeting the Educational Needs of Homeless Children," *Social Work In Education* 16, no. 1 (1994): 21–30.

8. Institute for Children and Poverty, *Job Readiness: Crossing the Threshold from Homelessness to Employment* (New York: The Institute for Children and Poverty 1999).

9. In 1995, one in three black men nationwide lived under some form of correctional supervision or control (prison, jail, parole, or probation). M. Maurer and T. Hurling, *Young Black Americans and the Criminal Justice System: Five Years Later* (Washington, DC: The Sentencing Project, 1995). In addition, an estimated 28.5 percent of black men will be admitted to prison during their lifetimes. T. Bonczar and A. J. Beck, *Bureau of Justice Statistics Special Report: Lifetime Likelihood of Going to State or Federal Prison.* (Washington, DC: U.S. Department of Justice, Office of Justice Programs, 1997).

10. Institute for Children and Poverty, *The Hidden Migration: Why New York City Shelters Are Overflowing with Families*, (New York: The Institute for Children and Poverty 2002).

11. Institute for Children and Poverty, *Homelessness: The Foster Care Connection* (New York: The Institute for Children and Poverty, 1997).

12. Institute for Children and Poverty, *Children Having Children: Teen Pregnancy and Homelessness in New York City* (New York: The Institute for Children and Poverty, 2003).

13. Institute for Children and Poverty, *Déjà Vu: Family Homelessness in New York City* (New York: The Institute for Children and Poverty, 2001); M. Kenning, A. Merchant, and A. Tomkins, "Research on the Effects of Witnessing Parental Battering: Clinical and Legal Policy Implications," in M. Steinman, ed., *Women Battering: Policy Implications* (Cincinnati: Anderson Publishers, 1991), 238.

14. Institute for Children and Poverty, *Déjà Vu*, 2001.

15. M. W. Edelman, "Children's Health Insurance: Stories from the Field," in *Child Defender* (New York: Children's Defense Fund, 2006).

16. L. M. Caruso and R. da Costa Nunez, *The American Family Inn Handbook: A How-to Guide* (New York: White Tiger Press, 2002), 31.

17. Ibid., 83.

Chapter Three

POLICING HOMELESSNESS

Ronald G. Burns

> It is not surprising that police are used to remove homeless people from affluent neighborhoods. This makes it possible to render the homeless invisible, thereby removing the disturbing evidence of a major human disaster.[1]

This opening statement acknowledges several problematic societal issues that require noteworthy attention. Of particular interest is the reference to the police as the primary social agents involved in handling the homeless. Furthermore, referring to homelessness as a "major human disaster" addresses, among other things, acknowledgment of the need for society to better address homelessness. To be sure, any discussion of the homeless requires recognition of their interaction with the police.

The police are tasked with the challenging burden of enforcing social control while maintaining concern for individual rights. Much of the controversial nature of policing in general stems from police practices that are seen by some as violations of civil rights, yet by others as justifiable acts of social control. Police shootings, traffic stops, and patrol practices are among the more common situations in which police practices are called into question. In recent history, police shootings in Cincinnati and New York prompted notable civil unrest among minority communities who felt the police unfairly targeted African-Americans. The same arguments are heard with regard to police traffic stops, as the term "racial profiling" has become an integral part of police vernacular and patrol practices, which focus primarily on the underclass.

Yet, there are two sides to every story. For instance, the police officers involved in the controversial shootings believed they were justified in behaving as such. Similarly, many officers will argue that profiling, whether it is based on race, gender, age, or related factors is not uncommon in policing and is an effective enforcement tool. Heavily policing the underclass is justified by arrest reports, which suggest overinvolvement in crime by those with limited means. Departments claim that their actions are within the law. Much of the controversy surrounding police practices stems from the difficult nature of policing.

Another controversial aspect of policing concerns officer interactions with and practices involving special populations, including the homeless. The atypical nature of the homeless population provides particular predicaments for officers who, again, must weigh individual rights with crime control as they perform their job. Homeless individuals spend most of their time abiding by the law, much like the domiciled; however, their mere presence draws the attention of the general public and the police. Although officers often recognize that the homeless generally do not pose immediate criminal threats, the public often requests the assistance of the police to respond to homeless individuals in their presence. Therein lies part of the challenges and controversy.

The following discussion of policing and the homeless is largely organized around the primary functions of policing: law enforcement, providing service, and maintaining order. The police perform many activities and are required to engage in a great deal of specialization and problem solving in their day-to-day functions. Aside from enforcing the law, they are tasked with responding to emergency medical situations, assessing and responding to mental illness and substance abuse problems, mediating disputes, educating, and many other related and challenging tasks. These and other functions as they relate to the homeless population are discussed throughout this chapter. The chapter concludes with a list of general considerations for policing this special population. The significance of policing the homeless cannot be understated, particularly in light of recent changes in police department orientation toward a community-oriented approach, and the fact that many departments do not have clearly defined policies and procedures to deal with the homeless.

POLICING THE HOMELESS: LAW ENFORCEMENT

Although police officers fall under the umbrella term "law enforcement agents," much of what they do falls outside of actual crime control activities. Despite what one sees on the popular television show *Cops*, police officers do not spend the majority of their time chasing down and wrestling suspects. Such activities, however, consume a portion of the job and are most often associated with policing. They also largely contribute to the controversy surrounding police practices.

Police officers must abide by procedural law when enforcing substantive laws. Procedural law guides and dictates officer behavior; it deals with the law as it pertains to enforcing social control. Substantive law pertains to the activities deemed illegal for everyone. Laws criminalizing burglary are an example of substantive law. Accordingly, the police must consider both sets of law when dealing with the public, and the laws become increasingly important when dealing with special populations such as the homeless. Specifically, being without a home and living on the streets is not illegal in most jurisdictions. Thus, it would be a violation of procedural law for some officers to arrest the homeless for no other reason than living on the streets as no substantive law has been violated. It is suggested that although police officers negatively view the homeless and hold them in low esteem, they do not view the homeless as dangerous criminals.[2] To some officers the homeless represent a nuisance that may or may not require attention.

The police, particularly as they operate in the current "community-oriented" period of policing, attempt to be responsive to public wants and needs, which may generate conflict with both procedural and substantive law. Community-oriented policing, which has been adopted by a majority of departments in the United States, encourages police cooperation with the public, including individuals and various groups. Such an approach focuses on quality-of-life issues and contrasts earlier police practices, most notably in the 1960s and 1970s when police departments concentrated primarily on law enforcement with limited assistance from the public. Claims that the police were disengaged from the public led to philosophical changes in many departments, leading many to re-engage the public in problem-solving and crime fighting. Citizen watch groups, drug education programs, and greater enforcement of zoning and code violations are part of the community-oriented approach. Needless to say, crime fighting certainly remains a priority for many police departments that have adopted a community-oriented approach.

Greater engagement with the public, for instance, through more frequently hosting neighborhood meetings in which police executives and officers converse with local citizens, enables the police to better understand citizens' concerns. Accordingly, many noncriminal issues are brought to the attention of the police at these meetings. Abandoned cars, neglected homes and yards, and the presence of the homeless are often noted as public concerns. Much of the serious, or simply criminal matters are brought to the attention of the police through calls for assistance and everyday police practices. Engaging with the public in a nonconfrontational manner enlightens the police to the "smaller" issues of concern to the public.

With regard to homelessness, several locales have reacted through legislation designed to crack down on the homeless population. There is notable evidence that the public has general disdain and even fears the homeless. Yet, being homeless is not illegal. Thus, what are the police to do? Should they do anything? It is well-established in the research literature that the homeless are more often represented in criminal statistics than the domiciled, yet much of their involvement in the criminal justice system stems from violations of minor laws, such as vagrancy, public urination, and trespassing.[3]

One study found that homeless individuals most often arrested for crime were under age thirty-five (although other studies identified an older homeless population[4]), had previous contact with the mental health system, and were on the streets for a longer period of time than their counterparts.[5] Substance abuse problems largely contribute to their involvement in the system as, for instance, national data suggest thirty-eight percent abuse alcohol and twenty-six percent abuse drugs.[6] Kenneth Peak argues that the street people who attract police attention are those who are primarily single males with drinking or drug problems whose survival is based on begging and theft. This particular group is responsible for a significant number of calls for police service. They "often panhandle, use intimidation, and generally are a problem for businesses and citizens using parks and public sidewalks."[7]

For several reasons the homeless are proportionately more represented in property crime statistics than the domiciled. Primary among the overinvolvement of the homeless in property crime statistics is their familiarity with the police. Part of the community policing approach involves having officers work in the same locales over a period of time, which facilitates their familiarity with the neighborhood culture and personnel. Officers working in particular areas soon become familiar with specific residents in the area and often know them by name. Officers may become aware of which homeless individuals are criminally active and which aren't.

Without "cover," the homeless individuals who engage in property crime are more likely to be exposed to police officers. The fact that the homeless may physically possess all of their belongings during their day-to-day activities enables officers to visually inspect their possessions, which facilitates the homeless population's involvement in property crime statistics. In other words, the stolen goods cannot be hidden in the trunk of a car or in a home.

The homeless are also at a disadvantage in escaping from police detection in that they are sometimes more easily identifiable than others. It is suggested that "homeless males are a stigmatized category in the eyes of the police" which "subjects them to closer scrutiny, increasing the possibility of arrest."[8] The stigmatization seems to be more enhanced for those who have spent more time living on the streets and the mentally ill.[9] For instance, a police report may come in stating that a homeless guy was seen shoplifting at a convenience store. With a working knowledge of the area and the homeless men living in it, officers already have an idea of where to begin their search for suspects. Such information enables the police to more easily apprehend the homeless shoplifter, than say, if they were searching for a domiciled male shoplifter.

Furthermore, the police may view arrest for property crimes as a means to get the homeless off the streets and appease the public's concern for their removal. Police maintain much discretion in their everyday activities, and their range of discretion is greatest with regard to lesser offenses, including many property crimes. Officers may be more likely to enforce the law when dealing with homeless suspects than with others, particularly when the victim has strong feelings for doing so. Police officers often base their decisions on the feelings of victims in using their discretion to arrest,[10] which could negatively impact those living on the streets and contribute to their overinvolvement in crime statistics. Finally, one cannot discount the need for survival absent appropriate means as a reason for the homeless to engage in property crime.

In light of these comments, it is not suggested that homeless individuals refrain from violent, or serious criminal behavior. One must bear in mind that the term "homeless" encapsulates many types of individuals facing varied problems. We would be ignorant to believe that, given the vast criminological literature highlighting the various causes of violent behavior, homeless individuals abstain from committing violent crime. For instance, Samuel Walker and Charles Katz refer to the "old homeless problem" and the "new homeless problem" to highlight changes in the nature of the relationship between homelessness and the police.[11] They cite the 1980s as a dividing point between the periods, suggesting that among the differences are members of the "new homeless problem" being more likely to commit predatory crimes. Public perception of violent crime committed by the homeless, however, seems distorted in that many believe most of the homeless are violent threats to public safety, when indeed they are not.

Prior to the "new homeless problem," police officers had a more complete grasp on the homeless population. The homeless were more easily identifiable to the police, enabling officers to engage in greater social control. The deinstitutionalization policies of the late 1960s and 1970s, which basically prevented individuals from being involuntarily institutionalized unless they posed a harm to themselves or others, led to changes in the homeless population and with that change came particular challenges for law enforcement. With greater numbers and more varied characteristics and problems, the new homeless were and are not as easily controlled by the police as they once were.

"Until a homeless person breaks the law by panhandling, trespassing, breaking into buildings, shoplifting, dealing drugs, or committing some other offense, police power to arrest that person is limited by statutes and laws."[12] Recent legislative changes in some jurisdictions have made it increasingly difficult for officers to simply ignore the homeless. Police sweeps, for instance, in response to a city expecting substantial media attention, and panhandling and sitting ordinances are among the recent efforts to remove the homeless from public view. Absent clearly defined policies and procedures, "departments depend on ordinances such as public intoxication, loitering, emergency mental health commitments, and other public disorder ordinances to contend with the homeless problem."[13]

"Although many cities seek constructive solutions to homelessness, other cities act in a hostile manner toward homeless people. In recent years, a growing number of cities have responded to the problem by passing or enforcing 'anti-homeless' laws or policies."[14] For instance, soon after being elected to the position in 1993, former New York City Mayor Rudy Giuliani generated substantial controversy with regard to his approach to the homeless. Giuliani's zero-tolerance approach to crime stressed enforcement of smaller offenses that arguably lead to larger offenses. Among other things, his emphasis on "personal responsibility" meant that the homeless were unwelcome on city streets and would be subject to greater police intervention. Among the targets of the zero-tolerance approach were those who engaged in subway fare evasion, public drinking, and public urination. Squeegee men, who clean the windows of automobiles stopped at red lights and demand payment, also became targets of law enforcement. Furthermore, Giuliani and then-Governor George Pataki instituted new shelter guidelines, which required the thirty-day eviction of homeless individuals for various reasons, including failure to cooperate with an assessment, violations of shelter rules, failure to comply with a service plan, or violations of other public-assistance requirements. Giuliani's enforcement approach, which he described as an act of love, set off a storm of protests and lawsuits from various religious, civil rights, and related groups.

Giuliani and other leaders around the country who have adopted similar enforcement-oriented approaches towards the homeless appear to have clearly identified the constituents they wish to appease. However, they fail to recognize several key issues, not the least of which involves individual rights and social justice. Put simply, their concern for cleaning the streets often interferes with civil liberties. Increasingly, it seems that municipalities are over-relying on the police to address a social issue that is beyond their scope.

POLICING THE HOMELESS: PROVIDING SERVICE

Providing service is a fundamental component of policing. We look to the police to provide numerous services in addition to law enforcement functions and order maintenance. Early police practices focused primarily on providing service to the public; however, the aforementioned concern for crime fighting in the 1960s and 1970s reduced the provision of police-related service. The recent shift towards community policing has recaptured some of the service-orientation of the police, and notable changes have occurred with regard to their handling of the homeless.

"Providing service" is a vague term that encapsulates many activities. Furthermore, providing service requires elaboration in terms of to whom is the service being provided. The police provide a service to the storeowner who wishes to have a homeless individual removed from his storefront. However, is this a disservice to the homeless individual? Officers confronting this situation, in practice, will look to the law, department policy, and/or personal beliefs regarding how to best handle the situation. Some officers may choose to ticket the individual for loitering, some may ask the individual to "move along," whereas others may take the individual to a homeless shelter or other social agency designed to address such a situation. It is possible that the individual needs treatment for mental illness, or alcohol or drug rehabilitation, which may also become options for the officer. The options of ticketing, moving along, and helping depict the three primary components of policing: law enforcement, order maintenance, and service provision, respectively.

To lump those who live on the streets into a category as vague as homeless says little of the individuals in that category. For instance, the temporarily homeless, whose situation typically stems from economic problems, seem to rarely draw attention from the police. The chronically homeless, however, are most likely to have mental illness and/or substance abuse problems and attract attention from the criminal justice system.[15] Furthermore, former chief of the Berkeley California Police Department, Daschel Butler, identified six types of homeless individuals living on the streets, "with each requiring a different tact to be taken in both approach and handling by police."[16] Particularly, he identified: (1) the service resistant, (2) the mentally disabled, (3) those who simply wish to live outdoors, (4) families with children, (5) the substance addicted, and (6) the professional panhandler posing as a homeless person. Each group poses particular challenges for law enforcement and highlights the varied nature of homelessness.

A blanket approach to such varied groups won't be effective. For instance, the services needed by the mentally disabled are different from those required by homeless families with children. Individuals become homeless for a variety of reasons, including financial losses, mental illness, having nobody to care for them, physical handicaps, chronic illness, and so on. Sure, we could say that in an ideal world we can solve the homeless problem by providing housing for them. To do so, however, would take immense resources and significant change in public attitude, among other things. Perhaps most important is the fact that many living on the street are there because of problems unrelated to housing. They require social services unrelated to the mere presence of a roof over one's head. This leads to the complex situation of the police providing service to the homeless, and the significance of multiple agency cooperation. Accordingly, it is argued that "social responses to homelessness should provide an integrated approach of mental health treatment, substance abuse counseling, social service, and employment assistance all in one setting—ideally a shelter."[17] However, many jurisdictions have limited available resources for the homeless, who, in turn, become the responsibility of the police.

The homeless population today is much different than years ago, for instance, because many more women and intact families live on the streets than in years past. These individuals may have taken different paths to life on the streets than the predominantly male population of homeless in earlier times. For instance, a sizable portion of the homeless includes undocumented aliens who avoid any contact with the police or any other authorities, making them increasingly vulnerable to victimization. Nevertheless, the undocumented may be brought to the attention of the police, leading to greater complexity in officer decision-making. Such increased diversity on the streets requires greater problem-solving skills and enhanced use of officer discretion.

Police must also view the homeless as potential victims of crime, because victimization among the homeless is problematic to say the least. It is suggested that the homeless are more often the victims of crime rather than the perpetrators,[18] which is explained, in part, by their inability to quickly report crime and their vulnerability because they sometimes possess most, if not all of their possessions. One study found that thirty-eight percent of the homeless have had possessions or money directly stolen from them. Another sizeable portion (forty-one percent) had money or belongings stolen while they were not present.[19]

Homeless youth pose additional problems for police officers because this group often engages in delinquent or criminal behavior for survival on the streets.[20] Accordingly, many homeless youth have had contact with the police, who are tasked with determining whether the interaction calls for formal intervention or not. The historical criminal justice approach of attempting to protect or nurture troubled youth has changed in recent years as society has adopted more of a law-and-order approach to juvenile crime. This change in orientation undoubtedly affects how police respond to homeless youth.

Officers must use their problem-solving skills when assessing whether or not to provide service to the homeless. It is hoped that proper pre- and in-service training has prepared the officer to act in an appropriate manner. "Police officers must be adept at recognizing the root cause of homelessness in each case and act accordingly. This is especially true because many homeless suffer from alcohol and drug abuse problems."[21] Officers will likely assess individual issues and personal characteristics prior to determining what type of service to provide, if indeed that is their orientation. Particularly, an officer will likely engage with the homeless individual and make a preliminary assessment of what service(s) is required. Drug rehabilitation? Financial counseling? Mental health treatment? Food? Shelter? Medical treatment? All of the above? Some jurisdictions provide hands-on service to the homeless; for instance, through having substance abuse counselors or mental health professionals ride along with officers on patrol.

As the social agents who most often come into contact with the homeless, it is important that officers have the ability to properly read and react to the various situations they encounter with the homeless. Officers will need to assess each situational and community-based factor surrounding a homeless individual, for instance, by recognizing whether or not the individual poses a threat to him/herself or others, and whether or not community resources are available to assist, and if so, what options exist. Police officer discretion is sometimes limited by the resources available, an issue which becomes increasingly important with regard to the homeless. For instance, without vacancy in a local shelter (or perhaps the presence of a local shelter), the police are limited in their ability to react to the homeless individual loitering in front of a building. Unfortunately, social services for the homeless are not always a priority for government leaders.

Providing service, in large part, assumes that services are available and the homeless wish to receive some type of service. With regard to the latter, some individuals choose to live on the streets; they are most comfortable being homeless and tend to view conventional life with disdain. Those who decline social services choose to do so for various reasons, including the crowded conditions at shelters and the mandatory counseling and treatment that may be required by shelters.[22] These individuals may provide frustration for the police officers willing to help; however, officers may soon realize that attempting to provide assistance to such individuals is futile and may subsequently direct their efforts elsewhere.

Nevertheless, others living on the street seek and appreciate officer assistance and support. As is the case with other social concerns, some jurisdictions maintain various options for police to provide services, yet others lag behind. Robert Langworthy and Lawrence Travis are among those who comment on the lack of shelter and treatment facilities to handle the large number of homeless individuals, suggesting that many homeless choose not to use such facilities.[23] While little can be done for those who reject assistance, it is important to recognize the need to alleviate the problems faced by the homeless who seek assistance. Given the nature of their work, the police most often encounter the homeless and are in a suitable position to find assistance for those who need and seek it.

Community policing, as noted, encourages police interaction and cooperation with various groups, agencies, and individuals. Prominent among the options for addressing homelessness are drug and alcohol rehabilitation facilities, mental health services, children's shelters, and hospital crisis units.[24] The police are in what would seem the most ideal situation to assess the problems of the homeless, given their familiarity with the community and their potential for understanding social problems. Officers can serve as referral agents with regard to information pertaining to services for the homeless, and perhaps any employment-related information that may help those seeking work.

It is expected that specialized "neighborhood patrol officers" or "community patrol officers," which are predominantly found in departments that have adopted a community-oriented approach, would make efforts to confront the homeless in their jurisdiction. The notable challenge to better address police-homeless interactions, however, involves asking (or requiring) all officers to provide a service-oriented approach.

One overlooked service police provide to the homeless and society in general involves listening. As agents of social control, the police often find themselves listening to the problems of others, which can be taxing on the officer. Nevertheless, providing service to the homeless could simply come in the form of listening to what they have to say. One fundamental human need almost always unfulfilled for the homeless is that they have no one to converse with, and few want to hear their stories.[25] If nothing else, listening to the homeless provides officers greater insight regarding the individual and perhaps the homeless in general.

POLICING THE HOMELESS: ORDER MAINTENANCE

Police officers are first and foremost human beings performing a job. As such, officers view the homeless in different lights. Some, like much of the public, may see the homeless as threats that require attention. Other officers may view the homeless as unfortunates who, unless they pose a clear violation to public safety, should be left alone. Still, other officers may be sympathetic to the homeless and act in a more accommodating manner towards the homeless than they do towards others. The discretion inherent in policing often enables officers to respond according to their preference.

Egon Bittner's earlier work on skid row provides contextualization for discussion of how the police have and continue to address the homeless population while maintaining order.[26] Bittner noted that police maintained the homeless population, which consisted largely of adult males who were down on their luck, by ensuring that they stayed within a particular area of the city, referred to as skid row, while intervening only when members of the group violated accepted social norms. Bittner referred to some police practices as peacekeeping, a term often used interchangeably with order maintenance. Although offered over a half-century ago, Bittner's observations are representative of the practices involving the homeless found today in many large urban areas.

Years ago police in many jurisdictions dealt with the homeless through providing lodging, ignoring them, or pushing them around through relocation efforts (e.g., providing transportation to the city limits). Some tried to arrest the problem. Early police efforts, prior to technological advances such as the automobile, involved the police being very familiar with their beats. Foot patrol was primarily used and officers had limited options other than to engage in human interaction. Accordingly, they were largely in touch with the members of the community and more aware of their concerns. They were also more aware of the homeless population, putting officers in a seemingly appropriate position to address public concerns and needs of the homeless.

The extensive integration of technological advances into police work changed police-community relations. As police distanced from the public, they became less aware of public concerns, and perhaps the plight of the homeless. For instance, officers in police cars are less likely to converse with the homeless, and the conversations they have are more likely to involve confrontation. Researchers found that the most common reasons for police interaction with the homeless involve citizens reporting a homeless person in their presence, officers observing a street person engaging in a problematic situation, and police responding to complaints from businesses.[27] Put simply, technological advances have certainly enhanced police practices, but there are notable areas where technology may have made the police less sensitive to the diversity of groups they encounter, which ultimately impacts how they keep the peace.

Much of what the police do involves maintaining order. What, specifically, constitutes "order" is highly subjective, so police operate according to accepted community norms and expectations. In some cases, maintaining order refers to removing the homeless from the streets. The mindset behind this approach is evidenced in the adage "out of sight, out of mind." Maintaining order could also refer to removing only the homeless individuals who negatively impact business practices, or only those who panhandle or commit crime, regardless of its seriousness. Maintaining order, or "normalcy," sometimes requires police intervention in noncriminal matters. Business owners, in particular, claim that homeless individuals located outside their buildings hamper their day-to-day operations because customers may be discouraged from entering out of fear of attack.

Jurisdictional size and the number of homeless individuals residing in an area can impact how police treat the homeless while maintaining order. For instance, one homeless individual in a small, homogenous town may face more harassment than those in large cities with more homeless and diverse populations. Maintaining the order in the smaller jurisdiction may involve officers being more cognizant of and responsive to general public wants than in large cities. In turn, the homeless individual in the small town may be dealt with more punitively and ultimately relocated, encouraged to relocate, or arrested. In summary, maintaining order, for instance with regard to the homeless, is dictated by community expectations, the nature of those expectations, and how closely the police abide by public wants.

WHAT CAN POLICE DO?

The police alone cannot solve the homeless problem, nor should we expect them to. They can, and do, play a pivotal role in dealing with the homeless, thus we should not overlook their ability to help. Unfortunately, a blanket policing approach to addressing homelessness isn't going to work. The homeless face many diverse, complex problems that the police are often ill-equipped to address. Accordingly, it is going to take cooperative and collaborative efforts from many individuals to adequately confront homelessness. But, what can the police do to help? How can the police more effectively deal with the homeless? Several departments have adopted proactive alternatives to arrest when addressing homelessness. "A common thread which runs through many of these alternatives is cooperation between cities and businesses on the one hand and homeless people and their advocates on the other."[28]

The Santa Monica Police Department's (SMPD) Homeless Liaison Program (HLP) demonstrates the complexities of the police role with regard to the homeless and identifies some options available to departments. In 1991, the SMPD created a four-person police unit to directly respond to the public's concern for homeless-related issues. The HLP presently involves two approaches: the traditional law enforcement approach and participation in social service efforts. The goals of the program include improving the quality of life for all, particularly through working with various social service agencies and placing the homeless in short-term shelter and hopefully in long-term housing. Evidence of the law enforcement approach is found on the SMPD website,[29] which includes links containing information pertaining to trespassing laws and how to deal with panhandling.

Research analyzing police department policies regarding the homeless sheds light on police-homeless interactions. The Police Executive Research Forum (PERF) has conducted a nationwide survey of police perceptions of the homeless and police policies with regard to the homeless. They found, among other things, that police executives do not view the homeless as a very significant problem in their communities. Respondents also noted the need for greater social assistance to the homeless even though they believe their departments had good working relationships with the available services. Respondents did, however, overwhelmingly note that the presence of street people increases public fear of crime, and roughly three-quarters of respondents believed that the conditions in which the homeless live posed public health hazards.[30]

With regard to police policies, the study found that less than ten percent had established formal policies for dealing with the homeless. Formal policies most often involved responses to severe weather conditions, providing victim assistance, addressing runaway youth, referrals, and substance abuse. Roughly half of the responding departments had not established training programs to deal with the homeless, and instruction, when it was provided, most often occurred during roll call. Training with regard to the homeless typically involved basic procedures and referral policies. Furthermore, only seventeen percent of respondents reported that their agencies had either full- or part-time personnel assigned to dealing with the homeless.[31]

In summarizing police approaches to homelessness, Finn notes that police primarily deal with the homeless via *strict enforcement*, or routinely arresting or disturbing the homeless through constant pressure, and *benign neglect*, through which officers ignore street people as much as possible and confront them only on an as-needed basis.[32] Neither approach alone appears overly effective.

In light of the challenges officers face with regard to the homeless, the question is asked: what can be done? The following suggestions are offered with consideration of historical and current challenges facing law enforcement in dealing with the homeless, and recent problem-solving efforts with regard to crime and justice. These suggestions are written from the comforts of my office and may seem idealistic in places. The limitations of applying thought to practice are certainly recognized, and to be sure, these suggestions are not the first of their kind. In general, they are offered as encouragement for police departments and, more generally, communities, to better confront police-homeless interactions. Key suggestions for better policing the homeless include:

- *Assessing the nature and extent of the homeless problem.* Addressing any problem begins with identifying and assessing the nature of the problem. Accordingly, we must ask questions such as "what is the problem and what do we wish to do?" It is argued that homelessness is often temporary and related to economics for most individuals living on the street. Those living on the streets because of economic issues are typically the most resourceful and will take advantage of resources available to them to get back on their feet.[33] Perhaps the assessment would encourage officers to provide more direct support to these homeless individuals.
- *Establishing department goals and policies regarding the homeless.* "Perhaps the most important component of a police response to the homeless is deciding upon the department's goals and policy regarding the problem. The first step here is to come to grips with the scope of the problem itself."[34]
- *Respecting individual rights.* It would seem that the police wish to appease the public and businesses by removing the homeless. They must simultaneously respect the individual rights of the homeless.
- *Protecting the homeless.* Those living on the streets are certainly entitled to police protection and their vulnerability to criminal victimization dictates that police pay special attention to their needs. "Just because the homeless have no votes, no PAC money, and no telephones should not mean they are excluded from police priorities."[35]
- *Identifying appropriate solutions.* Although legislation in some areas has given officers justification for removal of the homeless, one could argue that arrests do not attack the roots of the problem. In other words, arresting someone for loitering or panhandling does not end homelessness and associated problems. Thus, the concern for policing becomes how to best address the situation of public concern about the homeless absent the strict use of arrest.
- *Cooperating with outside agencies and groups.* Police departments must seek the assistance of social service agencies and others to determine the extent and nature of homelessness and address the problems they face. Cooperation among agencies is necessary in today's complex society. In the past we have primarily relied on the police to solve many social concerns; however, we have seen that police require the cooperation of others.

- *Assessing the level of existing resources and determining what is needed.* A needs-assessment evaluation will, among other things, help officers better use their discretion upon interacting with the homeless.
- *Better understanding of the homeless.* As mentioned, the homeless face many problems and come from various walks of life. In turn, a blanket approach of arresting the homeless is not the most effective. Instead, understanding the unique problems faced by these individuals and assessing the extent to which social services are available would help alleviate the problem. Helping the general public better understand homelessness would also provide beneficial results for all.
- *More effective police training with regard to the homeless.* Effective pre- and in-service training regarding sensitivity to the plight of the homeless would likely have positive impacts on police-homeless interactions. Unfortunately, "many departments do not provide the means, training, or tools necessary for officers to successfully reach out to the community's homeless."[36]
- *Thorough evaluation of department efforts.* It is important for departments to assess the effectiveness of their actions with regard to homelessness. For instance, have officers been able to assist the homeless? Have they been able to appease the public's concern for the homeless? The evaluation must be thorough, because it will likely, and hopefully, guide future efforts. Departments must be patient with regard to their efforts in this area, with the goal of avoiding quick judgments.

These suggestions will help provide for better police interactions with and protection of the homeless. At the very least, these suggestions offer direction for police involvement in addressing homelessness in manners other than invoking the law. Police actions directed toward assisting, instead of arresting, the homeless seem to show more promise. To do so would, among other things, reduce the divisiveness among involved parties, save criminal justice resources, and hopefully reduce the level of homelessness.

NOTES

1. T. Milton, "'The Law, in Its Majestic Equality, Forbids All Men to Sleep Under Bridges': Anatole France," *Journal of Public Health Policy* 23, no. 4 (2002): 501–2.
2. D. A. Snow, S. G. Baker, and L. Anderson, "Criminality and Homeless Men: An Empirical Assessment," *Social Problems* 36, no. 5 (1989): 532–49.
3. Ibid.
4. See, for example, P. Fischer, "Criminal Activity Among the Homeless: A Study of Arrests in Baltimore," *Hospital and Community Psychiatry* 39, no. 1 (1988): 46–51.
5. Ibid.
6. S. Klein, "Dealing with the Homeless and Improving Quality of Life," *The Police Chief* 67 (2000): 34–43.
7. K. Peak, *Policing America: Methods, Issues, Challenges*, 3rd ed. (Upper Saddle River, NJ: Prentice Hall, 2000), 196.
8. Snow, Baker, and Anderson, "Criminality and Homeless Men," 1989.
9. Ibid.
10. D. Smith and C. A. Visher, "Street-Level Justice: Situational Determinants of Police Arrest Decisions," *Social Problems* 29, no. 2 (1981): 167–77.

11. S. Walker and C. M. Katz, *The Police in America: An Introduction*, 4th ed. (Boston: McGraw Hill, 2002), 137–8.

12. H. M. Wrobleski and K. M. Hess, *Introduction to Law Enforcement and Criminal Justice*, 8th ed. (Belmont, CA: Wadsworth, 2006), 176.

13. R. Trojanowicz, V. E. Kappeler, and L. K. Gaines, *Community Policing: A Contemporary Perspective*, 3rd ed. (Cincinnati, OH: Anderson, 2002).

14. M. Foscarinis and R. Herz, "New Municipal Ordinances Regulating Homeless People," in M. L. Forst, ed., *The Police and the Homeless* (Springfield, IL: Charles C. Thomas, 1997), 29–41.

15. D. L. Carter and L. A. Radelet, *The Police and the Community*, 6th ed. (Upper Saddle River, NJ: Prentice Hall, 1999).

16. D. E. Butler, "Homelessness: Compassionate Enforcement," in M. L. Forst, ed., *The Police and the Homeless* (Springfield, IL: Charles C. Thomas, 1997), 88.

17. Ibid., 411.

18. L. S. Miller and K. M. Hess, *The Police in the Community: Strategies for the 21st Century*, 3rd ed. (Belmont, CA: Wadsworth, 2002).

19. Klein, "Dealing with the Homeless," 2000.

20. A. Munoz, L. B. Whitbeck, D. R. Hoyt, and B. J. McMorris, "Arrests among Homeless and Runaway Youths: The Effects of Race and Gender," *Journal of Crime and Justice* 28, no. 1 (2005): 35–58.

21. Trojanowicz, Kappeler, and Gaines, *Community Policing*, 2002.

22. Peak, *Policing America*, 2000.

23. See, for example, R. H. Langworthy and L. P. Travis III, *Policing in America: A Balance of Forces*, 2nd ed. (Upper Saddle River, NJ: Prentice Hall, 1999).

24. See, for example, Miller and Hess, *Police in the Community*, 2002.

25. M. Orton and T. McDonald, "Homelessness and the Police in Phoenix, Arizona," in M. L. Forst, ed., *The Police and the Homeless* (Springfield, IL: Charles C. Thomas, 1997), 181–96.

26. E. Bittner, "The Police on Skid-Row: A Study of Peace Keeping," *American Sociological Review* 32, no. 5 (1967): 699–715.

27. D. L. Carter and A. D. Sapp, "Police Experiences and Responses Related to the Homeless," *Journal of Crime and Justice* 16, no. 2 (1993): 87–108.

28. Foscarinis and Herz, "New Municipal Ordinances," 1997.

29. Santa Monica Police Department, available at: http://www.santamonicapd.org/units/hipteam.htm.

30. Carter and Sapp, "Police Experiences and Responses," 1993.

31. Ibid.

32. P. Finn, *Street People* (Washington, DC: U.S. Department of Justice, 1998).

33. Carter and Radelet, *Police and the Community*, 1999.

34. Trojanowicz, Kappeler, and Gaines, *Community Policing*, 2002.

35. Ibid., 248.

36. Miller and Hess, *Police in the Community*, 2002.

Chapter Four

THE CRIMINALIZATION OF HOMELESSNESS

Charles Crawford

According to a recent report by the U.S. Department of Housing and Urban Development, there are more than 750,000 homeless people on any given night in America.[1] Given the sheer number of people, being homeless in America raises numerous legal and social challenges around the use of public space and justice. Communities and policy-makers feel they have a right to control behavior in public spaces and should be able to outlaw activities such as panhandling and public sleeping to ensure that citizens are able to enjoy parks and other interaction spaces without annoyances. However, the claim to public space is complicated by the status of homelessness. As Margaret Crawford points out, for those that are homeless, the line between public space and private domestic and economic life are practically nonexistent; occupying parks, streets, sidewalks, and the lawns of public buildings, they claim the space necessary for their own personal and economic survival.[2]

The fight over public space and the sentiments expressed about homeless populations are intense and increasingly physical. A 2005 report from the Center for the Prevention of Hate Violence documented several incidents of threats of violence, property destruction, and sexual harassment directed towards homeless people. As one homeless man in the report states, "The sentiment is that the homeless should be hidden away from society. They, the 'dirty homeless people,' ought to be put somewhere where 'regular' people don't have to see them."[3] As the battle over public space continues with the homeless, many cities have turned to the criminal justice system and ever-increasing penalties for solutions to this complex problem.

THE CRIMINAL JUSTICE RESPONSE TO HOMELESSNESS

As cities across America increasingly turn to the criminal justice system to deal with quality of life and public space issues, numerous laws have been passed specifically targeting homeless populations. In a survey of 224 cities in America, the National Coalition for the Homeless (NCH) and the National Law Center on Homelessness and Poverty (NLCHP) reported the use of city ordinances as a tool to criminalize the homeless. The NHC and NLCHP survey found twenty-eight percent of cities prohibit "camping" in particular public places, whereas sixteen percent had citywide prohibitions on "camping," twenty-seven percent prohibit sitting/lying in certain public places, sixteen percent prohibit loitering citywide, forty-three percent prohibit begging in particular public places, and twenty-one percent have citywide prohibitions on begging.[4]

Furthermore, there appears to be a trend of passing more aggressive laws to remove the homeless from public spaces. Of the sixty-seven cities surveyed in both NCH and NLCHP's 2002 and 2005 reports, there was a twelve percent increase in laws prohibiting begging in certain public places, an eighteen percent increase in laws that prohibit aggressive panhandling, and an additional fourteen percent increase in laws prohibiting sitting or lying in certain public spaces.[5]

Proponents of stricter enforcement have cited various reasons for the involvement of the criminal justice system and the creation of new ordinances. Justifications such as preserving the economic viability of the city and the promotion of tourism are frequently mentioned by supporters.[6] These rationales reflect the impact a chronic public nuisance can have on citizens and cities. Truly aggressive panhandling can create fear in citizens, sidewalks that are made impassable by structures and tents clearly steer the public away from businesses and certain sections of town, and observing criminal behavior may be difficult for the public to ignore. The strong sentiments about how public space can be used are real; however, rather than dealing with the root causes of homelessness and the often intertwined social problems it is easier to create ordinances and focus on removing an unpleasant problem and improving the aesthetics of these spaces.

Laws that target homeless populations may take on many forms, even neutral laws such as open containers or loitering may be strictly enforced and become anti-homeless in their application. However, the ordinances and laws that criminalize homeless populations typically revolve around three areas: sleeping in public, panhandling and begging, and sweeps of city areas where homeless populations tend to gather or live. Each of these categories of ordinances presents unique legal and social challenges for homelessness.

As mentioned earlier, the most comprehensive report on the distribution of anti-homeless ordinances in the United States is the NCH and NLCHP survey of 224 cities. One of the topics included in the report is an analysis of the twenty meanest cities in the country. The cities are selected based on the number of anti-homeless ordinances, the enforcement of the laws, and the severity of penalties. Examining the narratives of select cities from the list in each of the main three areas of criminalization may help to illustrate the situations and battles that face many cities across the United States.

Prohibitions against Sleeping in Public

Of all the criminalization efforts of homelessness, the prohibition and restrictions on where citizens can sleep is at the heart of the battle over public space. For homeless populations there may be few alternatives for finding safe places to sleep. In 2005, nearly one-quarter of the requests for shelter in twenty-four major cities in the United States went unmet.[7] Clearly there is a population that has limited options and sleeping in public may be the sole choice that brings them into conflict with law enforcement and city ordinances. Numerous cities have ordinances against sleeping in public; however the vigorous enforcement by some helps to illustrate the concerns of criminalizing the status of homelessness.

The city of Sarasota, Florida, ranked number one on the twenty meanest cities list. City officials in Sarasota responded to complaints about homeless populations from downtown business owners by passing its first no-camping rule in 2002, along with prohibitions on public urination and aggressive panhandling. Currently the city bans sleeping outside in public or private settings without permission. Within five months of 2003, the police had made 120 arrests under the anti-camping ordinance.

Although the anti-camping laws have been challenged, Sarasota has proven to be persistent and sought to redraft ordinances as they were overturned. Under the latest version there is no pretense about who the law is meant to shift away from public space and sight, because one of the elements necessary for arrest under the new law is that the individual has several personal items and "has no other place to live." However, the new law does allow for police discretion and officers may take the homeless person to the Salvation Army instead of jail. The Sarasota police department came in contact with 4,500 transients and made forty-five arrests under the redrafted code.[8]

The city of Los Angles was ranked eighteenth on the list of the twenty meanest cities because of the city's attempt to "clean up" skid row. Los Angeles's skid row has the highest concentration of homeless people in the United States, with nearly 11,000 living within a few blocks. With the appointment of former New York Police Department Chief William J. Bratton in 2002, Los Angeles has essentially borrowed the broken windows strategy used by New York City during the 1990s by trying to enforce laws that deal with minor infractions in an effort to reduce crime throughout the city as well as making the city more attractive to visitors.

Within this context, the city of Los Angeles enforced a controversial municipal code that was one of the most restrictive in the country. The code was a twenty-four-hour ban on sleeping on public sidewalks as compared to other cities that restrict sleeping in public during certain daytime hours. The code has resulted in legal challenges from homeless populations. In 2003, six homeless people filed a lawsuit against the city of Los Angeles arguing that the law prohibiting sleeping on public sidewalks was unconstitutional and amounted to cruel and unusual punishment because the city did not provide adequate temporary shelter and there was essentially no other place to go. The federal appeals court ruled in the plaintiffs' favor, forcing the city to change its enforcement hours to 6 AM to 9 PM.[9] The ruling has been viewed as a major victory by legal advocates for the homeless, illustrating that anti-lodging laws can be challenged.

Nonetheless, the high level of enforcement has continued in Los Angeles. Since September of 2006, Bratton has added fifty additional police officers to the central division in an effort to target skid row. This has resulted in more than 5,000 arrests for various offenses and has prompted the American Civil Liberties Union (ALCU) to file an injunction against the tactics of the Los Angeles Police Department.[10] The enforcement of anti-camping and lodging laws has dire consequences for homeless populations. In addition to arrests, numerous citations are often issued that result in fines that impoverished citizens simply cannot pay. The city of San Francisco for example, issues roughly 2,000 citations for sleeping on streets or sidewalks, and another 2,000 under city park codes for sleeping under trees each year.[11] Failure to pay fines can result in additional arrests once contact with police has been made, expanding the criminalization of homelessness and pulling people further away from the services they desperately need.

Prohibitions Against Panhandling and Begging

Most pedestrians consider the occasional panhandler a minor annoyance; however, business owners may feel that panhandlers scare off potential customers, and some pedestrians may feel aggravated by the panhandler's plea and even fear depending on the aggressiveness of the person.[12] These concerns have pushed cities to address the issue of panhandling, so in addition to restricting the physical location of homeless populations, numerous cities across the United States have passed anti-panhandling laws essentially criminalizing what some see as free speech. During the late 1980s and early 1990s, cities such as Miami, New York, Seattle, and Minneapolis began passing aggressive panhandling laws often with stiff penalties attached for violation with fines of $500 and up to ninety days in jail.

The city of Atlanta was ranked fourth on the list of the twenty meanest cities because of its recent passing of a comprehensive ban on panhandling and begging. The law makes panhandling illegal in what is viewed as the "tourist triangle" of the city, which covers most of the downtown hotels and tourist spots, including the new $200 million Georgia Aquarium. Furthermore, the ordinance prohibits panhandling within fifteen feet of an ATM, bus stop, taxi stand, pay phone, public toilet, or train station anywhere in the city effectively banning panhandling in Atlanta.

The passing of the ordinance was contested as advocates for the homeless in Atlanta voiced their opposition at a city council meeting. The heated debate at the meeting resulted in two arrests and several opponents being escorted away by the police.[13] The case of Atlanta's prohibition of panhandling raises several concerns. The ACLU of Georgia has planned to fight the ban, calling it too broad and a possible violation of free speech. Beyond the legal issues, the context of Atlanta's homeless population must be considered. In 2006 there were more than 6,000 homeless in Atlanta, with the typical homeless person being an African-American male between the ages of thirty-six and forty-five,[14] which raises the issue of race and class in the enforcement of this law. Anita Beatty, executive director of the Metro Atlanta Task Force for the Homeless, summarized the concern over race: "The real issue here is the business community exaggerating people's fear in order to sweep the city clean of poor African-American males. It's a racist, classist agenda."[15] This concern does have historic validity, as Bass points out, "For the better part of our history, race has been a central determinant in the definition, construction, and regulation of public spaces."[16]

The city of San Francisco was ranked eleventh on the list of meanest cities because of its voters overwhelmingly passing panhandling restrictions in 2004. Under the ordinance, panhandling and solicitation are prohibited near ATM machines, in parking lots, on public transit, median strips, and freeway on-ramps. One section of the ordinance did attempt to divert people who panhandle into mental health and other rehabilitation programs when properly assessed. Violations of the panhandling ordinance typically result in citations; after three violations, future infractions are classified as misdemeanors that can result in incarceration. Although the mayor's office and proponents promised the proposition would not result in panhandlers being incarcerated, violators have been receiving jail time.[17] At the very least, violators may rack up numerous citations and fines further criminalizing their status.

In addition to restrictions of location for panhandling, several cities have taken the unusual step of trying to regulate panhandlers through licensing procedures. The interest in such actions is reflected in the Criminal Justice Legal Foundation publication of a booklet that provides information to cities, mayors, and police chiefs seeking advice on how to curb panhandling.[18] Cities such as Dayton and Akron, Ohio, require people to obtain a registration issued by the chief of police to have a license to panhandle. Under the Akron ordinance, the potential panhandler must meet the basic requirements, submit to fingerprinting, have a photograph taken, and is required to wear the city-issued identification at all times while panhandling.[19] To date, Dayton has issued 186 licenses with sixty-six current, and has made forty-four arrests since the program began. Police officials in the city feel the registration program has eliminated panhandling at night and curbed the amount of panhandling during the day.[20]

It should be noted that citizens do have a valid concern about being free of aggressive solicitation in public places, but requiring registration does raise several issues. For example, this places a burden not only on those who wish to panhandle, but it also requires city tax dollars to process the information, take photographs and fingerprints, and run background checks. This leads one to wonder, might tax dollars be better spent dealing with root causes or more helpful interventions with homelessness?

Although the topic is serious and touches on numerous social issues, a recent article by Larry Elders sheds a humorous reflection on the subject of having homeless panhandlers register for a license and may spur some thought from city officials. In discussing the city of Cincinnati's proposed passing of a panhandling registration, Elders pointed out the contradiction:

> The Cincinnati panhandling application asks for: Home? Apartment number? Phone number? Driver's license? Assuming a panhandler possesses all these things, why panhandle? Oh, well, no doubt the enlightened Cincinnati government will figure it out.[21]

Sweeps of Homeless Areas

Of the three areas of criminalization, it is sweeps of homeless areas that are the most unsettling. Sweeps essentially bring the full power of city officials and law enforcement down upon homeless encampments, raising issues of citizenship, use of space, and constitutional rights. Advocates for homeless rights and services point to the numerous tent cities that have grown across the nation as a glowing indictment against poverty and the lack of affordable housing. Supporters of sweeps look at tent cities as potential health hazards, crime hotspots, and gritty eyesores particularly as they spread into the park like settings of the suburbs. There is little doubt that city officials and workers have the right and duty to keep public areas clean and safe, but what happens when cleaning a public area may involve seizing or destroying someone's shelter and personal property?

The city of Las Vegas was ranked fifth on the twenty meanest cities list for its use of habitual police sweeps of homeless encampments. In 2005, the city began a multi-agency effort to relocate a 125-person homeless encampment located under a downtown bridge. The coordinated effort was supposed to be an attempt to find housing for the people, but transportation spokesperson Bob McKenzie stated the reason for the cleanup was the Clark County Health District declared the site a health hazard because of the homeless urinating and defecating near the encampment.[22]

Although the project was understood to be a coordinated effort to remove the encampment while simultaneously finding shelter for the residents, there appeared to be little planning involved in the undertaking. The metro police told members of the encampment a few days prior to the cleanup that they needed to leave and find shelter by the following Tuesday at 8:00 A.M. By the weekend before the cleanup, forty-five people had found temporary shelter. The remaining eighty residents, some of whom struggled to find assistance and temporary shelter under the time constraints, simply lost all of their worldly possessions including items of survival such as tents, sleeping bags, donated blankets, and medication, as well as personal items such as family photographs.[23]

The transportation spokesperson was quick to point out that there should be assistance available for the homeless; however, public safety should be taken care of first. Advocates for the homeless had to remind the officials that the homeless are a part of the public also and removing them from temporary shelter and destroying personal items does little to help.[24]

Homeless encampments can be elaborate and resemble small towns, which can make sweeps even more dramatic. These tent cities can morph and shift areas depending on the season and the level of law enforcement activity. To date, Seattle and Portland are the only two cities in the United States to legally sanction tent cities. Seattle currently has four such settlements. These tent cities have their own community rules and norms. For example, some residents of Tent City 4 in Seattle claim that the community's strict rules against drug and alcohol use have helped to keep them sober.[25]

The city of Dallas, Texas was ranked sixth on the twenty meanest cities list in part because of the city officials' repeated efforts to remove one of Dallas's most elaborate homeless encampments. The homeless camp in Dallas contained cardboard shacks, tents, portable toilets, and a power source that was tapped from a nearby billboard sign and used to power a community microwave. Dallas officials raided the camp and the structures were bulldozed. The city officials hoped that the demolition would encourage residents to seek help for alcohol, drug, and metal health issues. These efforts were repeated in 2006 as the encampment grew to two sites containing more than 180 residents; these tent cities were also bulldozed.[26] The city devised a new approach for the 2006 effort in which social workers were on hand before the settlement was leveled to ask people on the spot if they wanted to be taken to drug and alcohol or mental health treatment. Ten people were taken away for help, others signed up for later appointments, most refused help and simply packed what they could carry and walked away.

In addition to the razing of homeless encampments, city officials in Dallas tried a different tactic to deal with tent cities by passing an ordinance in 2005 that prohibits churches and other organizations from distributing food to the needy outside of designated areas in the city. The penalty for the violation is a fine up to $2,000. It would appear that the net widening of the criminalization of homelessness has begun as officials felt that mobile feedings simply enable homeless encampments and may contribute to public health problems. However, some charity organizations such as millionaire Phil Romano's Hunger Busters state that they intend to violate the ordinance and feed the homeless wherever they are.[27]

City officials often find themselves walking a thin line between public interest and the Fourth Amendment rights of the homeless. The cleanups and sweeps do temporarily relive communities of the eyesores and smell of human waste, garbage, and criminal activity that may go along with some homeless encampments. Yet most members of these homeless communities return after the destruction to rebuild, as is the case in Dallas, leaving city officials and activists pondering how to break the cycle.

FINDING A REASONABLE RESPONSE TO HOMELESSNESS

By all accounts, the use of ordinances and the criminal justice system to address homelessness is merely a Band-Aid solution. The extreme diversity of the homeless population, which may include people with mental health, drug, and alcohol problems as well as those facing the hardships of poverty, requires a multitude of social services for this multifaceted problem. The need for overlapping services was made clear in a recent study of administrative databases from the San Francisco County jail system.

Of the 12,934 people that were booked into jail during a six-month period, one of every six episodes of incarceration involved a person who was homeless. Furthermore, homeless inmates were significantly more likely than those who were not to receive a psychiatric diagnosis and were more likely to be given diagnoses of substance-related disorders, schizophrenia, and personality disorders.[28] The use of the criminal justice system typically results in higher incarceration rates for those that are arrested for petty crimes such as sleeping in the subway or panhandling. The research also found that homeless inmates had a jail stay that was 4.5 days longer than those that were not homeless.[29]

The Criminal Justice Approach

Clearly the criminal justice system is not designed to provide the types of social services needed to deal with such a complex problem. Although the narratives of several cities have been offered as examples of the criminalization trend and extreme measures, others provide good examples of how to create a constructive and balanced response to the associated problems of homelessness. In 1989, Public Defender Steve Binder helped organize the nation's first homeless court in an effort to assist homeless veterans in San Diego.

The Homeless Court Program (HCP) is essentially special court sessions held in local shelters or convenient locations and is designed to help homeless defendants resolve outstanding misdemeanor cases and citations. The cases typically stem from the quality of life offenses that have been described in the selected narratives from the meanest cities list. As the NHC and NLCHP report illustrates, homeless people are typically caught up in the daily struggle for food, shelter, and basic survival and with few resources to deal with criminal infractions the misdemeanor warrants and citations are often ignored further compounding their criminal justice problems.[30] The resolution of the criminal justice case in the homeless courts serves several purposes. Homeless people are often fearful of courts so the HCP offers a more comfortable setting to deal with the criminal justice problems. In addition to this, the HCP also eases the court case backlog.[31]

The HCP operates a progressive plea bargaining system with an alternative sentencing structure. Most importantly, the program assures no custody. Sentencing substitutes in the HCP may include counseling, participation in shelter programs, and public service. The larger goal here is not to have the criminal justice system install more roadblocks between the needed services and homeless populations. For example, in a traditional court case a homeless defendant may end up with a criminal record, which may preclude them from participation in counseling and treatment programs, living in low-income housing, or obtaining public benefits.

The San Diego HCP appears to be successful, with over 700 cases processed between 1999 and 2001. Survey data collected from participants showed the HCP increased positive attitudes towards law enforcement and satisfaction with the court process, staff, and services.[32] The HCP has served as a model for others and has been replicated in over twenty cities across the country with an additional fifteen communities developing homeless courts.[33] Although these court programs do not address the root causes of homelessness, they do appear to be balanced criminal justice responses to a difficult problem. These are programs that should be explored further in communities that face such challenging issues.

In addition to the court system there are examples of police departments redefining their role and interaction with homeless populations. The city of Fort Lauderdale, Florida, has a population of 150,000 residents and a police force of 500 sworn officers. Within this context there are roughly 5,000 homeless people countywide.[34] The Fort Lauderdale Police Department (FLPD) admits that in the past they used a traditional response, not unlike the many of the departments in the twenty meanest cities. They conducted strict enforcement of the laws and often carried out "bum sweeps" in which officers worked overtime in the early mornings to sweep the homeless from beaches, parks, and downtown.[35]

The major shift in attitude and policy came as advocates for the homeless began to threaten civil lawsuits to fight the criminalization of homelessness.

The FLPD was approached by the Broward Coalition for the Homeless, which offered to assist officers with creating a better response to homeless populations. This sparked the change. The Coalition created a two-hour training program for police officers called Homelessness 101, in which officers were given a greater awareness of the causes and consequences of homelessness. This effort has resulted in the department clearly stating in their policy that homelessness is not a crime.[36]

The FLPD and the Broward Coalition for the Homeless have formed a partnership and created a team made up of police officers and outreach workers who were formerly homeless. The team has been successful. In its five years of operation it has had contact with over 20,000 homeless citizens and placed more than 11,000 in shelters. Most importantly, estimates suggest that the partnership and redesigned police response has resulted in 2,400 fewer arrests each year.[37]

Other city police departments have also shown some innovation in designing a moderate response and avoiding criminalizing homelessness. For example, the Pasadena Police Department created a partnership with the Los Angeles County Department of Health in 2002 to create a H.O.P.E. (Homeless Outreach Psychiatric Evaluation) team. The Pasadena police department details several roles for the team to play, including crisis intervention, mental health calls for service, and most notably to maintain a homeless outreach program. According to the Pasadena police department, the benefits of the homeless outreach program is that it provides referral services for the homeless, reduces future calls, and prevents unnecessary incarceration and hospitalization of the homeless.[38]

Each team consists of a Pasadena police officer and a Los Angeles County Department of Mental Health licensed clinician. The concept of the team is to avoid arrest unless a serious felony has been committed. Most of the minor crimes that have been highlighted in this chapter are viewed as symptoms of other issues such as drug and alcohol dependency. One representative from the health department stated the object is to better care for the homeless and mentally ill, and "rather than throw them into the criminal justice system, we will try and shift them to the social system."[39] The program appears to be paying dividends in numerous ways. According to Police Chief Bernard Melekian, since 2002 H.O.P.E. teams have handled more than 3,000 calls, saving patrol officers more than 2,700 hours.[40]

Chief Melekian reiterated the importance of avoiding arrest and searching for long-term solutions. He stated that in 2004 the city of Pasadena used a traditional criminal justice response in dealing with one chronically homeless person. The city reacted with police, fire department, and paramedic responses along with subsequent hospitalizations that totaled more than $600,000.[41] Clearly criminalizing homelessness has a dollar cost associated with it that should make most citizens, criminal justice, and city officials reevaluate the traditional justice response. The creative approach Pasadena has used in dealing with homelessness has been recognized, as the International Association of Chiefs of Police presented the department with a community policing award for seeking long-term solutions to the city's problems rather than just jailing the homeless.

The West Hollywood Police Department has also created a constructive response to homelessness. In 1995 the West Hollywood Police Department partnered with a West Hollywood homeless organization in an attempt to address citizen's concerns about homeless people in public and private spaces as well as treating homeless citizens respectfully and avoiding traditional sweeps and arrests. The department maintains a five- to six-officer outreach team that travels with service workers from the homeless organization. The officers essentially remain in the background unless there is a clear threat or criminal activity occurring. This partnership has two purposes. First, it allows the service worker to travel in remote parts of the city to reach homeless encampments and deliver counseling/assessment during early morning or late night hours. In addition, it provides balance for law enforcement by keeping officers from resorting to unwarranted traditional tactics such as citations and arrests. According to representatives from both the police department and homeless rights advocates, the program has been successful in both reducing unnecessary police involvement and providing assistance to West Hollywood's homeless population.[42]

CONCLUSION

Very few groups challenge the concept of public space more than homeless populations. Cities do have the right to be concerned about public health and the safety of its citizenry. Although some of the behaviors that cities target may appear trivial or minor, when there is a large number of people engaged in the same behavior (e.g., sidewalk sleeping, aggressive panhandling, or setting up camps) it can affect hundreds of people per hour in any given city. From this standpoint the use of the criminal justice system would seem like a reasonable response to most citizens, and it may be hard to deny the surface-level effectiveness of this approach. Sweeps and aggressive enforcement do tend to move homeless populations out of sight, but they turn our city's centers into battle zones and areas of social drama.

Resorting to coercion and heavy-handed enforcement to remove the homeless is nothing new. Once the populations have been removed through sweeps or other measures, the issue becomes what services are in place to assist this dislocated population? For most cities it is difficult and complex work designing a balanced response to ensure that citizen feelings of safety, free enterprise of business, and appropriate services for homeless populations are all met. Given these constraints it is simply easier for most officials to give into citizens and business owners by locking up the homeless or moving them along.

It has been made clear throughout history that trying to use technical solutions to solve social problems typically results in failure or exacerbating the problem in unforeseen ways. The temperance movement of the early twentieth century and the subsequent prohibition of alcohol, and the crack cocaine "fiasco" of the 1980s and its well-documented impact on minority defendants in federal sentencing are only two examples. Social problems real, created, or imagined are rarely resolved through law enforcement. Fortunately, for each of the cities that have been ranked one of the twenty meanest by the NCH and NLCHP, there are other cities across the nation that can serve as examples of balanced approaches.

The problems that are enmeshed in homelessness are typically beyond the scope of any one city's government. To deal effectively with homelessness it will take local and national governments, volunteers, private sources of aid, and a mix of various social and emergency services in a coordinated effort that not only addresses the issues of affordable housing, but also the mental health system. As Gregg Barak points out, policies that hide the problem, instead of those that attempt to come to grips with the underlying causes of homelessness and the housing crisis, are clearly not the policies needed.[43]

As cities begin to understand their homeless populations, the multiple problems and sheer diversity of the group may appear to make a reasonable balanced response difficult to achieve. Trying to end the spatial war zones and battles in many downtown areas and homeless encampments may appear to be an arduous task. However, sweeping the problem away and criminalizing the surface actions of survival for some is not a feasible or long-term solution. To paraphrase Barak and Bohm, it is time we stop doing things "to" and "for," and begin to do things "with" homeless populations in a team effort to help.[44] It is a difficult balancing act because there are multiple claims made on public spaces, but clear examples exist and can serve as starting points for designing, evaluating, and improving multi-agency and system-wide responses, with problem-solving as the long-term goal rather than criminalization and punishment.

NOTES

1. Housing and Urban Development, "Annual Homeless Assessment Report (AHAR)," 2005, http://www.hud.gov/offices/cpd/homeless/ahar.cfm.

2. M. Crawford, "Contesting the Public Realm: Struggles over Public Space in Los Angeles," *Journal of Architectural Education* 49, no. 1 (1995): 4–9.

3. Center for the Prevention of Hate Violence, "Homeless and Hated: Bias Motivated Violence, Degradation and Discrimination Against Maine's Homeless," 2005, 19, http://www.preventinghate.org/publications/homeless.htm.

4. National Coalition for the Homeless and the National Law Center on Homelessness and Poverty, "A Dream Denied: The Criminalization of Homelessness in U.S. Cities," 2006, 9, http://www.nationalhomeless.org/publications/reports.html.

5. Ibid.
6. M. Foscarinis, K. Cunningham-Bowers, and K. Brown, "Out of Sight—Out of Mind? The Continuing Trend toward the Criminalization of Homelessness," *Georgetown Journal on Poverty Law and Policy* 2 (1999): 145–59.
7. U.S. Conference of Mayors, "Hunger and Homelessness Continues to Rise in U.S. Cities," 2005, http://www.citymayors.com/features/uscity_poverty.html.
8. M. Saewitz, "Sarasota Collects 'Meanest City' Title," *Herald Tribune,* January 12, 2006.
9. H. Weinstein and C. M. DiMassa, "Justices Hand L.A.'s Homeless a Victory," *Los Angeles Times*, April 15, 2006.
10. R. Winton and M. DiMassa, "ACLU Seeks Court Injunction in Skid Row Cleanup," *Los Angeles Times,* March 2, 2007.
11. K. Fagan, "L.A.'s Homeless Law Ruled Unconstitutional," *San Francisco Chronicle*, April 15, 2006.
12. R. Ellickson, "Controlling Chronic Misconduct in City Spaces: Of Panhandlers, Skid Rows, and Public-Space Zoning," *Yale Law Journal* 105, no. 5 (1996): 1165–1248.
13. L. Copeland and C. Jones, "Atlanta Puts Heat on Panhandlers," *USA Today,* August 15, 2005.
14. Crossroads Ministry, "Who is homeless in Atlanta?" http://www.crossroadsatlanta.org/.
15. Copeland and Jones, "Atlanta Puts Heat on Panhandlers," 2005.
16. S. Bass, "Policing Space, Policing Race: Social Control Imperatives and Police Discretionary Decisions," *Social Justice* 28, no. 1 (2001): 156–76.
17. R. Brown, "Busting Beggars," *San Francisco Bay Guardian,* July 20, 2005.
18. K. Scheidegger, "A Guide to Regulating Panhandling," 1993, http://www.cjlf.org/publctns/Panhandling/Pcvr_bio.htm.
19. City of Akron News Releases, "Curbing Panhandlers," 2006, http://www.ci.akron.oh.us/News_Releases/2006/0612.htm.
20. S. Russell, "License to Beg," *Downtown Journal*, 2005, http://www.downtown-journal.com/index.php?publication=downtown&page=65&story=3293.
21. L. Elders, "Coming to a City Near You ... License to Panhandle?" 2003, http://www.jewishworldreview.com/cols/elder071703.asp.
22. T. Pratt, "About 125 Homeless Displaced," *Las Vegas Sun*, January 19, 2005.
23. Ibid.
24. Ibid.
25. C. Rowe, "Tent City Residents are Homeless on their own Terms," *Seattle Post-Intelligencer Reporter,* December 11, 2004.
26. K. Horner, "City Razes Homeless Camp Downtown," *The Dallas Morning News,* May 11, 2005.
27. T. Korosec, "Dallas Law Cracks Down on Feeding the Homeless," *Houston Chronicle,* August 7, 2005.
28. D. McNiel, R. Binder, and J. Robinson, "Incarceration Associated with Homelessness, Mental Disorder, and Co-occurring Substance Abuse," *Psychiatric Services* 56, no. 7 (2005): 840–6.
29. Ibid., 843.
30. National Coalition for the Homeless and the National Law Center on Homelessness and Poverty, "Dream Denied," 2006.
31. California Collaborative Justice Programs, "Homeless Courts," 2007, http://www.courtinfo.ca.gov/programs/collab/homeless.htm.

32. Ibid.

33. National Coalition for the Homeless and the National Law Center on Homelessness and Poverty, "Dream Denied," 2006.

34. B. Pusins, "The Fort Lauderdale Model: Police Response to Homelessness," 2000, http://ci.ftlaud.fl.us/police/homeless5.html.

35. Ibid.

36. Ibid.

37. National Coalition for the Homeless and the National Law Center on Homelessness and Poverty, "Dream Denied," 2006.

38. Pasadena Police Department, "Field Operations Division: H.O.P.E. Team," 2007, http://www.ci.pasadena.ca.us/police/Div_FieldOps/HopeTeam.asp.

39. E. Parker, "HOPE Instead of Handcuffs," *San Gabriel Valley Tribune,* January 19, 2002.

40. E. Parker, "Helping the Homeless," *Star-News,* October 5, 2005.

41. Ibid.

42. "Operation Outreach: Homeless, Helpless, or Hopeless?" *Sheriff Times* 1, no. 2 (1996).

43. G. Barak, "Homelessness and the Case for Community-Based Initiatives: The Emergence of a Model Shelter as a Short Term Response to the Deepening Crisis in Housing," in H. E. Pepinsky and R. Quinney, eds., *Criminology as Peacemaking* (Bloomington: Indiana University Press, 1991), 65.

44. G. Barak and R. Bohm, "The Crimes of the Homeless or the Crime of Homelessness? On the Dialectics of Criminalization, Decriminalization, and Victimization," *Crime, Law and Social Change* 13, no. 3 (1989): 275–88.

Chapter Five

THE BEST OF TIMES, THE WORST OF TIMES: REFLECTIONS OF A SERVICE PROVIDER

Michael Chesser

Winter, 1995. The house meeting had just gotten started with the usual banter among the men in the Transitional Housing Program. As the group settled in, the common complaint seemed to be how tired everyone was—tired of work or tired from work, tired of the daily cares—just, well, tired. And, as usual, being tired, like many other things, got related to religion. Ronnie said he was ready for the Lord to come back and set up his new heaven and new Earth. Anthony said it wouldn't be a new heaven and new Earth—he said our perception would change and the old heaven and the old Earth would still be around, we'd see it differently. Erwin was adamant—hopeful of a new heaven and a new Earth—it had to be so, he insisted—it just had to be, because as he told us all, "he wasn't doing so well in this heaven and this Earth."

Homeless people not doing well in this heaven and Earth? How can that be what with all the money we spend and the programs we have to assist homeless people?

WHAT DOES IT MEAN TO BE HOMELESS?

It's doubtful that home always carries fond memories for everyone. Surely, home can be the place of both great joy and great sorrow. Such, though, is to be expected, for home is the place where we grow up and there is always great joy and great sorrow in growing up. Home is never idyllic; but then neither is life and home is part of life. But home is home, more than house, less than Eden.

Whenever one asks a homeless person what he or she wants most, the answer is, invariably "a place of my own." And that, of course, is home. A place of my own: a place where, for a few hours a day, we can close the door on the world. It is a place where we rule, that is ordered by our thoughts and priorities and values. It is a place of safety and security. It is a place where we learn to get along, to resolve conflict, to be responsible, to honor our obligations, to serve, to love, and to be loved, and be served. It is the place where our holiday traditions and rituals are established and perpetuated. It is the place of familiarity where the rules of living are known and that creates a sense of security and belonging, connectedness, and meaning.

These are precisely the things a homeless person does not have. These are precisely the things a homeless child does not experience. Homeless means being disconnected, not belonging, being insecure, and unsure. It means following the rules, values, and priorities of others—it means being unfree, a captive, and a stranger in the land. And the unfree, by definition, are dependent. In dependency, honor, integrity, and one's sense of worth are forfeited.

What does it mean to be homeless? It means there is no meaning to life. It means life is a series of disconnected, transient events held together by the occasional hot shower and the daily meal at the local soup kitchen.

WHAT ARE THE CAUSES OF HOMELESSNESS?

If we are being honest, we probably do not know why people become homeless. What we do know is twofold. First, homelessness is not a career choice for ninety-nine percent of homeless people. (We do not address the one percent for which it is.) Second, the things we label as causes are no more than contributing factors. There is not "a cause" of homelessness.

We would probably like to say that the root cause of homelessness is poverty. Yet, even that is not the cause. Although it is true that many homeless people grew up in poverty, many, nay most, people experiencing poverty are permanently housed. Also, a good number of homeless people grew up in the middle class. Economic class is not the cause of homelessness.

We would probably like to say that the lack of a good, marketable education is the cause of homelessness. Again, it is true that many homeless people lack good education, read and spell poorly, and are dismal failures at arithmetic, but then, that is also true of a lot of college graduates. I have worked with homeless men who hold PhDs and/or master's degrees in engineering, economics, and other disciplines. It is not unusual to find the college graduate among the homeless. Lack of education is not the cause of homelessness.

This little exercise with economic class and education has a point. In every discipline, we have fallen in love with the cause and effect relationship. If we can identify the cause and know the effect, surely we can provide the solution. And that fable permits us to reduce human life to the mechanical; and that will not change lives. We want to hold on to the cause and effect relationship because it is simple, because we do not really want to think, because we really do not want to engage the whole person. We want the cause and effect relationship to hold because it is neat and clean. But life is messy and sometimes, even sordid. Life is confusing and mysterious and, far more than we want to admit, beyond our control.

We want the cause and effect relationship to hold, we use the mechanistic, resort to reductionism, and fail to engage the whole homeless person for a reason. We do all of that so we do not have to examine our own lives. To engage the wholeness of another, we must also engage our own humanness. And that can be a fearsome task.

The training of our new case managers engages these notions. Our task at this point is to create in the new case manager a sense of humility—a lost virtue in our society. For without humility, a case manager can never truly be a catalyst for change.

If there is no "cause" of homelessness, what are the contributing factors? There are of course, the obvious things: poor education, lack of job skills and work experience, chemical dependency, lack of coping skills, lack of stress management techniques, lack of personal discipline, lack of a developed sense of responsibility, poor credit history, lack of direction and goals, poor decision making skills, inability to see the likely consequences of an action, domestic abuse, poverty, and so forth. The contributing factor is—life. How does one live in a complex, modern, technological, "aspiritual" society? Most of us live in it because we do not think about it. In working with the homeless, we must get them to think about it.

Transitional Housing

It is not reasonable to expect a homeless person to address the issues of living and make the effort to hold body and soul together. Our transitional housing program is designed to permit a person to deal with the issues in their life without having to work. We pay the rent, the utilities, and the telephone bill, and we provide child care and a host of other supportive services. The homeless person's full-time job is to resolve the difficulties that have led to their homeless status.

Our folks come to us by referral from other human service agencies: the Drug and Alcohol Commission, emergency shelters, halfway houses, mental health agencies, outreach teams, departments of social services, and others. Once referred, we begin a rather lengthy assessment period. We require a psychological evaluation, a physical examination, and, if there is a history of chemical dependency, a drug and alcohol assessment. While these things are being done, we gather a social history and assess their educational background, work experience and history, as well as job skills. A case manager coordinates all of these assessment tools. During the assessment period, the case manager will assign the homeless person several small tasks: arrange transportation to the medical exam, call for an appointment to establish food stamp eligibility, and the like. The homeless person's actions in these tasks will often demonstrate their level of commitment. If they are not willing to do these small tasks, their chances of self-sufficiency are very limited.

Once the assessment is complete, the case manager determines if the program will benefit the homeless person. Although many are needy, not all will benefit. Once accepted into the program, a case plan is developed in conjunction with the homeless person. Goals are established with appropriate time frames and the game is on. Please be aware that although housing is provided, ours is not a housing program. We provide housing so that a person has an opportunity to develop the skills and resolve their personal issues to become self-determining. To do that, we may work with a person for as long as two years.

The Reality of the Work

Transitional housing programs exist in order that homeless people may gain the skills necessary to be self-determining. The ultimate goal is that the homeless person will become permanently housed. This is accomplished through intensive case management. Our case managers have a small caseload, usually around ten persons/families. Case managers are required to make daily contact and have at least one in-home visit per week. The case manager's task is to coordinate all of the services the assigned client needs to fulfill the case plan: arrange transportation, establish interview times for things such as psychotherapy, and a host of other duties.

In the first days, all generally goes well. Clients keep appointments, are cooperative, and have the best of intentions. But about the sixth week of residency, things begin to unravel: work is missed, appointments are broken, plans change abruptly without notifying the case manager, and program rules are violated. Now, we really do not know why this occurs. We suspect it has to do with the first attempts by the homeless persons to assert themselves—to live by their own rules, values, and priorities. Surely, that is a positive step—the desire to be independent emerges. It is negative in that the homeless person is not ready to embrace that freedom.

One might think a homeless person would be appreciative and grateful for the opportunity they have been given, that they would be compliant, eager to make the necessary changes in their lives. That is not the case. The problem of change has been an issue among theologians, psychologists, sociologists, governments, and revolutionaries for ages.

Change is a fearsome thing. The goals for which change is made are often too far away. To go from being homeless on the street to a responsible, permanently housed person is a huge leap. Change, of course, means doing things differently. Doing things differently means a change in the rules, it means living in the unfamiliar, and it means not really knowing the outcome. Change is very hard work. We would rather live in chaotic familiarity than serene uncertainty.

But change must occur for the homeless person. They must face their fear, overcome anxiety, and be willing to fail. At this point, the case manager becomes a cheerleader. A small success, for example, setting up a payment plan on a long overdue bill, is saluted and hailed as a major accomplishment.

In these kinds of programs, the general rule is failure not success—at least not meaningful, lasting success. Most homeless folks cannot sustain the force for change and resort to the familiar comfortable ways of the past. Because failure is the rule and not the exception, it raises some interesting problems. Case managers, in very real ways, foster failure. Not intentionally of course, but as an outgrowth of their jobs and, perhaps, misguided societal norms. Homeless people are notoriously impatient; they want what they want when they want it. Case managers are also notoriously impatient; they want immediate success for their clients. Society is notoriously impatient and demonstrates what Kahn has referred to as the "brown butterfly syndrome"—easy and comfort without effort, right now. Therefore case managers must be patient.

Patience, though, is problematic. When does patience become indifference and tolerance license? Traditionally, transitional housing programs have a maximum stay of two years. A forty-year-old single mom with two children has to reorder forty years of experience and alter forty years of perception in two. Case managers are under the gun—hurry up because the clock's ticking. Hurry up, but do not be impatient. Consequently, case managers often face the prospect of becoming cynical and calling into question the meaningfulness of what they do.

The question becomes "Am I doing these folks any good?" It would seem, on the surface, to be a rhetorical question. But the issue is far deeper. Compliance from the client is often only conditionally forthcoming—to remain in the program. No real learning occurs. Second, what the client receives from the program is, in most cases, more than they will be able to maintain on their own. They receive housing; utilities; telephone; medical, dental, and psychological care; child care; transportation; and more. With the exception of psychological care, these are the necessities of life. They cannot be sustained in a job that pays seven dollars per hour. Perhaps as telling is the philosophy. What are we teaching them that has lasting value and meaning?

We preach freedom and responsible choice, and, equally important, we teach the acceptance of the consequence of choice. Only in decision and the acceptance of the consequence of decision is there freedom. If we have, own, possess stuff (houses, cars, washers, televisions, etc.) these soon become the master of our lives. We must repair the car; we must have the car to get to work, church, play, get the kids, and so on. The same is true of all the stuff we accumulate—we forfeit our freedom. But it is not a choice. Without an automobile (especially true in our community, which lacks an effective public transportation system), one cannot engage the life of the community or expand one's own life beyond walking distance.

The question is: "Are we, in an effort to prepare homeless people to be self-sufficient, in effect setting them up for failure, or at best to be second class citizens?" We often talk of these things among ourselves. We make an effort at self-condolence by suggesting that we offer an opportunity—in reality that's what we do. We offer homeless people an opportunity to partially correct the consequences of the past, to re-learn, to change perceptions. We want this opportunity to provide hope for a better future. Privately, we wonder if the opportunity is really an opportunity and if the hope is not false.

An Excursus: Economic Reform

I am not trained in economics, but in theology. Yet, the practical experience of working with the homeless people I am called to serve has led me to see the need for a re-allocation of our nation's economic resources. There is no doubt that welfare was in need of reform. The reports we are getting lead us to believe the success of reform. But our efforts at welfare reform do nothing to attack poverty. If programs such as ours are to be successful, we need as a nation to provide the necessities of modern living to the poor; and we need to do so at little or no cost to them.

Above, we briefly addressed the transportation crunch. The private automobile is a most ineffective way to get to and from work, and it is not available to the poor. In my community, many higher paying jobs are in suburban industrial parks. Our local transportation system maintains sporadic, first-shift hours to these jobs. They are not accessible to the poor, especially on off-shifts.

Services needed by the homeless are located in the inner city—DSS, drug and alcohol services, free medical clinics, community health centers, and so forth. Low-income housing (which is all a program like ours can afford) is located in or very near the city. Rare is the grocery, pharmacy, doctor, or library located near low-income housing—the neighborhoods have the wrong image. If we are to address poverty, if we are to offer the current population of homeless people real hope and opportunity, we need a public transportation system that effectively matches the advantages of the private automobile. Public transportation needs to be readily available (no more than thirty minutes between pick-ups) and serve the job market on all shifts.

The same is true of child care. Single parents could afford to work at lower-paying jobs if child care was available at nominal or no cost. They could afford to work the off-shift if off-shift child care was available. If we want to provide people with an opportunity to be self-sufficient, we need to provide the services that make that possible. Certainly, we have the resources to do this. Whether we have the will and courage to do that is another question.

A Miscellany of Problems

One thing we learned early on in our adventure is, in addition to the normal problems our folks bring with them, there are always special individual problems as well. These "out of the ordinary" situations bring groans and variety to our work. Working with recently released prisoners is very difficult. Working with the illegal alien raises lots of groans, for example, or the homeless man who spoke only Polish, had no green card, was present in the United States on a tourist visa that had expired eight years earlier. Finding an interpreter in order to communicate with him took three weeks. Working with the pedophile brought special dangers and liabilities. Having homeless clients sell illegal drugs from one of your homeless shelters is always interesting. Having a former drug abuser relapse and sell the furniture from the homeless shelter always adds to the variety of daily life. Working with the pregnant thirty-seven-year-old illiterate female who had five children and no work history or skills was most challenging.

You get the point. There is no such thing as the routine homeless case. They all bring special problems and concerns to our desks. A case manager must be all things to all people—equipped to deal with the most "routine" problem and equipped to use imagination to handle off-the-wall problems.

THE BEST OF TIMES

The work can be and often is depressing, frustrating, and tedious. Service providers must be able to survive on a minimum of success. But the joys are real, the pleasure is intense, and the fullness of being human is present when, for example:

- Sherry got her teeth fixed and came by to give me one of the most beautiful smiles I have ever seen. Her self-confidence just soared.
- John finally trusted me enough to sit sobbing in the park and tell me how afraid of life he was.
- Peter, age twenty, got his first full-time job working with a landscaping company. He was finally, "like all men should be."
- Latoya, aged six, Latrissa's daughter, got her first puppy.
- Joanne took into her small two-bedroom home a stray, full-grown St. Bernard. The homeless sheltering the homeless.

Our folks do succeed and life does flourish. From time to time, there is even peace.

THE OTHER SIDE

The fun part of working with the homeless is being a case manager. Despite the sorrow and frustration, the short-lived success, this is where the action is. But we do not pay case managers much, so if human services is to be the career that allows us to live the life we see on television, one must become an *administrator*. Overnight—effective with the day of "promotion" one becomes resident expert in all things, great and small. The administrator knows all of the answers, knows where all of the land mines are hidden, knows every person of influence in town, knows every applicable public law, and is expert in double-entry accrual accounting. The workday is now long—sixteen hours is a good start and dreams should lead to new methods of fundraising.

Grant Writing

Writing a grant is like shooting in the dark. Grant writers write for grant readers. The language used is specialized jargon like "human services delivery system" (where to go for help), "seamless system" (all of the bases are covered), and "Continuum of Care" (we have involved everyone we could think of in this project). Language, which used to be a method of communicating an idea clearly, has no place in grant writing. Know the jargon. Cloak the project in language acceptable to the reader (whom you have never met). Close reading of the NOFA (notice of funding availability) or RFP (request for proposal) can supply the writer with language clues.

NOFA's usually arrive at one's office three days before the application deadline. By the time the mail has been date-stamped (an essential agency action: it verifies that the NOFA is real) and finally gets to the grant writer's desk, two days are left before the application deadline. Reading the NOFA takes half a day. Contacting the grantor for clarification takes half a day, if they can be reached (grant readers, in anticipation of all that reading, usually take a vacation the week before application deadlines).

Developing the budget to bring the project to reality, if funded, is always an adventure. Grant writers know that cost effectiveness is critical to being funded. They also know grantor's rarely fund at the requested level. This makes an interesting game. Grant writer: how much can I pad the budget and still be cost-effective? Grantor: how much have they padded the budget and given the appearance of being cost-effective? Usually the grantor wins. What is funded is rarely enough to do the work.

Most funding cuts are directed at staff salaries. Do with less people. But human services work is labor intensive. Most program participants, or recipients, or clients, or customers need close, directive support. Caseloads need to be very restricted so that the case manager can actively follow the customer daily. But the cost of one case manager runs between $50,000 and

$60,000 a year. What's included? Salary, fringe benefits, travel, training, office space, supplies, telephone, and supervision.

The next place cuts are made is in the area of supportive services. In homeless programs, supportive services are essential. Affordable housing and living wage jobs are important, of course. But unless supportive services are available, the homeless person is destined to remain in or return to their homeless state.

Here's an example. In my community, services are available to a single person free of charge if their annual income is less than $8,400. That's about $190 a week, gross. After taxes, it is about $152. If a single homeless person seeks drug and alcohol treatment and makes more than $190 a week they must pay for the service. Now, a homeless person seeking drug and alcohol help is probably actively using. They are not going to have the resources to pay for treatment. They aren't going to have fifty dollars up front for assessment, orientation, and staffing. On the other hand, drug and alcohol treatment centers must pay staff and operating expenses. They simply cannot afford to provide pro bono for all who are in need. And, in this example, the sad part is that those who suffer drug and alcohol problems rarely become sober and rarely abstain the first time treatment is provided. They are simply not ready. One strike and you're out is punitive—three strikes and you're out is better, but in some cases still inadequate.

It is not that grantors are ignorant of the problem. Their responsibility is to fund as many programs as possible. The U.S. Department of Housing and Urban Development (HUD) has recently drawn fire for continuing to provide supportive services as an eligible activity for its national Supportive Housing Program (SHP) competition. The criticism is that supportive services, if funded at all, should be funded by the U.S. Department of Health and Human Services (HHS). HUD should be concerned with housing. At least HUD, for all its flaws and missteps, understands the issue. If such legislation is passed, many very good, sound, effective homeless programs will die. Why? Housing is, as I have repeatedly emphasized, critical, but not the overriding issue. Their objective is addressing and resolving the contributing factors of drug and alcohol abuse, education, job training, transportation, and child care. So if one applies to HUD for housing, one must also apply to HHS for services: twice the work. HUD may fund, HHS may not, or vice versa. So an agency may be left with a housing program and no services or a host of services and no housing. Sometimes, it seems, we step over quarters to pick up nickels.

Working with Other Agencies

The trend today is to involve as many agencies as possible in a given project. Grantors love to see a page of involved agencies as part of their application. This is called concerted community involvement. Now, concerted community involvement brings together in one room many resident experts who are very important and very busy and indispensable. A 1:00-PM meeting usually convenes by 1:30. Such meetings are well attended. The need to establish one's importance and visibility is essential. Without fail, the one person who truly knows something is being important and visible at a meeting about which he/she knows nothing. The meeting is usually convened by the most senior administrator present with something like "While we wait for Jane/John, let's rehearse the known parameters of the population this Continuum intends to bring into the delivery system under the HUD SHP initiative delineated by this NOFA." This is immediately followed by some important, highly visible person's cell phone ringing. Everyone waits sharing knowing smiles, using the time to consult their Daytimers.

It is easy to poke fun at the egos that make up these community-building meetings. But the truth is they are necessary—both the egos and the meetings. Funders are pleased when the involvement in a project appears to cover a broad spectrum of the community: human service providers, business, banks, religious organizations, volunteers, and government. The concept is good; the reality is something less. Usually, the bulk of the actual work falls to a few people, generally those who are most concerned and most knowledgeable about the project underway. These meetings do create new ventures, more cooperation among a wide variety of enterprises, and keep people informed.

Duplication of services and the elimination of such is a key issue in the human services arena. But, I think it is a false issue. Duplication of services exists when the service supplied exceeds the demand. When the demand for a service is equal to or exceeds the supply, duplication does not exist. Now to mandate that a service be consolidated under one provider may be justified, but often is not feasible. A given agency may not have space or staff to meet the need. The agency may not want to expand for reasons of mission or limiting their service areas. What may be advantageous in consolidation is decreasing overhead and supervisory staff.

What is really needed is a universal (at least a community-wide) criteria for access to services, waiting periods before a person may re-enter the system in the event of noncompliance, common in-take forms, and general access to this information. If homeless people knew that every agency and religious organization in town operated under the same regulations, procedures, and waiting periods there would be less effort to beat the system. Duplication is not the issue; having a universal system is. Why isn't such a system in place? It calls for change.

Working with Funders

The lifeblood of any human service project is funding. As public contributions are only a fraction of what is needed, most agencies rely on government and foundations. Funders do not fund what they are not interested in. In that respect, working with funders is easy—there exists common ground and common goals.

Some funders set their regulations in place, provide technical assistance for compliance, audit once a year or so, and leave you to do the work. The U.S. Department of Housing and Urban Development (HUD) is an example of this. It is a pleasure to work with the local field office of Community Planning and Development (CPD)/HUD. They want your program to succeed and often find ways to enhance program directions. Personal relationships based on common objectives are built and support is received. Unless one does something really stupid or attempts to deceive, one can enjoy these relationships.

Other funders, far too many, want to micromanage the program. They delve into program criteria, attempt to set limits on duration of services, limit services to "acceptable" persons (no homosexuals for example), and even want to reshape management techniques. They often visit program sites several times a year and do so en masse—five or six people in the party. No program has yet been known to satisfy these funders. Why bother with them? Without money, nothing gets done. It is a fact of human services life, inescapable, mandatory. Consequently, keeping funders happy is essential.

Administrators often feel like hypocrites. It is hard to be open and honest, to maintain personal integrity and honor when one really must be all things to all people. It is a constant strain having to choose language that will not offend, cloak answers in half-truths, be aware of the personal agendas of those with whom one speaks, and be aware of their hot buttons and areas where they feel threatened. Adult people are fragile, egos are easily dented, feelings are hurt—our "touchy-feely," yet radically "bottom-line" society has made it so.

So we are wary of funders, yet play the game. It seems senseless and more profoundly, meaningless. There are too many people in need of so much, with too few resources and too many "hoops" to make the work worthwhile. But, from time to time, one hears again the call—people are worth the effort. The call may revisit us as a spiritual confirmation, or a sense of human dignity, or the stark realization that one must work to eat. I think, though, for the most part, people want to help people. The need is there—it is endless and eternal, and some step into the breach and make the effort. The trick is to know that you are not defined by success or failure or the necessary hypocrisy. The trick is to know you must play the game—the trick is to admit the games one plays. Devastation and loss of one's person happens when we come to believe we are not playing a game.

Reporting

Every funder requires program reports. These are not bad in themselves because funders need information and programs need to know where they stand. Reports are necessary and valuable, even if they are (and they definitely are) time consuming to generate. From an agency standpoint, the problem is that all funders want different information. A problem is that reporting periods differ from funder to funder—some monthly, quarterly, or annually. Some want quantitative reports whereas others want qualitative reports and still others want both.

Now, the information necessary to generate a report begins at the in-take and case-management level. These people must gather data, assess, staff, plan, and keep score. Keeping score is a low priority (rightly so, I think) for them, but a very high priority for administrators. Administrators cannot get enough information. A natural conflict exists between administrators and case managers. A good case manager has more to do than they can accomplish; yet, they can provide really good, accurate information. So we try to schedule office days—days for paperwork and the compiling of information. Usually, case managers are sick on these days. Threats to their personal well-being are effective cures. Information is amassed, usually in illegible form—only doctors have worse handwriting. Usually colleagues will help colleagues, and the information is gained. Now the task is to put it in the form that the funder requests. Formats differ, information requested differs, and time of submission differs. An administrator could spend their life generating reports—that is why there are administrative assistants.

Let me address one critical area of reporting. In this age of accountability, funders are requiring outcome-based goals as part of the application. An outcome-based goal for a homeless program might be something like this: fifty percent of all people who complete their case plan will become permanently housed for at least one year. Sounds very good, professional, and certain. The funder needs to have some assurance some good will come from their money. Programs need some objective ways to measure productivity and effectiveness.

However, the premise of outcome-based goals is wrongheaded. It assumes one can control and predict outcome, which, in fact, one cannot do. The old, time worn adage, "You can lead a horse to water, but you can't make it drink" has special relevance here. We can provide the services; arrange drug and alcohol treatment, mental health intervention, job training, child care, life skills courses, and more, but we cannot make it "take." That is beyond our control. To require accountability where one has no control is akin to making one responsible to see that a task is done, but granting no authority to get it done. It is senseless.

What are possible are input goals. Such a goal might read: 100 percent of all homeless persons enrolled in the program will receive at least ten hours of instruction in the South Carolina Landlord-Tenant Act. Such instruction will be given during the first three months in residency. This is a measurable goal. This can be controlled. If a person does not receive the necessary instruction within the mandated time period, administration/management can determine why and hopefully rectify the error.

Working with Local Government

This is the black hole of human services work. Local government does not trust service providers who, in turn, do not trust local government. This quality relationship stifles productive work. Local government does not have the resources to determine the areas of need within the community or the intensity of the problem. They rely on service providers to inform them. But they know service providers need money, so government has a tendency to view the information provided askance. Government believes agencies inflate the need and overdramatize its intensity. And there is some truth to that, especially because there is no effective way to present numbers in an unduplicated manner.

Agencies may provide service to the same person. Each agency counts that as a person served and that, of course, inflates the number. What government needs to understand is there is no intentional attempt to deceive. Inflated numbers grow out of requested reports. Such numbers do, however, put us on notice with regard to the intensity of the problem. The problem for those who are homeless is probably greater than we understand if they are seeking services from so many agencies.

The truth is there is not a good method to determine the number of homeless people in a given community. How many homeless people are there? A lot. Is that a good enough answer? Probably not. But providing numbers isn't either. Numbers are either too high or too low. Numbers, at best, are only approximate: even good, well-thought out, methodologically sound surveys won't provide complete accuracy.

The natural conflict between service providers and local government officials sets the stage for the more serious problem. Distrusting the information given by service providers, local officials rely on their personal opinion of homeless needs, problems, and solutions. These are, at least in our community, ill-informed and stereotypical: The homeless are hobos and tramps, lazy beggars who could take care of themselves if they'd quit drinking or drugging or conning. Consequently, public policy is developed and public funds expended on the basis of the local officials' usually uninformed opinion, which is why service providers distrust local government officials.

Accurate information is necessary. An understanding of the problem is essential. The admission that a socially unacceptable problem (homelessness) exists is critical. We need the support of local government to assist us in these areas. A good start would be for units of local government (ULG) to meet and develop uniform reporting criteria and time frames, then meet for a frank discussion of the problem, then determine which ULG will assume responsibility for a certain portion of the problem, for example, housing or transportation or services. Perhaps then, we could get on with it.

CONCLUSION

There are real joys, heartaches, frustration, and success in working with the homeless. It is not easy work. It requires some expertise in a wide arena of subjects: programs, politics, time management, funding, administration, human relations, accounting, and management.

From a program standpoint, I don't think we really know what works. If the homeless person is truly motivated, most any program will be of benefit. If not, probably none will. How to motivate people, especially those who are oppressed by poverty and their own poor choices, is critical. I am not intelligent or wise enough to know, universally, what works. Some things work with some people, some of the time. Is that acceptable? You must decide.

That raises our final consideration: what does the public (you) have a right to expect from the expenditure of public monies on homeless programs? Let me suggest a realistic expectation. Perhaps twenty-five percent of homeless people will go on to be self-sufficient and permanently housed. Perhaps. Most will become permanently housed for six months or so and then become homeless or precariously housed again. It is unreasonable to expect that everyone can live effectively in a society as complex as ours. And I am not so sure that those who can are better for it. What I think justifies such programs as ours (and the huge monetary expense associated with it) is our national belief that everyone deserves an opportunity and, often, several. In reality, that's what we are about—we offer, with your money, an opportunity to people who have failed, to people who may not even know how to take advantage of an opportunity. Programs like ours say a lot about the kind of nation, and, consequently, the kind of people we are.

Will we continue to fund such programs or not? I don't know. What's important—the bottom line or people? You must decide and the choice will be painful.

So are homeless people doing well in this heaven and this earth?

Chapter Six

CLEANING UP THE STREETS: COMMUNITY EFFORTS TO COMBAT HOMELESSNESS BY CRIMINALIZING HOMELESS BEHAVIORS

Amy M. Donley and James D. Wright

Homelessness has been a major social policy issue in the United States for well over two decades.[1] Estimates of the size of the homeless population in any given year in America range from 300,000 to 3.5 million,[2] with about a million annually being a commonly accepted consensus guess.[3] Although it is estimated that as many as three percent of Americans experience an episode of homelessness in a given five-year period,[4] in 2005 fourteen percent of all emergency shelter requests went unfilled. As a result, many homeless individuals and families are forced, literally, into living on the streets.

The lack of available shelter beds for all who need them coupled with the hesitance of many homeless persons to avail themselves of shelter services[5] mean that many or most urban public places in the United States harbor a population of homeless people. This has proven to be a source of great aggravation to downtown business people, residents, and urban politicians, especially in areas that are being revitalized or "gentrified." Those seeking "new urban lifestyles" rarely include encounters with homeless people among the urban diversities they wish to experience. The result in cities everywhere has been a great deal of political pressure to "do something" about the homeless hordes, to "clean up the streets," or in short, to be rid of homeless people by whatever means necessary. In all too rare instances, this has meant some effort to address the larger issues of poverty and low-income housing from whence homelessness springs. Far more commonly, the effort is focused on criminalizing the behaviors that annoy us. We are resolved, it seems, to dealing with the homeless problem by making homeless behaviors illegal. What this lacks in cleverness or compassion it makes up in sheer spite.

This chapter reviews recent efforts in many cities to reduce or eliminate the visible portion of the homeless problem by either enacting new legislation or calling for more aggressive enforcement of existing legislation to prohibit such things as panhandling, loitering, and public intoxication. The use of "Greyhound therapy" has also been employed in many smaller communities where the homeless are simply supplied a bus ticket to somewhere else. Some initiatives target those who want to assist the homeless as opposed to targeting the homeless themselves. For example, Orlando and Las Vegas have enacted ordinances restricting the feeding of homeless people.[6] These and related efforts are also reviewed.

A 2006 joint report by the National Coalition for the Homeless and the National Law Center on Homelessness and Poverty reports that criminalization initiatives are on the rise. Comparing the most recent report with a similar one conducted in 2002, the authors found a three-percent increase in laws that prohibit loitering, loafing, or vagrancy; a fourteen-percent increase in laws that prohibit sitting or lying down in specific public spaces; and an eighteen-percent increase in laws prohibiting aggressive panhandling. According to the 2004 report by the National Coalition for the Homeless (NCH) entitled, *Illegal to be Homeless: The Criminalization of Homelessness in the United States:*

> The underlying assumption behind these actions is that homelessness is a "public safety" issue. Therefore, cities attempt to eliminate visible homelessness through enforcing "quality of life" ordinances, which seek to improve the "quality of life" of housed and higher-income individuals by removing from sight those people who look poor and homeless. Arrest and incarceration have become an expedited way of removing individuals from sight. Unfortunately, many people justify criminalization as a "benevolent" means of coercing individuals into treatment and other services that are not voluntarily available.[7]

Another facet of the criminalization of homelessness involves the violence that homeless people have endured on the streets of American cities. Assaults against homeless individuals are apparently on the rise. A report issued by NCH compiles all of the known cases of homeless victimization. The NCH reports 142 violent acts against homeless persons occurring in 2006, including twenty deaths. Many homeless advocates believe that the attacks against homeless people demonstrate the effects of the homeless being unwanted in America. It is this link between criminalization and victimization that we explore.[8]

Scholars have given relatively short shrift to the criminalization of homelessness and as such, there is not an abundance of academic studies focused on the topic. Thus, we review recent local initiatives to criminalize homeless individuals and their behaviors and discuss some recent significant court decisions in this area. We also rely more heavily than we would otherwise prefer on data, statistics, and trends produced by various advocacy organizations. Although academic literature is included where relevant, the majority of our literature comes from the homeless advocacy community. But that has also allowed us to review what local advocacy groups are doing to combat initiatives that have been passed throughout the country.

SOME HISTORICAL PERSPECTIVE

Attempting to deal with the problem of homelessness through the brute force of law has a long if inglorious tradition in the United States (and, of course, elsewhere, but the focus here is domestic). Every major economic dislocation in the nation's history has been accompanied by an increasingly visible homelessness problem, and "decent people" throughout our history have urged that the problem be resolved by shooing the homeless away, institutionalizing them in poorhouses, orphanages, and homes for "fallen women," or by tossing them in jail.

The homeless problem in America dates back at least to the Colonial era,[9] when there were sufficient numbers of what were called the "wandering poor" to raise popular alarm and lead to the enactment of legal measures to deal with them. In Massachusetts, the chosen mechanism was the process of "warning out" (i.e., warning people to leave town). Names of transients, along with information on their former residences, were presented to Colonial courts. After judicial review, the person or family could then be warned out. A corollary process was that of "binding out," in which transients could be in essence indentured to families that needed laborers or servants.

The American Revolution at the end of the eighteenth century left masses of homeless ex-soldiers in its wake. According to Markee, "rising numbers of vagabonds were noted in urban areas in the wake of the Revolutionary War. New York City Mayor Richard Varick noted in 1784 that "vagrants multiply on our hands to an amazing degree, and overcrowding in jails, workhouses, and almshouses led to the construction of a new four-story facility [to house vagabonds] in 1796."[10]

DePastino points out that in the years following the Civil War, a "veritable army of homeless men" swept across America, creating a counterculture that he refers to as "hobohemia," a deviant culture much celebrated in the pulp fiction of a later era that extolled the romanticism of an unfettered life on the road.[11] Many of the pejorative terms used to refer to the homeless, for example, "tramp," "bum," and, of course, "hobo" itself, date to the Civil War era.[12] According to DePastino, hobo culture was explicitly acknowledged as a "danger to civilization" and popular thinking about what to do with the hoboes influenced the "creation of welfare state measures, the promotion of mass consumption, and the suburbanization of America."[13]

Indeed, in an important sense, homeless people founded America. Hard as it may be for the contemporary generation of students to believe, when the *Mayflower* pulled up on the Massachusetts shore, it was not lined with beachfront condos or expensive single-family homes. No, these were literally homeless people fleeing religious persecution and looking to start a better life. The inscription at the base of the Statue of Liberty invites the world to "send these, the homeless, tempest-tost to me. I lift my lamp beside the golden door." In the nineteenth and early twentieth centuries, hundreds of thousands of homeless immigrants passed through Ellis Island and into the nation's heartland to populate the cities and build a modern society.

To be sure, homeless people have rarely been seen as builders of nations at any point in American history. More commonly, they have been dismissed or vilified as derelicts and bums, hopeless alcoholics, insane or otherwise dangerous people, or social parasites deserving of contempt—in short, as beyond help, responsible for their own misery, or socially unworthy. Rarely has popular thinking about "what to do about homelessness" extended much beyond removing them from our midst, least of all the "unworthy" homeless, whose miseries (we like to believe) are self-inflicted and who are, therefore, beneath contempt.

The Great Depression marked the last major wave of homelessness in this country before the 1980s resurgence. Rossi has pointed out that in 1933 the Federal Emergency Relief Administration housed 125,000 people in its transient camps around the country.[14] Another survey of that period, also cited by Rossi, estimated that the homeless population of 765 select cities and towns was on the order of 200,000, with estimates for the entire nation ranging upward to 1.5 million.[15] Most of the homeless in the depression were younger men and women moving from place to place in search of jobs.

The outbreak of World War II ended the depression and created many employment opportunities for men and women alike, an economic boom that continued throughout the 1950s and 1960s and caused the virtual extinction of homelessness, at least as a public problem. Certainly, residual pockets of homelessness remained in the skid row areas, but the residents of skid row came less and less to be the economically down and out and more and more to be broken-down alcoholic men. In view of the urban renewal efforts of the 1960s and the obvious aging of the skid row population, the impending demise of skid row was widely and confidently predicted.

Skid row, of course, did not disappear. The postwar growth in real personal income ended in about 1967, and economic times have been troubled ever since. The national poverty rate—the percentage of Americans living at or below the official federal poverty line—which declined in the 1960s and held steady in the 1970s, began to climb back up in the 1980s, retreated somewhat in the boom times of the 1990s, and has begun to climb back up again. This year, we will have more poor people in the United States than at any time since the onset of the War on Poverty in the early 1960s. Even more troubling, the rate of chronic poverty has also increased, and with it the problem of homelessness. Thus, the 1980s resurgence of homelessness, a resurgence with which we are still struggling, is only the latest phase of a cycle that extends back for three centuries.

Panhandling

Of all the behaviors associated with homelessness in the public mind, beggary is evidently the most offensive; thus, panhandling and the criminalization of begging behavior are at the forefront of the effort to "clean up the streets." Never mind that empirical studies of the phenomenon report with great consistency that "contrary to common belief, panhandlers and homeless people are not necessarily one and the same. Many studies have found that only a small percentage of homeless people panhandle, and only a small percentage of panhandlers are homeless."[16] Although exact numbers are unavailable, estimates of the percentage of homeless people that engage in panhandling range from five to forty percent, that is, a minority of the total homeless population.[17] And many panhandlers are not homeless, as evidenced by Goldstein's study in New Haven, Connecticut, where only one-third of panhandlers were indeed homeless. Despite the consistency of these sorts of findings, panhandling and homelessness are intimately linked in public thinking.[18]

Ordinances attempting to ban or regulate panhandling are often viewed as a way of removing the homeless from public view. As one commentator has put it, the purpose of anti-panhandling ordinances "… is to permit people to use streets, sidewalks, and public transportation free from the borderline robbery and pervasive fraud which characterize so much of today's panhandling."[19] The idea that panhandlers are not "really" needy, that beggary is some sort of scam, and that aggressive panhandlers rake in improbably large sums of money only to drive home at the end of the day in shiny Cadillacs is so widespread in contemporary American society that it has attained the status of an urban myth.

Empirical studies of panhandlers do not depict the activity as highly profitable.

> Most evidence confirms that panhandling is not lucrative, although some panhandlers clearly are able to subsist on a combination of panhandling money, government benefits, private charity, and money from odd jobs such as selling scavenged materials or plasma. How much money a panhandler can make varies depending on his or her skill and personal appeal, as well as on the area in which he or she solicits. Estimates vary from a couple of dollars (U.S.) a day on the low end, to twenty to fifty dollars a day in the mid-range, to about $300 a day on the high end.[20]

The high end "estimates" of hundreds of dollars a day are almost certainly exaggerated. Realistically, when combined with other income-generating activities panhandling would normally provide a subsistence income at best.

Panhandling has been ruled by the U.S. Supreme Court to be legally protected behavior under the First Amendment, which guarantees free speech and freedom of religion. One can no more ban people from asking for spare change than one can ban people from asking for the time of day (free speech), and likewise, the asking for and giving of alms is constitutionally protected religious behavior. Thus, numerous efforts simply to ban panhandling have been stricken down as unconstitutional. But the Court has also ruled that regulations concerning the "place and manner" of panhandling are not unconstitutional, and this has led to several anti-panhandling ordinances that the courts have allowed to remain in place.

Of these, the most common are laws prohibiting "aggressive panhandling." Most panhandling is in fact passive, not aggressive,[21] and the definition of what constitutes "aggressive" panhandling remains unclear. But these points have not deterred cities from targeting this specific form of panhandling or prevented "no aggressive panhandling" ordinances from being enacted all across the country.[22]

Necessarily, every jurisdiction wishing to ban aggressive panhandling has to develop some definition of what aggressive panhandling entails. In Cleveland, for example, the definition of aggressive solicitation, which is illegal, specifically prohibits panhandling in any of the following places:

- Within twenty feet of a bus stop, rapid-transit shelter, or bus shelter;
- Within twenty feet of a line of pedestrians waiting to obtain access to a building or event;
- Within twenty feet of the area of the sidewalk used by an outdoor restaurant;
- Within twenty feet of a valet zone;
- Within fifteen feet of any pay telephone;
- Within fifteen feet of the entrance or exit of any public toilet facility;
- On public property within ten feet of an entrance to a building; or
- On public property within ten feet of an entrance to a parking lot.[23]

Many anti-panhandling ordinances follow the Cleveland lead in specifying places where panhandling is not allowed. Other cities, such as Seattle, attempt to define specifically prohibited panhandling methods and behaviors. For example, the Seattle definition of aggressive panhandling includes the following specific behaviors:[24]

- Confronting someone in a way that would cause a reasonable person to fear bodily harm;
- Touching someone without his or her consent;
- Continuing to panhandle or follow someone after he or she has refused to give money;
- Intentionally blocking or interfering with the safe passage of a person or vehicle;

- Using obscene or abusive language towards someone while attempting to panhandle him or her; and
- Acting with intent to intimidate someone into giving money.

In 2004, the city of Orlando, Florida, passed an ordinance requiring panhandlers to obtain a permit from the municipal police department; this too is not an uncommon strategy in various American cities.[25] The Orlando ordinance further makes it a crime to panhandle in the commercial core of downtown Orlando, as well as within fifty feet of any bank or automated teller machine, except in specially designated blue boxes that have been painted onto downtown Orlando sidewalks. Thus, downtown Orlando panhandlers must have a police permit and stay inside the designated blue boxes. (In fact, hardly any do.) It is also considered a crime in Orlando for panhandlers to make false statements, to disguise themselves, or to use money obtained with a claim of a specific purpose (e.g., food) for anything else (e.g., alcohol). So in Orlando, if you tell someone you are hungry if in fact you are not, then take the money you are given and use it for a pack of cigarettes, you are in technical violation of the Orlando panhandling ordinance.

As shown above, definitions of aggressive panhandling may not only restrict how one can panhandle but where one can do so as well. Ordinances generally include the specific word "aggressive" and most of these laws restrict locations where panhandling is allowed and the way in which solicitations may be pitched.[26]

As might be anticipated, these anti-aggressive-panhandling ordinances have often evolved into enforcement nightmares. As Scott notes, "Enforcing aggressive-panhandling laws can be difficult, partly because few panhandlers behave aggressively, and partly because many victims of aggressive panhandling do not report the offense to police or are unwilling to file a complaint."[27] Many of these laws require police discretion (who's to say, for example, that someone has been confronted "in a way that would cause a reasonable person to fear bodily harm?") and therefore invite selective enforcement, which then leads to citizen and business owners' complaints that the police are letting panhandlers get away with too much.

Because of dissatisfaction with the results obtained in efforts to ban aggressive panhandling, many cities (literally from Savannah to Evanston to San Diego) have begun to experiment with solutions that attempt to control the behavior of the *givers*, not the behavior of panhandlers themselves. The implementation of such measures entails public education to discourage giving money directly to individuals and instead encouraging people to donate their spare change to area service providers. In Scott's view, this can be part of "an effective and comprehensive response" to the panhandling problem. In Baltimore, the "Make a Change" campaign provides collection boxes inside area hotels and businesses for people to deposit money that would have otherwise gone to panhandlers (http://www.godowntownbaltimore.com).[28] Similarly, in

Athens, Georgia, among other places, parking meters have been converted into donation kiosks where people can deposit spare change that is then given to local homeless service providers.[29]

Obviously, there is nothing in the Constitution to prevent municipalities from trying to encourage citizens *not* to respond positively to panhandlers' requests. As Scott points out, "Most studies conclude that panhandlers make rational economic choices—that is, they look to make money in the most efficient way possible."[30] In other words, if people can be persuaded to stop giving, panhandlers will stop panhandling and go somewhere more lucrative. This, of course, does not solve the problem but it successfully displaces the problem to somewhere else. And for many cities, that is good enough. So cities such as Savannah, Memphis, Baltimore, Evanston, Nashville, and many others have embarked on various versions of these "Do Not Give" information campaigns.

Savannah's version involves posting signs in high-traffic areas that read,

> Help discourage panhandling in Savannah by refusing those who ask for change on the street. By doing this you will foster a better environment for all. Avoid supporting what is, in many cases, an alcoholic and destructive lifestyle. Numerous resources are available through support agencies for those who wish to utilize them. Please help curtail the harassment of visitors by refusing to give money to panhandlers.

Other cities post signs encouraging citizens to report panhandling to the police or urging people not to feel guilty for saying no.

In almost all cases, these Do Not Give campaigns have stirred up some resentment among local homeless advocates and no city has managed to eliminate nuisance panhandling by any of these means. But most cities report some modest successes in reducing the most abusive cases. In Evanston, for example, there was a documented reduction in the number of panhandlers working the streets, a reduction in the number of citizen complaints, and survey results documenting an upturn in citizen perception of the downtown area as a safe place to shop and work. Scott has concluded,

> Most researchers and practitioners seem to agree that the enforcement of laws prohibiting panhandling plays only a part in controlling the problem. Public education to discourage people from giving money to panhandlers, informal social control, and adequate social services (especially alcohol and drug treatment) for panhandlers are the other essential components of an effective and comprehensive response. The state of the economy, at the local, regional and even national level, affects how much panhandling occurs. As the economy declines, panhandling increases. As government benefit programs become more restrictive, panhandling increases. At least as important as economic factors, if not more so, are social factors. The stronger the social bonds and social network on which indigent people can rely for emotional and financial support, the less likely they are to panhandle. Thus, the weakening of social bonds throughout society affects the indigent most negatively.[31]

For most Americans, panhandling "represents the most tangible expression of contemporary homelessness."[32] For most business owners, panhandling is a problem that can negatively affect business. Regardless of which method or methods are used, initiatives to curb panhandling do not seem to be abating. As downtowns continue to "revitalize" all across the country, measures to reduce or eliminate as much panhandling as possible seem nearly certain to increase.

Loitering

Another issue related to (and often enforced concomitantly with anti-panhandling laws) is loitering, of which municipalities often find it necessary to legally disapprove. These ordinances come in the form of "anti-sitting" laws or laws regulating where a person can lie down. In Olympia, Washington, the panhandling and anti-sitting laws are subsumed under the same ordinance, entitled "pedestrian interference." Under this ordinance "a person is guilty of pedestrian interference if, in a public place, he or she ... obstructs pedestrian or vehicular traffic ... in a pedestrian walking lane," the latter meaning that "portion of any sidewalk, street or alley located within the downtown area and: (a) within six (6) feet of the edge of any building or structure located immediately adjacent to the sidewalk or alley, or the edge of the right-of-way, if no building or structure exists."[33]

The NCH and the National Law Center on Homelessness and Poverty annually rank U.S. cities in terms of their "meanness" towards the homeless, on the basis of many factors including the number and enforcement of anti-homeless laws, the severity of penalties for violating those laws, and the existence of pending or recently enacted criminalization measures in the city. In 2005, Sarasota, Florida, was named the meanest city in America mainly because of the Sarasota ordinance that banned, among other things, sleeping "without permission on city or private property, either in a tent or makeshift shelter, or while atop or covered by materials."[34]

In the previously cited report, *Illegal to Be Homeless*, twenty-eight percent of the 224 surveyed cities prohibit "camping" in certain public places and sixteen percent had citywide bans on camping. Twenty-seven percent of the surveyed cities prohibit sitting or lying down in some public places. Thirty-nine percent prohibit loitering in specific public areas, and sixteen percent prohibit loitering anywhere in the city.[35] Although having laws against loitering is not new, it is the selective enforcement of such laws that portend criminalization. If the law against sleeping on park benches is ignored when affluent businessmen catch a few winks after their luncheon martini but enforced aggressively against raggedy, broken-down homeless people, that selectivity implies that the simple fact of being homeless has been operationally defined as a criminal act.

By definition, people without housing have nowhere to go during the day, so if they are to seek respite from their daily activities, practically anything they do can be seen as loitering. Most emergency shelters for homeless people are only open at night. Some initiatives have been undertaken to assist homeless people during the day and to give them an alternative to being on the streets. In Glendale, California, the police department created a "day labor center" that offers such classes as computers and English for non-native speakers. And many cities either have created or are in the process of creating "drop-in" shelters open during the day where homeless people can get off the streets, perhaps shower or do laundry, take a meal, watch television, or see a social worker or case manager.

Street Sweeps

Street sweeps consist of homeless people being targeted when they are living or loitering out of doors in public locations. A "sweep" entails law enforcement officers coming through an area, rousting homeless people, making them "move on," and often confiscating or destroying their things (nine times in ten, on the bogus grounds that the "stuff" of homeless people is trash or litter). Often times the police work with other local government employees to clear an area of homeless, or apparently homeless people, often in conjunction with major local political or sporting events, appearances by visiting dignitaries, or other occasions that bring tourists and media attention to a particular area of a city.

In New York City, Mayor Bloomberg announced in July 2006 that the city would erect barriers blocking access to makeshift camps as well as disallowing homeless people from sleeping under highways and near train trestles as a way to help homeless people gain shelter.[36] This occurred at the same time there was a forty-four percent increase among sheltered homeless New Yorkers while rents in the city continued to rise.[37]

Sweeps of homeless people and encampments have become common across the nation. In Honolulu, Hawaii, in 2003, police conducted sweeps in a park and an airport three times a week for six weeks.[38] In Cleveland in 1999, the city ordered police to focus on criminals as well as panhandlers and homeless sleeping on the sidewalks so that shoppers "will have a peaceful shopping season."[39] According to NCH, sweeps and other forms of criminalization are usually conducted under "quality of life" ordinances and their purpose is to move the homeless out of sight.[40]

The Fourth Amendment protects people from unreasonable search and seizure and street sweeps are often challenged on the grounds that they are violations of homeless peoples' Fourth Amendment rights. Sometimes these challenges are successful and some sort of redress or restitution is ordered. In the extreme case, the courts have used police violations of court orders against sweeps to order massive increases in local services for the homeless, as in Miami in the aftermath of the *Pottinger* decision. Pottinger was one among several homeless people living under Miami's highway overpasses whose belongings had been confiscated and destroyed over and over by the Miami police, despite repeated court orders to desist in the behavior. The court ruled that homeless people were not homeless by choice, homelessness was an involuntarily assumed status, and, as such, laws against survival behavior by this group (loitering, public urination, sleeping in public, etc.) were unconstitutional. When the city lost its challenge against the court ruling, it was forced to enact a special food and beverage tax to pay for the expanded shelter capacity and homeless services that the court ordered into existence.[41]

Dumping

"Dumping" is the elegantly simple strategy of putting troublesome people on a bus to somewhere else with the hope that they don't find their way back (the modern-day equivalent of the Colonial era "warning out"). The dumping of "troublesome persons" by police officers has been documented throughout American history.[42] Homeless people are not the only troublesome element that municipalities will try to dump, but certainly they have experienced their share, and more, of dumping. In some cases, dumping has been practiced so egregiously that neighboring cities or concerned advocacy groups have sued the "dumping" city for their behavior.[43]

The police agencies are not the only ones that engage in dumping. In 2006 in Los Angeles, city prosecutors charged area hospitals with dumping homeless patients in the infamous skid row area.[44] There is no hospital in any American city of appreciable size that has not seen its emergency room utilization figures jump up with cases of "uncompensated care" (i.e., people without health insurance or a fee source to pay for their hospitalization). And although the hospitals are required by law to offer emergency care to anyone in need regardless of their ability to pay, the sooner the poor and homeless can be stabilized and released, the less they cost the hospital. At the Coalition for the Homeless facility in Orlando, taxi cabs have pulled up and discharged homeless people who were still in hospital gowns and had IV lines attached to their arms. So common is "dumping" by hospitals that the behavior has been given a name: GOMER (as in: "What happened to the broken leg in 3-B?" "He was GOMERed.") GOMER stands for Get Out of My Emergency Room!

Although dumping is probably not a very common reaction to homeless individuals, the use of "Greyhound therapy" appears to be more widespread. Greyhound therapy refers to the issuing of bus tickets to homeless individuals so they can leave town. Although these "relocation" programs have been widely criticized, as recently as January 2007, the mayor of Daytona Beach announced that his city was instituting a program in which homeless individuals would be given bus tickets so they could, in the mayor's belief, be "reunited with friends and family." Local homeless advocates pointed out that many of the Daytona Beach homeless are originally from the Daytona area and many more have no family or friends who would provide them with shelter.

Some programs take this concept a step further. In Reno, Nevada, the Homeless Evaluation Liaison Program (HELP) is a program run by the local police force. Homeless individuals may apply once per lifetime for a bus ticket to reunite with friends and family. The officers call the person that will be receiving the homeless individual in the other location to make sure that someone will in fact be taking them in. However, the homeless individual is not provided any services, only a bus ticket.[45]

Many advocates for the homeless contend that programs such as these do nothing but move homeless individuals around, never addressing the root problems.[46] To be sure, every city will have some homeless people who are homeless because they got stranded, ran out of money, and have no way to get back to wherever it is they came from, and for these unfortunate few, a bus ticket may indeed be all their homelessness requires. This cannot possibly describe more than a percent or two of the homeless population in most cities. Nevertheless, the popularity of these relocation programs is growing in many cities, including Orlando, Florida, where a program modeled on Reno's HELP is being discussed as a potential addition to the spectrum of homeless services within the city.

Restrictions on Feeding

Restrictions on the feeding of homeless people have also been enacted in several cities. These initiatives are unique because they focus on those that are supplying the food, not the homeless clients who receive it. In Las Vegas, Nevada, a federal judge blocked a law that banned serving food to the poor in city parks.[47] However, similar laws still exist in other cities. In Dallas, Texas, feedings are limited to certain designated areas and providers must obtain a permit and attend food safety training.[48]

The recently enacted restrictions on feeding homeless people in Orlando are some of the most stringent in the country. Under the new law, which is being challenged by several organizations including the American Civil Liberties Union (ACLU), a person or group cannot feed more than twenty-five people at a time without obtaining a permit. This permit can only be obtained twice a year. At first, the Orlando police simply ignored the ordinance as unenforceable, and then tried to work with local organizations to assure that homeless people were being fed in lots of twenty-four or less. But in March 2007, bowing to pressure from downtown residents and business interests, the Orlando police arrested an activist from the organization Food Not Bombs after he was filmed violating the feeding ordinance by undercover officers. His arrest was the first effort to enforce this controversial ordinance, which is supported by the majority of the local business community, particularly those located near the park where the feedings and this arrest took place. Feedings continue weekly despite the arrest.[49] The ACLU has challenged the constitutionality of the feeding ban in a suit that is still percolating through the system. In fact, there are numerous feeding programs for homeless people in the downtown Orlando area and most service providers have pleaded with the Food Not Bombs people to work with existing programs as an outlet for their charitable impulses, so far to no avail.

Victimization

As we have seen, cities all over the country are enacting measures to "clean up the streets" by driving away or locking up the visible homeless of the area. Although these measures are rarely effective, are often found to be unconstitutional, and generally do nothing to address the real problems of homeless people, their popularity grows as the urban areas try to attract shoppers, tourists, and residents, none of whom seem comfortable having homeless people around. Michael Stoops, director of NCH, argues that one notable consequence of the effort to criminalize homeless people and their behaviors has been to foster a generalized disregard for the civil rights of the homeless and that, Stoops argues, has had a direct effect on their victimization and on the stunning increase in what can only be described as hate crimes perpetrated against them.[50]

Hate crimes against homeless people have burgeoned in recent years and have become a nationwide problem. Since 1999, NCH has issued an annual report on these trends. The most recent in the series, *Hate, Violence, and Death on Main Street USA*, covering the years through 2006, is available at the NCH home page (http://www.nationalhomeless.org).[51]

According to the 2006 report, "over the past seven years (1999–2005), advocates and homeless shelter workers from around the country have seen an alarming, nationwide epidemic in reports of homeless men, women, and even children being killed, beaten, and harassed."[52] The NCH data only include incidents from newspaper stories in which victims are identified as homeless people and their assailants are known. Thus, the vast majority of these crimes must escape attention.

Still, between 1999 and 2005, 472 violent hate-crime attacks against the homeless were documented, resulting in 169 deaths. Incidents have been recorded in 165 cities in forty-two states and Puerto Rico. In 2006, Florida experienced the greatest number of attacks with forty-seven incidents, with Arizona second with sixteen. Often it is assumed that Florida simply has more homeless people, which accounts for the higher number of attacks. However, this is not the case. California has nearly three times the number of homeless persons as compared to Florida and nowhere near as many assaults.[53] Victims range from four-month-old babies to elderly people in their seventies. Most perpetrators are young males ages fourteen to nineteen.[54]

Although no one knows for sure why these attacks are increasing, advocates for the homeless believe that as a society, America is sending the message that homeless people do not matter. The NCH report notes, "The term 'hate crime' generally conjures up images of cross burnings and lynchings, swastikas on Jewish synagogues, and horrific murders of gays and lesbians."[55] Interestingly, homelessness is not included in the federal definition of a hate crime. Attacks on people because of their religion, race, ethnicity, beliefs, or sexual orientation can be prosecuted as hate crimes and the penalties are more severe. Homelessness does not enjoy the same legal protection, although in fairness several states, including Massachusetts, California, Maryland, and Florida, are proposing legislation that would include housing status in the hate crime definition.[56]

RAYS OF LIGHT

American cities are not unanimous in their efforts to criminalize the behaviors of people experiencing homelessness and not all of them post signs at the city limits that read, in effect, "Homeless people not welcome. No sitting, lying, leaning, panhandling, loitering, camping, obstructing the sidewalk, sleeping in public or storing your stuff in public places. Poor people should register with the local police." NCH has identified three "model cities"—Minneapolis, Philadelphia, and Fort Lauderdale—that have made serious efforts to buck the criminalization trend.[57]

In Minneapolis, several anti-homeless ordinances have been repealed, the police have been trained in how to link homeless people to the services they need rather than just roust them or toss them in jail, a Decriminalization Task Force was created to review all of the local laws and practices, the effect of which, if not the intent, was to criminalize homelessness, and an aggressive long-term effort to address the housing needs of homeless people was undertaken. In Philadelphia, police officers that encounter homeless people are required to contact social workers that respond within twenty minutes, and homeless people who are sleeping outside (in violation of local ordinances) are referred to local shelters and transitional housing services rather than being fined or arrested. In Fort Lauderdale, police and city officials have created outreach teams comprised of police officers and formerly homeless people to encounter and assess individuals on the street and make appropriate referrals.[58]

These and other examples suffice to make the important point that there are creative and humane ways of addressing local homelessness problems that do not necessarily require oppressive, discriminatory, and unconstitutional measures. We conclude with a point made in the title of a book by the Romanian author, Dmitry Sokolov: *You Cannot Drive Tramps off the Street with a Club!*

Evidence shows that many homeless people will respond positively to services, outreach, health care, or anything else that seems to represent an alternative way of living. But there is practically no evidence anywhere to suggest that they respond positively to threats, intimidation, or enforcement of laws that attempt to prohibit or criminalize their behaviors.

NOTES

1. M. Burt, L. Aron, E. Lee, and J. Valente, *Helping America's Homeless* (Washington, DC: The Urban Institute Press, 2001).
2. D. S. Cordray and G. M. Pion, "What's Behind the Numbers? Definitional Issues in Counting the Homeless," *Housing Policy Debate* 2, no. 3 (1990): 587–616; G. Glisson, B. Thyer, and R. Fischer, "Serving the Homeless: Evaluating the Effectiveness of Homeless Shelter Services," *Journal of Sociology and Social Welfare* 28, no. 4 (2001): 89–98.
3. National Coalition for the Homeless and the National Law Center on Homelessness and Poverty, *Dream Denied: The Criminalization of Homelessness in U.S. Cities* (Washington, DC: The National Coalition for the Homeless and The National Law Center on Homelessness and Poverty, 2006).
4. B. Link, E. Susser, A. Stueve, J. Phelan, R. Moore, and E. Struening, "Lifetime and Five-Year Prevalence of Homelessness in the United States," *American Journal of Public Health* 84, no. 12 (1994): 1907–12.
5. Burt et al., *Helping America's Homeless*, 2001; J. Wright, D. Edelen, A. Donley, A. Freeland, and C. Bolden, "Living Rough: A Qualitative Study of Homeless People in Outdoor Camps in East Orange County, Florida," Final Report, 2007.
6. T. Lewan, "Orlando's Homeless Laws Spark Debate," *Washington Post,* February 3, 2007.
7. National Coalition for the Homeless, *Illegal to be Homeless: The Criminalization of Homelessness in the United States* (Washington, DC: National Coalition for the Homeless, 2004).
8. National Alliance to End Homelessness, *Homelessness Counts*, (Washington, DC: National Alliance to End Homelessness, 2006).
9. J.D. Wright, *Address Unknown: The Homeless in America* (Hawthorne, NY: Aldine de Gruyter Publishing Co, 1989).
10. P. Markee, "War and Homelessness: How American Wars Create Homelessness Among United States Armed Forces Veterans," 2003, http://www.coalitionforthehomeless.org/top/CFTH/news/War_and_Homelessness.html.
11. T. DePastino, *Citizen Hobo: How a Century of Homelessness Shaped America* (Chicago: University of Chicago Press, 2003).
12. K. Kusmer, *Down and Out, On the Road: The Homeless in American History* (Cambridge: Oxford University Press, 2002).
13. DePastino, *Citizen Hobo,* 2003.
14. P. Rossi, *Without Shelter* (New York: Priority Press Publications, 1989).
15. Ibid.
16. M. S. Scott, *Panhandling* (Washington DC: U.S. Department of Justice, Office of Community Policing Services, 2002).

17. B. A. Lee, C. A. Farrell, and B. G. Link, "Revisiting the Contact Hypothesis: The Case of Public Exposure to Homelessness," *American Sociological Review* 69, no. 1 (2004): 40–63.

18. Ibid.

19. K. Scheidegger, "A Guide to Regulating Panhandling," *Criminal Justice Legal Foundation*, 1993, http://www.cjlf.org/publctns/Panhandling/Pcvr_bio.htm.

20. Scott, *Panhandling*, 2002.

21. Scott, *Panhandling*, 2002; B. A. Lee and C. A. Farrell, "Buddy, Can You Spare a Dime? Homelessness, Panhandling, and the Public," *Urban Affairs Review* 38, no. 3 (2003): 299–324.

22. National Coalition for the Homeless and the National Law Center on Homelessness and Poverty, *Dream Denied*, 2006.

23. Cleveland Codified Ordinance, section 605.031, http://caselaw.lp.findlaw.com/clevelandcodes/cco_part6_605.html.

24. G. L. Kelling and C. M. Coles, *Fixing Broken Windows: Restoring Order and Reducing Crime in Our Communities* (New York: Free Press, 1996).

25. Orlando Municipal Code, section 43.86.

26. National Coalition for the Homeless, *Illegal to Be Homeless*, 2004.

27. Scott, *Panhandling*, 2002.

28. City of Baltimore, MD, "Make a Change," http://www.godowntownbaltimore.com.

29. Scott, *Panhandling*, 2002.

30. Ibid.

31. Ibid.

32. Lee and Farrell, "Buddy, Can You Spare a Dime?" 2003.

33. Olympia Municipal Codes, Section 09.16.180, http://olympiamunicipalcode.org/.

34. National Coalition for the Homeless and National Law Center on Homelessness and Poverty, *Dream Denied*, 2006.

35. National Coalition for the Homeless, *Illegal to Be Homeless*, 2004.

36. D. Cardwell, "City to Clear Homeless Encampments," *The New York Times*, July 18, 2006.

37. National Coalition for the Homeless and the National Law Center on Homelessness and Poverty, *Dream Denied*, 2006.

38. H. Altonn, "City Homeless Sweeps Draw Concern: Advocates Say More Needs to be Done to Provide Adequate Services for the Needy," *Honolulu Star Bulletin*, February 14, 2003.

39. R. Amster, "Patterns of Exclusion: Sanitizing Space, Criminalizing Homelessness," *Social Justice* 30, no. 1 (2003): 195–222.

40. National Coalition for the Homeless, *Illegal to Be Homeless*, 2004.

41. Ibid.

42. W. R. King and T. M. Dunn, "Dumping: Police-Initiated Transjurisdictional Transport of Troublesome Persons," *Police Quarterly* 7, no. 3 (2004): 339–58.

43. Ibid.

44. Lewan, "Orlando's Homeless Laws," 2007.

45. Reno City Website, "Homeless Evaluation Liaison Program (HELP)," http://www.cityofreno.com/res/police/det/help.php.

46. J. Fabyankovic, "Alternatives to Homeless Criminalization," *Law and Order*, 2000, http://action.web.ca/home/housing/resources.shtml?x=66853.

47. E. Bazar, "Cities Set Limits on Serving Food to Homeless People," *USA Today*, March 26, 2007.

48. E. Bazar, "The 'Lord's Table' Illegal in Dallas," *USA Today*, March 26, 2007.
49. "Florida Police Arrest Activist for Feeding Homeless," *Reuters*, April 5, 2007, http://www.reuters.com/article/topNews/idUSN0517193520070405.
50. National Coalition for the Homeless, "Hate, Violence, and Death on Main Street USA," 2006, http://www.nationalhomeless.org.
51. Ibid.
52. Ibid.
53. Ibid.
54. A. Fantz, "Teen 'Sport Killings' of Homeless on the Rise," 2007, http://www.cnn.com/2007/US/02/19/homeless.attacks/index.html?eref=rss_latest.
55. National Coalition for the Homeless, "Hate, Violence, and Death," 2006.
56. Ibid.
57. Ibid.
58. Ibid.

Chapter Seven

THE FUTURE OF HOMELESSNESS: TRENDS IN ASSESSMENT AND SERVICE UTILIZATION

James Petrovich and Emily Spence-Almaguer

Since the late 1970s, the face of homelessness and our understanding of it have changed dramatically. Single males, previously understood to be the dominant group experiencing homelessness, are now being joined by emerging groups of single women, families, and unaccompanied youth. Homelessness is also spreading beyond larger urban centers and becoming more prevalent in rural areas. Caucasians, who once represented the largest ethnic group of homeless people in the United States, are now being replaced by African-Americans, while the average age of all people who are homeless decreases. Additionally, the influence of larger, structural factors in the creation and perpetuation of homelessness has also been more readily acknowledged. Although older, more conservative understandings seemed to focus on individual factors including substance abuse and mental illness, or attempt to explain homelessness away as a lifestyle choice, the influence of larger social and economic trends has also been identified.

As these subgroups have emerged and larger causal factors have been acknowledged, the nation has been challenged to abandon a "one-size-fits-all" approach to interpreting and addressing homelessness. The diversity present among people who are homeless demands a thoughtful approach to assessing the nature of homelessness and an equally diverse approach to providing services. Consequently, researchers, service providers, and policy-makers have been forced to confront the challenges inherent in researching homelessness, shape public discourse to reflect a more contemporary understanding of homelessness, develop and evaluate intervention strategies, and secure the resources required to adequately implement them.

In addition to these shifts in thinking, communities have also been challenged to re-assess their understanding of homelessness as well. As our general conceptualization of homelessness continues to acknowledge its increasing scope, complexity, and diversity, older ideologies regarding homelessness must be challenged. Where it has been common in the past to speak of homelessness using uninformed stereotypes or make reckless generalizations about the causal nature of homelessness, contemporary insights are making these one-dimensional interpretations highly inappropriate. It is important for communities to understand that homelessness represents a confluence of personal vulnerabilities contributed to and exacerbated by larger environmental conditions.[1]

It is also essential for communities to understand that in any legitimate attempt to address homelessness, an organized community effort is essential. Although no one can predict the future, certain trends have and will continue to play a role in the success of efforts to relieve homelessness in the United States. These include the manner in which homelessness is assessed and the factors that influence homeless people to use services. This chapter intends to address two interrelated issues: the manner in which we attempt to measure homelessness as a social problem, and issues that influence the use of services by people who are homeless. Although there are other issues that are equally important and should be addressed, these have been selected due to their influence on our understanding of the nature of homelessness, our reaction to people who are homeless, and the ability to develop effective services. From a more philosophical perspective, these issues also speak to how we assign responsibility for homelessness, how some groups may be considered more worthy of assistance than others, and how attempts are made to reduce the visibility of homeless people and mediate their impact on mainstream society.

ASSESSMENT AND PROGRAM PLANNING

Many factors guide the development of the local, state, and federal policies designed to respond to homelessness in the United States. Among these factors, assessment strategies have a tremendous impact on our understanding of homelessness as a social problem and a significant influence of the development of local, state, and federal policies designed to respond to it. However, initiating a dialogue about assessing homelessness must also include an exploration of the values and beliefs that underlie our understandings of it. Too often, community decision-makers design interventions in a context that dehumanizes people who are homeless, relegating them into problem-centered criterion such as "mentally ill," "addicts," and "criminals." The underlying assumptions are that some kind of character flaw separates those who are homeless from those who are not.[2]

Thus, assessment efforts become driven by the desire to identify these flaws, count them, and to provide interventions to fix them. This often results in a tremendous waste of resources when people who are homeless fail to utilize these interventions or when services produce no meaningful results.

As social service resources become scarcer, the demand for greater accountability and effective interventions has increased. Along with this desire to conserve resources has come a greater recognition that social service delivery is not a one-way transaction from provider to recipient. Ultimately, it is the recipients of services who make the key determination whether or not a program will succeed or fail. Furthermore, many programs are indicating that involving potential recipients and other stakeholders in the early stages of assessment and program planning will likely result in the identification of better outcomes at evaluation. Some communities and service delivery models take this a step further by shifting their focus from fixing deficits to enhancing existing strengths and resiliencies.[3] Currently, some of the trends influencing the assessment of homelessness and program development include strengths-based practice, consumer participation, client-centered needs assessment, and evidence-based practice.

Evidence-Based Practice

The Substance Abuse and Mental Health Services Administration (SAMSHA) in the U.S. Department of Health and Human Services has fueled much of the evidence-based practice movement by linking grant funding to the adoption and testing of evidence-based models, as well as the development and maintenance of the National Registry of Evidence-Based Programs and Practices (NREPP). The NREPP was first created in 1997 and ten years later was enhanced through its conversion to an online, searchable database. NREPP provides the following description of what they mean by evidence-based programs and practices:

> In the health care field, evidence-based practice (or practices), also called EBP or EBPs, generally refers to approaches to prevention or treatment that are validated by some form of documented scientific evidence. What counts as "evidence" varies. Evidence often is defined as findings established through scientific research, such as controlled clinical studies, but other methods of establishing evidence are considered valid as well. Evidence-based practice stands in contrast to approaches that are based on tradition, convention, belief, or anecdotal evidence. One concern is that too much emphasis on EBPs may in some cases restrict practitioners from exercising their own judgment to provide the best care for individuals. For this reason many organizations have adopted definitions of evidence-based practice that emphasize balancing the "scientific" with the "practical." NREPP does not attempt to offer a single, authoritative definition of evidence-based practice. SAMHSA expects that people who use this system will come with their own perspectives and contexts for understanding the information that NREPP offers. By providing a range of objective information about the research that has been conducted on each particular intervention, SAMHSA hopes users will make their own judgments about which interventions are best suited to particular needs.[4]

As a corollary to evidence-based practices, data driven decision-making has become central in all federal funding streams targeted for homeless populations, including those affiliated with the U.S. Departments of Housing and Urban Development (HUD), Health and Human Services (HHS), and Veterans Affairs (VA). Strong evidence of this occurred in 2001 when Congress issued a directive to HUD to guide the implementation of Homeless Management and Information Systems (HMIS) at the local level. Their purpose in undertaking this significant effort was to "improve the delivery of services to homeless clients and to increase understanding of their characteristics and needs at the local and national levels."[5]

HUD's first national annual HMIS report to Congress was published in February of 2007 and although many communities have yet to accurately capture data on homelessness using HMIS, this report summarizes the efforts of eighty regions. These data are helping HUD to make progress on establishing unduplicated counts of homeless service users, tracking patterns of service delivery usage, and to some extent, capturing basic details on service user characteristics. Thus, at the federal level these simultaneous efforts to gather information at the front end and measure "evidence" of program outcomes highlights an overall emphasis on data collection and data-driven decision-making.

Client-Centered Needs Assessment and Consumer Participation

Although many would agree that making decisions using sound data is preferable over using anecdotal or other less reliable and valid sources of information, gathering data without alienating clients and further burdening already overtaxed service providers presents significant challenges. The unique circumstances of people who are homeless provide additional complications. For example, HMIS often uses social security numbers and birthdates as a means to "de-duplicate" databases and obtain unduplicated counts of service users. However, for some homeless people, the factors that contributed to their homelessness may also serve as a reasonable justification to resist community efforts to collect such precise, identifying information. Domestic violence survivors who are fleeing abusive ex-partners, persons with criminal warrants, people experiencing delusional beliefs, and undocumented immigrants may all have seemingly valid reasons to either provide false information to HMIS data gatherers, or refuse to utilize services that require HMIS participation. For these reasons, among others, the valuable ideals of HMIS may meet significant resistance with front users (clients and service providers).

The Client-Centered Needs Assessment (CCNA) models first articulated by Devillaer,[6] as well as the general philosophies of consumer participation, provide means to both strengthen HMIS data gathering and offset some of its limitations by adding alternative data sources. The CCNA was developed to enhance substance abuse service delivery systems in Ontario, Canada.[7] The model was driven by the recognition that typical needs assessment methods (key informant interviews, service utilization data, tracking of social indicators, focus groups, and community surveys) are each limited in their ability to provide data specific enough to guide program planning, tend to rely on point-in-time community profiles, and are subject to being overly skewed toward the perspectives of planners and service providers.

To offset these limitations, the CCNA involves collaborative data gathering and service planning between providers and clients in agency settings. It honors the knowledge and skills of both practitioners and clients, maximizing the expertise of each individual to envision "ideal" solutions. The ultimate goal is to use the clients' vision of "success" as the guide to determine what the pathway towards that success (e.g., the intervention) will look like. At the macro level, community planners will aggregate the data collected through individually developed "ideal" plans to assess whether or not there are sufficient resources in the community to carry out those plans.

Thus, in a CCNA the determination of community needs is not done in isolation of front-user perspectives by relying simply on counts of clients and their characteristics. For example, community needs assessments of the homeless often count the problems that people have (e.g., the numbers of mentally ill, substance abusing, domestic violence victims, ex-offenders, etc.). The basis for program planning then becomes how big or small these proportions of problems are in the data set, with assumptions being made as to what types of interventions will work. Although adopting evidence-based solutions will increase the chances that services will be effective, there remain numerous factors at the community level that can influence the success of even a well-tested evidence-based model. These include historically-based perceptions that clients have of particular agencies, methods used for client outreach and engagement, the adequacy of agency infrastructure to implement the model, the ability to monitor intervention fidelity (e.g., the degree to which practitioners adhere to the model), and other sociocultural influences unique to that community.

Although it cannot address all of these issues, the CCNA model of assessment and planning can alleviate some by examining the service delivery system through the perspectives of the users and frontline providers. Gathering data about clients' willingness to use certain services, understanding their own perceptions of what is "effective," and being able to view the entire service system through the eyes of the user can shed light on why certain programs haven't worked or why others failed to engage their target populations.

Beyond the partnership that can be established between clients and their service providers in the CCNA model, consumer participation can be observed in several other facets of assessment and program planning. Belcher, DeForge, and Zanis[8] make a strong argument for the use of a

Participatory Action Research (PAR) framework for homeless research, in which those most affected by the problem (e.g., people who are homeless) play a central role in planning research designs and helping to promote policies and programs that have the capacity to address the "context of poverty, stigma and discrimination, isolation, and a socioeconomic system that creates the social conditions of joblessness and unaffordable housing."[9] Thus, a PAR approach can extend the dialogue on homelessness beyond individual "deficits" to a more complex analysis of the inter-relationships between individual, community, sociocultural, and economic influences. Including other stakeholders in this process, such as community members, representatives of businesses, government, law enforcement, and faith organizations, will further serve to understand and address this complexity.

A final trend with important implications for assessment is the development of programs and interventions that maximize and build on the strengths and assets of individuals, groups, and organizations in communities. Kretzmann and McKnight[10] have played a strong leadership role in shifting the focus of needs assessments from being deficit-based to asset-based. Their work highlights the success of communities that have utilized high degrees of consumer participation to make positive macro-level changes. Central to this approach is an emphasis on what is "working" in communities and building on that to promote further success. At the micro-level, strengths-based approaches have been steadily increasing in social service settings[11] and have been implemented with people who are homeless.[12] At the federal level, SAMSHA has begun to promote a strengths-based philosophy in some of their programs and policies. When SAMSHA identified strategies to improve mental health service delivery, they incorporated strengths-based language into their purpose statement:

> Ensure that mental health services and treatments (1) are consumer and family-centered and (2) focus on increasing consumers' ability to successfully manage life's challenges, on facilitating recovery, and on building resilience.[13]

Interestingly, similar strengths-based or consumer-oriented language is noticeably absent from their Strategic Action Plan for Homelessness, in which the emphasis is clearly problem-focused:

> Prevent or reduce homelessness among persons with mental illnesses and/or substance abuse disorders by providing outreach, mental health, substance abuse prevention and treatment, and other supportive services to individuals who are homeless or at risk of becoming homeless ... Many homeless individuals, in particular those who experience chronic homelessness, tend to have disabling health and behavioral health problems. One-half of homeless adults have histories of alcohol abuse or dependence and one-third have histories of drug abuse. About twenty to twenty-five percent of homeless adults have lifetime histories of serious mental illness. Between ten to twenty percent have a co-occurring substance abuse/mental health disorder.[14]

A Community Case Example

Building strengths-based and client-centered practices into assessment and program planning requires a fundamental shift beyond this predominant perspective of homelessness being centered on mental health, substance abuse, and disabilities. In two urban cities in North Texas, we have conducted assessments in an attempt to incorporate client-centered and strengths-based principles and practices. Although our assessments have in fact measured problems faced by people who are homeless, such as substance use and mental health—we have extended our analysis to include numerous other life experiences as well. Furthermore, we have continued to strengthen our focus on evaluating survival skills, social networks, and experiences with community members and organizations, and capturing perspectives about what they see as viable solutions and opportunities to improve their life conditions.

Our first CCNA for people who are homeless was based on interviews conducted at two large social service organizations: a faith-based facility serving daily lunches and providing transitional housing; and a daytime facility that provided laundry, showers, television, limited case management, and part-time access to other service providers in the community. Clients were invited to participate in in-depth interviews that lasted one to three hours and involved closed- and open-ended questions. Over an eighteen-month period, nearly 175 interviews were conducted. The results of the first 104 were analyzed and a report was presented to organizational staff, board members, and clients. The specific focus on gathering clients' perspectives and information about their strengths helped us understand that the homeless experience could not be explained through the assessment of mental and physical disabilities. We learned that many clients have faced a complex trajectory of life traumas, disappointments, and experiences that can both trigger and aggravate mental health symptoms and substance using behaviors. Furthermore, the societal context of increasing poverty and unemployment rates, as well as a lack of affordable housing clearly provides a setting that facilitates homelessness and serves as a barrier to obtaining economic stability. We also found that an elaborate social network was in place in this geographic region where people who are homeless help each other navigate the limited social service resources available and provide each other with significant support, protection, and basic assistance.

Our second implementation of the CCNA involved further adaptation of the interview protocol, expanded outreach practices, broader community participation, and a better refinement of questions intended to assess strengths and resiliencies. This project is in its final stages of completion. It has included interviews with 100 people who are homeless, with a considerable portion recruited directly from the streets. The perspectives of community members, business representatives, and service providers were also collected through surveys and focus groups. These multiple sources of data will be triangulated and used to help inform a municipalities' development of a ten-year strategic plan to end homelessness. It is believed that this approach offers a more contextualized understanding of homelessness and insight that cannot be gained through other assessment approaches. Gathering data from relevant stakeholders including service providers, the general public, and people who are homeless, allows for an understanding of homelessness in this geographical area, the capacities of the current assistance network, insight into public perceptions of homelessness, and what efforts they support to address it. Ultimately, communities attempting to address homelessness in their area will require this information. National trends regarding homelessness and en vogue service models all help point communities in the right direction, but in the end subtle—and sometimes not so subtle—economic, social, and political factors specific to each community must be acknowledged.

SERVICE USE BY PEOPLE WHO ARE HOMELESS

Current research illustrates that although people who are homeless are a diverse group united by a common need for shelter, they differ considerably in regards to demographic characteristics, the path taken into homelessness, and services needed to assist them.[15] Consequently, a variety of efforts have been attempted at the local, state, and federal levels with federal funding for homelessness assistance approaching $1 billion per year. Unfortunately, it appears that the results are mixed in some areas; the number of emergency shelter beds has doubled or even tripled over the last twenty years and one-third of the general homeless population report being homeless for two years or more.[16]

Obviously, this large population of individuals experiencing protracted homelessness is disconcerting and seems to suggest that a gap exists between services and the needs of people who are homeless. Given this evidence, it seems to indicate that a challenge in assisting people who are homeless is not always to make concrete assistance services available, but also engaging people to make use of them.

A considerable amount of research has investigated the service utilization behaviors of people who are homeless and the outcomes of assistance services. Unfortunately, transferring these findings to a practice environment is not always a simple process. The reality of providing services to people who are homeless is that the scarcity of resources, the complexity of the issues they are presented with, and the sheer volume of need can make providing assistance an overwhelming task. For research to be helpful to service providers, it should provide findings that are readily transferable to a variety of settings and offer practical suggestions to increase service use and improve the effectiveness of services. Given access to these resources of information, it would be possible for service providers to efficiently evaluate their practice and programs and make adjustments that could improve utilization and outcomes.

In an effort to identify research that would inform an understanding of service utilization and outcomes, a helpful perspective would be to evaluate research that sought to understand why people who are homeless do not use services. This question seems to provide a direct conduit to a better understanding of why people who are homeless may underutilize or refuse services in addition to offering insight into how to increase program utilization. Thankfully, research has addressed this question and the results of these findings are informative. What follows is a brief discussion of a sample of this literature and its application to providing services to people who are homeless.

Empirical Research

The reasons why people who are homeless may underutilize or refuse services vary, but some common themes can be identified. Fountain, Howes, Marsden, and Strang[17] found that reasons for not using services included the prevalence of substance abuse, violence, chaos, and because participants did not know where the services were located. Elderly homeless people are noted by O'Connell et al.[18] to often have difficulty with crowds, restrictive environments, and have difficulty tolerating and navigating the bureaucracy often found in accessing services. Comparing sheltered and unsheltered groups of people who are homeless, Nyamathi, Leake, and Gelberg[19] discuss that street-dwelling people who are homeless often experience barriers in obtaining services. Because these participants may not use shelter services, they generally cannot access the drop-in medical care, case management, or mental health and substance abuse treatment provided to residents at these facilities. In a similar comparison, Larsen, Poortinga, and Hurdle[20] identify that many homeless are unwilling to use shelter services because they fear being committed for mental health treatment and their dislike of shelter restrictions that typically prohibit the use of alcohol.

Investigating the influence of the social interaction of people who are homeless on their use of services has also yielded relevant findings. Shiner[21] acknowledges that a distinct culture develops among people who are homeless and that this culture must be considered in attempts to develop assistance services for people who are homeless. For street-dwelling individuals, the act of sleeping unsheltered was understood to redefine an individual's attitudes toward health and illness. In terms of their physical environment, Shiner[22] discusses that people who are homeless may view their environment as a threat to their physical health instead of a protector, and through a process of adaptation begin to accept an increased level of ill health in the midst of their homelessness. Additional findings identify that the unsheltered homeless assess the perceived costs and benefits of service use and that in general, "they did not seek care because they could see little benefit is doing so."[23] Street culture is also acknowledged, with the author discussing that:

> The accounts given by respondents included in this study point towards the existence of a distinct street culture which, based on shared knowledge of what it means to be homeless, emphasized powerlessness and marginality. Sleeping rough transformed respondent's relationships with mainstream health care providers and, it has been argued, rendered inappropriate the rules of thumb that govern health and illness behavior in wider society.[24]

In an article investigating begging as a form of legitimacy and indicator of social exclusion, Kennedy and Fitzpatrick[25] discuss that individuals did not utilize shelter services because they wanted to be with their friends on the street as well as being barred from shelters because of rent arrears, violence, or substance use. Additionally, people remained unsheltered because of the unwillingness of some shelter providers to accommodate certain groups including couples and people with pets. A final assessment revealed "a number of interviewees had rejected hostels because of their previous poor experiences of this type of accommodation, including restrictive rules, violence, intimidation, and high levels of drug use."[26]

Two qualitative articles focusing on military veterans are also relevant to our discussion of why some homeless people underutilize services. Higate,[27] within a study investigating the high number of ex-servicemen among the unsheltered homeless in the United Kingdom, noted that the military-oriented ideology of fierce pride, independence, and stoicism serve to influence how veterans decide to use or refuse services. Higate elaborates that:

> The recurrence of the rough sleeping theme appeared to be linked to the participant's shared knowledge of outdoor survival techniques, and the high levels of fitness fostered through the demands of Army "regulation" physical tests, measured both "in the field" and in the gym.[28]

In assessing barriers to service use encountered by homeless veterans, Applewhite[29] identifies that negative feelings of self-worth had a significant effect on their ability to cope with being homeless. Additionally, restrictive rules implemented at shelters, the lack of hygiene facilities, and transportation also presented barriers that were difficult for these individuals to overcome. Finally, public perception problems such as stigma and "false generosity of paternalism"[30] seemed to present more considerable barriers to exiting poverty and homelessness. The study participants also indicated that service providers at times demonstrated a "lack of respect for their human dignity, apathy, indifference, callousness, service-connected labeling, degrading comments, and put downs."[31] Organizational policies and procedures also presented barriers in that age discrimination, limits placed on assistance, dehumanizing rules and regulations, and address requirements pose considerable obstacles to obtaining services. Finally, barriers present within the social service delivery system were noted to include its unwieldiness, inadequacy, and inaccessibility.[32]

Research regarding the use of services by people who are homeless has also focused on the adolescent homeless population. Ensign and Panke[33] assert that the concept of cultural competency is essential in recognizing and appreciating the lifestyle, beliefs, and adaptive attitudes of homeless youth. They confront the perception of homeless youth as being deviant and advocate for training personnel that interact with this population to assist in understanding the health of homeless youth. Specific findings of the study identify: "that the biggest structural barriers present at many hospitals … were questions over consent of care, being asked to provide addresses and an identification card, and source of insurance or payment."[34] Additionally, lack of transportation, money, and social support were identified as being individual issues that affected the use of services. Finally, characteristics of organizations, providers, and communication issues were identified as affecting the use of services by female youth who are homeless.

Raleigh-DuRoff[35] has expanded this body of research with an investigation into the factors that influence homeless adolescents to leave or stay on the streets. Findings of the study discuss that a sense of freedom, community, distrust of authority, no chance for success, and a sense of adventure made it difficult for homeless adolescents to leave the streets.

Finally, DeRosa et al.[36] note in their research that "youth did not tolerate the strict rules and regulations set forth by youth shelters, or found them counterproductive. In addition, some youth described shelter rules as degrading, frustrating, or infantile."[37] Additionally, "requirements for disclosure of personal information, lack of confidentiality, and extensive paperwork constituted barriers to shelter utilization for many youth."[38] Other research with implications regarding service utilization involved the manner in which self-perceptions affect the use of services. Boydell[39] noted that several respondents identified themselves as being "introverted and stated that they did not like to talk and they kept everything inside." In addition, many respondents referred to themselves as being independent, which influenced their ability to reach out to others for support in the midst of their homelessness. Finally, those who were chronically homeless tended to put themselves down by stating that they were "unreliable, unaccomplished, and irresponsible. Several admitted that they were pretty violent, and a couple of individuals used the term disgust to describe how they felt about themselves."[40]

In the midst of these findings, there are perspectives of homelessness and practice models that would increase the use of assistance services and promote positive service outcomes. In terms of developing a more sophisticated perspective of contemporary homelessness, the ecological systems perspective proposed by Toro, Trickett, Wall, and Salem[41] is useful because it acknowledges that "homelessness is now recognized as a complex and multifaceted phenomenon involving broad social policies, economic shifts, service system deficiencies, disruptions of social support, and individual and family differences in access to resources and coping styles."[42]

The authors also discuss the essential features of an ecological perspective including the principles of adaptation, the cycling of resources, interdependence, and succession. These principles help to make the person-environment connection inherent in homelessness accessible and assist in understanding homelessness and taking action to address it. In addition to the structural components, the authors also discuss the importance of a collaborative and empowering professional style, noting that the inclusion of homeless people themselves in "the design, execution, and analysis of data will increase the range, depth, and relevance of information."[43] Additionally, this professional stance is also proposed to extend beyond interactions with homeless people in that:

> If we wish to develop interventions that provide a long-lasting resource to the community, local involvement and collaboration should increase the chance that the intervention will be indigenously supported and that it will be structured in a way that is acceptable to the community.[44]

Several practice models offer insight into addressing the needs of people who are homeless. Cohen[45] identifies that "many homeless mentally ill individuals avoid contact with others, particularly members of the mental health profession, who are often viewed as having power to exert authoritarian control over their lives."[46] The author then discusses that the process of engagement is a critical aspect in encouraging the use of services by the mentally ill that include: (1) the offering of voluntary services, (2) offering services that meet the client's perceived needs, (3) the building of connections between clients themselves, and (4) the empowerment of the client. All of these are proposed as strategies to increase the involvement of the homeless mentally ill in the use of services.[47] Similarly, Belcher and Ephross[48] discuss that:

> Homeless mentally ill face a highly institutionalized, bureaucratized, and complex mental health system. To obtain help, they must negotiate this system ... workers must understand how the needs of this population fit with community-based services as well as policy decisions and program designs that can potentially solve their problems.

In pursuit of this understanding, the authors advocate for a model refocusing assessment "from the level of pathology of an individual to the nature of the 'fit' between the person and the environment that is causing stress."[49] Advocating for a radical reconceptualization of practice, the authors go on to discuss the need for flexibility in agency service hours, a restructuring of the manner in which services are counted and billed, the relationship between the social worker and psychiatric service providers, and the involvement of the social worker in the role of the advocate for the client.[50]

The alternative approaches discussed by Cohen,[51] as well as those discussed by Belcher and Ephross[52] are expanded upon by Sheridan, Gowen, and Halpin[53] as they discuss characteristics of a practice model for the homeless mentally ill. In this article, the authors note, "Although it is necessary to address assertively the multiple needs of the homeless mentally ill, it is equally important to recognize and utilize their many strengths and resources."[54] Eight ideal practice characteristics are identified, which include the use of a client-centered and individualized practice, empowerment of the clients, enhancement of decision making, flexible and creative service approaches, a responsiveness to the client's cycle of needs, and a focus on client's strengths.[55] Additional principles include respecting client diversity, the use of natural support systems, and the creation of a bridge to existing services as well as advocating for additional services. The authors also discuss the importance of the worker themselves in the process of treating the mentally ill homeless. Effective staff expressed a sense of fulfillment for their work, possessed a specialized knowledge of mental illness and homelessness, a knowledge of intensive case management and other service approaches, skills in relationship building and communication, collaboration and advocacy skills, and other personal attributes and attitudes that enhance services provided to clients.[56] Finally, the authors discuss the importance of agency characteristics on the delivery of services to the homeless mentally ill. Generally, the authors identify the need for comprehensive services, coordination and integration, accessibility, and the creation of a viable Continuum of Care. In more detail, the importance of clinical and program supervision, training and networking opportunities, and adequate salaries and benefits are noted to be worker-level agency supports that facilitate engagement and service use. Client-level supports include concrete services and consumer involvement.[57]

Advocating an effort to reconfigure the traditional approach to service provision to the homeless mentally ill, Rowe, Hoge, and Fisk[58] discuss that:

> Mental health professionals and researchers have begun to explore the use of a new approach to providing treatment, rehabilitation services, and housing to homeless mentally ill persons who often avoid contact with traditional mental health programs because of the past difficulty in obtaining access to care, demands from clinicians for treatment, or having been hospitalized against their will.[59]

The authors emphasize that special strategies are required in serving the mentally ill and identify three general areas, including: (1) location and scheduling of the work, (2) client choice vs. clinician control, and (3) bureaucratic norms. Strategies include the selection of staff that "enjoy interdisciplinary work and are more temperamentally suited to 'negotiated partnerships' with clients than is the norm in office-based practice"[60] as well as the need for staff training in specific outreach and engagement skills. An additional strategy is the use of a hands-on management style by administration, which enhances their credibility to staff in the field and allows them a more accurate perspective of the work their employees do.[61]

In the midst of these perspectives on assisting people who are homeless, the discussions by Levy[62] offer additional insights into increasing the use of service by the homeless. Levy's conceptual article discussing homeless outreach asserts "homeless persons with severe mental illness will partake in services, if the service system can break out of the mold of traditional service provision and become responsive to their needs."[63] Additionally, in reference to the homeless mentally ill, the author notes that "Kuhlman states, 'that a psychotic person might develop a sense of identity and fit within a street-culture which makes this person more resistant to treatment warrants more serious consideration than it has been given thus far.' "[64]

Consequently, the author advocates for a pretreatment approach with the mentally ill homeless that utilizes a psychosocial developmental and ecological perspective. Additionally, the principles of harm reduction and an emphasis on the creation of a common language between the outreach worker and the client are stressed.[65] In support of this proposed model, the author goes on to identify five pretreatment principles that constitute the foundation of the outreach model. These principles include: (1) the promotion of safety, (2) the formation of a relationship between workers and clients, (3) the development of a common language, (4) the promotion and support of change, and (5) an acknowledgement of cultural and ecological effects.[66]

In a later article, Levy[67] goes into more detail on the need for a common language between outreach workers and clients who are homeless. A three-stage model of outreach with the mentally ill homeless were proposed to result in an increased use of services. The importance of this incremental approach is discussed in the article as:

> A homeless person's sense of immediacy and basic need often conflicts with the extended process of treatment, as well as with an office culture of scheduled appointments. Further, the street culture devalues treatment and often characterizes it through negative stereotypes. Even homeless individuals who recognize the potential benefits of treatment may reject it because of bad experiences with clinicians, inclusive of involuntary hospitalizations.[68]

Levy[69] goes on to further emphasize the need for a more patient, client-centered outreach approach by discussing that "the outreach clinician's initial goal is not to provide treatment, but rather to build relationships with homeless individuals that promote trust while not threatening their sense of autonomy."[70]

In the midst of this discussion, the author identifies the challenge of developing a common language in the midst of significant differences in culture and life experience, the identification of a common language, and the building of a bridge that allows the worker to connect with the client, as well as assist other providers in understanding the language that is used by people who are homeless. Ultimately, this model asserted to:

> Help demystify the engagement process and can provoke further discussion on the crucial task of facilitating good communication between outreach workers and homeless individuals. Ultimately, the goal of outreach is to reside in the same house as the homeless individual, thereby fostering a "being there" connection. It is within this context that a homeless person and outreach clinician can consider the possibility of change from a common frame of reference.[71]

It is important to note that there are contemporary intervention models that seem to acknowledge the factors that influence individuals to avoid assistance services and make efforts to minimize them. Two of the more prominent include the Assertive Community Treatment (ACT) model[72] and the Housing First supportive housing model.[73] These approaches are demonstrating their effectiveness with people who are homeless and mentally ill through their emphasis on client-choice, collaborative partnerships, and streamlined access to services. The Housing First model has placed homeless individuals into housing at a higher rate and demonstrates higher retention rates than more conventional linear treatment models.[74] This model also appears to contribute to a decrease in psychiatric symptoms due to an increase in perceived choice.[75]

Similarly, ACT is demonstrating higher client satisfaction levels, less time homeless, increased use of community resources,[76] and larger social networks that include social service professionals.[77] This model also confronts long-standing notions regarding agency-based services and a *train–place* approach to housing and employment; notions that remain very entrenched in some approaches to independent housing and supportive services. In practice, ACT places an emphasis on providing a comprehensive range of services using interdisciplinary teams that maintain small caseloads. Acknowledging the need to promote service use through streamlined access and an in vivo approach to service provision, the ACT teams work in the community and actively prioritize advocacy in linking clients to services.[78]

CONCLUSION

Considering the earlier discussion regarding the strategies used to assess homelessness and an investigation into the reasons why people who are homeless may underutilize services, the links appear evident. The methods used to assess the incidence, prevalence, and severity of homelessness have a considerable impact on the development and provision of assistance services and the ultimate success of these programs. By emphasizing a more client-centered approach, it would be possible for communities and assistance agencies to gain insight into the experience of homelessness and identify barriers to services. Additionally, by incorporating these models of assessment and their findings into the ongoing development of evidence-based practice, more efficacious policies and services can be developed. Involving people who are homeless in the initial assessment process, the development of social policy, and the design of assistance services, it would be possible to minimize many of the barriers influencing the use of services. Obviously, this presents challenges to the current hierarchy that often exists when service providers assist people who are homeless. An integral piece of any attempt to improve dialogue and promote collaboration will require that deficit-based understandings of homelessness be abandoned. To value the opinions of people who are homeless, we have to value them as people first.

NOTES

1. P. A. Toro, E. J. Trickett, D. D. Wall, and D. A. Salem, "Homelessness in the United States: An Ecological Perspective," *American Psychologist* 46, no. 11 (1991): 1208–18.

2. J. Blau, *The Visible Poor* (New York: Oxford University Press, 1992).

3. C. Schauer, A. Everett, and P. delVecchio, "Promoting the Value and Practice of Shared Decision-Making in Mental Health Care," *Psychiatric Rehabilitation Journal* 31, no. 1 (2007): 54–61.

4. Substance Abuse and Mental Health Services Administration, "National Registry of Evidence based Programs and Practices," http://www.nrepp.samhsa.gov/about-evidence.htm.

5. U.S. Department of Housing and Urban Development, *The Annual Homeless Assessment Report to Congress* (Washington DC: U.S. Government Printing Office, 2007).

6. M. Devillaer, "Client-Centered Community Needs Assessment," *Evaluation and Program Planning* 13, no. 3 (1990): 211–9; See also M. Devillaer, "Establishing and Using a Community Inter-agency Client Monitoring System to Develop Addictions Treatment Programs," *Addictions* 91, no. 5 (1996): 701–10.

7. Ibid.

8. J. R. Belcher, B. R. DeForge, and D. A. Zanis, "Why has the Social Work Profession Lost Sight of How to End Homelessness?" *Journal of Progressive Human Services* 16, no. 2 (2005): 5–23.

9. Ibid.

10. J. P. Kretzman and J. L. McKnight, *Building Communities from the Inside Out: A Path Toward Finding and Mobilizing Communities' Assets* (Chicago, IL: ACTA Publishers).

11. D. Saleebey, "The Strengths Perspective in Social Work Practice: Extensions and Cautions," *Social Work* 41, no. 3 (1996): 296–305.

12. D. Polio, S. M. McDonald, and C. North, "Combining a Strengths-Based Approach and Feminist Theory in Group Work with Persons on the Streets," *Social Work with Groups* 19, no. 3–4 (1997): 5–20.

13. Substance Abuse and Mental Health Services Administration, "SAMSHA Strategic Action Plan for Mental Health Systems Transformation," 2006–2007, http://www.samhsa.gov/matrix/SAP_mh.aspx.

14. Ibid.

15. L. Larson, E. Poortinga, and D. E. Hurdle, "Sleeping Rough: Exploring the Differences Between Shelter-using and Non-using Homeless Individuals," *Environment and Behavior* 36, no. 4(2004): 578–91.

16. G. Sullivan, P. Koegel, and A. Burnam, "Pathways to Homelessness Among the Mentally Ill," *Social Psychiatry and Psychiatric Epidemiology* 35, no. 10 (2000): 444–51.

17. J. Fountain, S. Howes, J. J. Marsden, and J. Strang, "Who Uses Services for Homeless People? An Investigation Amongst People Sleeping Rough in London," *Journal of Community and Applied Social Psychology* 12 (2002): 71–5.

18. J. J. O'Connell, J. S. Roncarati, E. C. Reilly, C. A. Kane, S. K. Morrison, S. E. Swain, J. Strupp-Allen, and K. Jones, "Old and Sleeping Rough: Elderly Homeless Persons of the Streets of Boston," *Care Management Journal* 5, no. 2 (2004): 101–6.

19. Adeline M. Nyamathi, Barbara Leake, and Lillian Gelberg, Sheltered versus Nonsheltered Homeless Women." *Journal of General Internal Medicine* 15, no. 8 (2007): 565–72.

20. Larson, Poortinga, and Hurdle, "Sleeping Rough," 2004.

21. Michael Shiner, "Adding Insult to Injury: Homelessness and Health Service Use," *Sociology of Health and Illness* 17, no. 4 (1995): 525–49.

22. Ibid.

23. Ibid., 540.

24. Ibid., 545.

25. C. Kennedy and S. Fitzpatrick, "Begging, Rough Sleeping, and Social Exclusion: Implications for Social Policy," *Urban Studies* 38, no. 11 (2001): 2001–16.

26. Ibid., 2007.

27. P. R. Higate, "Tough Bodies and Rough Sleeping: Embodying Homelessness Amongst Ex-Servicemen," *Housing, Theory and Society* 17 (2000): 97–108.

28. Ibid., 98.

29. S. L. Applewhite, "Homeless Veterans: Perspectives on Social Services Use," *Social Work* 42, no. 1 (1997): 19–30.

30. Ibid., 24.

31. Ibid.,. 25.

32. Ibid.

33. J. Ensign and A. Panke, "Bridges and Barriers to Care: Voices of Homeless Female Adolescent Youth in Seattle, Washington, USA," *Journal of Advanced Nursing* 37, no. 2 (2001): 166–72.

34. Ibid., 169.

35. C. Raleigh-DuRoff, "Factors that Influence Homeless Adolescents to Leave or Stay Living on the Street," *Child and Adolescent Social Work Journal* 21, no. 6 (2004): 561–72.

36. C. J. DeRosa, S. B. Montgomery, M. D. Kipke, E. Iverson, J. L. Ma, and J. B. Unger, "Service Utilization Among Homeless and Runaway Youth in Los Angeles, California: Rates and Reasons," *Journal of Adolescent Mental Health* 24, no. 3 (1999): 190–200.

37. Ibid., 196.

38. Ibid., 196.

39. K. M. Boydell, P. Goering, and T. L. Morrell-Bellai, "Narratives of Identity: Representation of Self in People who are Homeless," *Qualitative Health Research* 10, no. 1 (2000): 26–38.

40. Ibid., 31.

41. P. A. Toro, E. J. Trickett, D. D. Wall, and D. A. Salem, "Homelessness in the United States: An Ecological Perspective," *American Psychologist* 46, no. 11 (1991): 1208–18.

42. Ibid., 1208.
43. Ibid., 1214.
44. Ibid., 1214.
45. M. B. Cohen, "Social Work Practice with Homeless Mentally Ill People: Engaging the Client," *Social Work* 34, no. 6 (1989): 505–9.
46. Ibid., 505.
47. Ibid.
48. J. R. Belcher and P. H. Ephross, "Toward an Effective Practice Model for the Homeless Mentally Ill," *Social Casework* 70, no. 7 (1989): 421–7.
49. Ibid., 424.
50. Ibid.
51. Cohen, "Social Work Practice with Homeless," 1989.
52. Belcher and Ephross, "Toward an Effective Practice," 1989.
53. M. J. Sheridan, N. Gowen, and S. Halpin, "Developing a Practice Model for the Homeless Mentally Ill," *Families in Society* 74, no. 7 (1993): 410–20.
54. Ibid., 413.
55. Ibid.
56. Ibid.
57. Ibid.
58. M. Rowe, M. A. Hoge, and D. Fisk, "Critical Issues in Serving People who are Homeless and Mentally Ill," *Administration and Policy in Mental Health* 23, no. 6 (1996): 555–65.
59. Ibid., 555.
60. Ibid., 560.
61. Ibid.
62. J. S. Levy, "Homeless Outreach: On the Road to Pretreatment Alternatives," *Families in Society* 81, no. 4 (2000): 360–8.
63. Ibid., 360.
64. Ibid., 366.
65. Ibid.
66. Ibid.
67. J. S. Levy, "Pathway to a Common Language: A Homeless Outreach Perspective," *Families in Society* 85, no. 3 (2004): 371–8.
68. Ibid., 374.
69. Ibid.
70. Ibid., 372.
71. Ibid., 378.
72. A. S. Young, M. J. Chinman, J. A. Cradock-O'Leary, G. Sullivan, D. Murata, and J. Mintz, "Characteristics of Individuals with Severe Mental Illness who Use Emergency Services," *Community Mental Health Journal* 41, no. 2 (2995): 159–68.
73. S. Tsemberis, "From Streets to Homes: An Innovative Approach to Supportive Housing for Homeless Adults with Psychiatric Disabilities," *Journal of Community Psychology* 27, no. 2 (1999): 225–41; S. Tsemberis, L. Gulcur, and M. Nakae, "Housing First, Consumer Choice, and Harm Reduction for Homeless Individuals with a Dual Diagnosis," *American Journal of Public Health* 94, no. 4 (2004): 651–6.
74. Ibid.
75. R. M. Greenwood, N. Schaefer-McDoniel, G. Winkel, and S. J. Tsemberis, "Decreasing Psychiatric Symptoms for Adults with Histories of Homelessness," *American Journal of Community Psychology* 36, no. 3–4 (2005): 223–38.

76. M. Johnsen, L. Samberg, R. Calsyn, M. Blasinsky, W. Landow, and H. Goldman, "Case Management Models for Persons who are Homeless and Mentally Ill: The ACCESS Demonstration Project," *Community Mental Health Journal* 35, no. 4 (1999): 325–46.

77. R. J. Calsyn, G. A. Morse, D. W. Klinkenberg, M. L. Trusty, and G. Allen, "The Impact of Assertive Community Treatment on the Social Relationships of People who are Homeless and Mentally Ill," *Community Mental Health Journal* 34, no. 6 (1998): 579–93.

78. Ibid.

Chapter Eight

THE EVOLUTION OF HOMELESSNESS: TRENDS AND FUTURE DIRECTIONS

Maria Foscarinis

Homelessness has been a major social problem in the United States for the past three decades. Although it has a long history, contemporary homelessness grew dramatically in size and scope beginning in the early to mid-1980s. The resulting crisis spurred advocacy efforts for solutions at all levels of government and a variety of responses by both public and private sectors.

This chapter reviews major policy trends in responding to homelessness, focusing both on advocacy and on government responses. The chapter suggests that responses to homelessness over the past twenty-five years or so fall into four rough stages. First, early in the 1980s, advocacy focused primarily on local crisis response, and advocacy for a right to shelter met with some success in several cities. Later in that decade, a second stage emerged as advocacy shifted to the national level with a push for congressional and agency action, and culminated with the enactment in 1987 of the landmark Stewart B. McKinney Homeless Assistance Act. In the 1990s, advocacy focused on implementation and enforcement of the new law; the decade also marked the beginning of national advocacy for longer-term solutions, with some government response. At the same time, however, local governments began cutting back aid to the poor and implementing harsh laws and policies aimed at homeless people living in public places. Currently, much advocacy is focusing on longer-term solutions, primarily permanent housing and access to "mainstream" social welfare programs. National (and some local and state) government policy is making a rhetorical shift in support of such solutions; however, the policy reality is often far different. The paucity of law recognizing economic rights in general, and housing rights in particular, makes advocacy for these longer-term resources particularly challenging.

Looking toward the future, the chapter discusses recent efforts to develop a united national advocacy agenda to press for new policies to put longer-term solutions in place. The chapter also discusses recent initiatives that incorporate advocacy for the human right to housing as part of a strategy to build a firmer foundation for such solutions. This approach has generated interest among advocates and is building momentum, and may also help to build political will for long-term solutions to homelessness.

INTRODUCTION: HOMELESSNESS IN THE UNITED STATES

Recent estimates are that on any given night more than 800,000 people experience homelessness in the United States, and that over the course of a year, 2.5 to 3.5 million people will experience homelessness.[1] A study published in 1994 indicated that 7 million Americans had experienced homelessness between 1985 and 1990, and that as many as 12 million Americans, or 6.5 percent of the U.S. resident population in that year, had been homeless at some point in their lives.[2] The current homeless population is diverse, marking a shift from the predominantly middle-aged white male alcoholics who populated skid rows in the post-war era. According to the most comprehensive national survey of U.S. homelessness to date, thirty-four percent of homeless people are members of homeless families; about twenty-three percent of the total population consists of children.[3] Thirty-two percent of the population is female.[4] In addition, forty-four percent of homeless adults worked at some point in any given month.[5] Some thirty-nine percent reported indicators of serious mental illness.[6]

Lack of affordable housing is a primary cause of homelessness in the United States.[7] The gap between poor households in need of rental housing and the availability of affordable housing is 4.7 million; some 13.7 million households, or fourteen percent of all households, live in substandard housing or spend more than fifty percent of their incomes on housing, far in excess of the thirty percent federal affordability standards and putting them at substantial risk of homelessness.[8] At the same time, full-time work at the minimum wage is not sufficient to afford fair market rent, on the basis of these affordability standards, for an efficiency apartment (an apartment consisting of one room only) in any of the fifty largest cities in the United States.[9] Mental and physical illness and addictions—and the lack of services to address them—are also significant factors contributing to homelessness, along with domestic violence[10] and low levels of education.

Homelessness has a devastating effect, and it is particularly damaging to families and children. A recent survey found that in fifty-five percent of major U.S. cities surveyed families may have to break up in order to be sheltered.[11] Homeless children suffer several additional harms. Because they lack a permanent address, homeless children may be illegally denied access to school, and many do not attend school regularly or receive appropriate educational services.[12] Numerous studies document the serious emotional and developmental problems that these children suffer, which may persist long past the period of homelessness and increase the risk of adult homelessness.[13]

EFFORTS TO ADDRESS HOMELESSNESS: STRATEGIES AND TRENDS

The most important elements of both long-term and immediate solutions to homelessness are housing, jobs, and social services.[14] Indeed, there is growing consensus within advocacy and government communities that these are the elements necessary for true solutions to homelessness. But implementing such solutions—and marshalling the resources to fund them—has been a challenge. Litigation has also played an important role in protecting rights and providing some aid to some groups of people. But there is little or no constitutional basis for requiring the creation of systems that end and prevent homelessness, reflecting a legal system that commonly protects civil and political rights, but not economic or social rights. Legislative and regulatory advocacy has led to the creation of important new laws and programs, but not to a degree sufficient to solve the problem; more is needed to provide material aid to homeless people as well as recognize and protect their rights. New research can play an important role in supporting such advocacy. Political organizing, public outreach, and media education are crucial as well.

Early Advocacy—Response to Crisis

As the incidence of homelessness began to grow in the late 1970s, advocates pressed city governments to respond by providing emergency shelter. One of the earliest advocacy strategies aimed at addressing homelessness was litigation to secure a right to shelter under state and local law. Initially successful in winning aid for homeless people, the early right-to-shelter advocacy in many ways defined the nature of government response to homelessness for years to come. At the same time, media attention to the rapidly growing crisis of homelessness—especially the increasing numbers of homeless families and children—focused tremendous public attention and sympathy on the issue.

The first right to shelter case was filed in 1979 in New York City. In *Callahan v. Carey*, a class of homeless men in New York City filed suit in state court seeking to require the state and city to provide them with shelter and meals and arguing that the defendants' failure to do so would cause them irreparable harm, including possible death from exposure during the winter months. Relying on a state constitutional provision requiring the state to provide for the "aid, care and support of the needy," the court held that "the Bowery derelicts are entitled to Board and lodging."[15] The court found that the then existing shelter spaces were not sufficient for "all of the destitute and homeless alcoholics, addicts, mentally impaired derelicts, flotsam and jetsam, and others during the winter months," and issued a temporary, emergency order requiring the city to provide shelter pending further consideration of the claims.

Following that order, the plaintiffs and the city negotiated a consent decree; as a result, no final, definitive court ruling on the right to shelter was made. The consent decree obligated the city to provide overnight shelter to every eligible homeless man, set minimum shelter standards, and defined the process by which application for shelter was to be made and addressed. Shelter standards included the width and construction of shelter beds; provision of soap, towels, and toilet paper; storage facilities and security; and defined maximum capacity levels for existing shelters. The decree foresaw the construction of new shelters and set out for standards for them as well.

Subsequent cases in New York City established similar shelter rights for women and for families.[16] A successful case was also brought to enforce shelter rights for homeless families under the then-federal welfare program, which provided federal funding to states.[17] Advocates in other parts of the country brought suit to establish similar rights, on the basis of state statutes, with some success, including in New Jersey, West Virginia, and California.[18] In Washington, D.C., the Right to Overnight Shelter Act of 1984 was passed as a ballot initiative with seventy-two percent of the vote; it guaranteed "safe, sanitary, and accessible shelter space, offered in an atmosphere of reasonable dignity."[19]

Advocates had few options, however, for litigation to establish shelter—or housing—rights under the U.S. Constitution. In a 1972 case, *Lindsey v Normet*, the Supreme Court held, in the context of a landlord-tenant dispute, that there is no right to housing of a particular quality. Although it is possible to argue that the ruling is limited to its particular facts, as a practical and political matter, prospects for establishing a constitutional right to shelter or housing were rightly seen as extremely limited, and such litigation was not actively pursued.

Beyond the Local Response—National Advocacy

By the early to mid-1980s, homelessness was clearly a national crisis.[20] The administration then in office, however, denied this reality. According to then-President Reagan, homelessness was a "choice" made by those who preferred that "lifestyle."[21] According to this view, homelessness was a concern for charity or, at most, local government; it was not an issue for national policy. Beginning in 1983, funds for emergency food and shelter were appropriated on an ad hoc basis through the disaster relief program administered by the Federal Emergency Management Agency (FEMA), but no permanent legislation was authorized.[22] In this context, advocacy began to focus on eliciting a national response.

In the mid-1980s, a group of legal advocates working on an array of poverty issues came together to draft model legislation designed to address homelessness. As finally drafted, it contained three titles, focusing on emergency, preventative, and long-term solutions to homelessness. The model bill, styled the Homeless Persons' Survival Act (HPSA), was based in part on the needs identified by legal services lawyers seeing homeless or near-homeless clients. Efforts to secure sponsors to introduce and champion the legislation in Congress initially met serious obstacles. Homelessness was generally not viewed as a national policy issue, and even sympathetic members of Congress claimed that supporting the bill would be politically risky given upcoming elections and the political powerlessness of homeless residents of their district, sometimes noting bluntly that "homeless people don't vote."[23]

Nevertheless, following concerted lobbying, the HPSA was introduced in both the House and Senate in 1986 and, later that year, a small part of it was enacted as the Homeless Eligibility Clarification Act. This new law provided that homeless people could receive certain federal benefits, including Supplemental Security Income (SSI), Medicaid, Aid to Families with Dependent Children (AFDC), and food stamps, without having to supply an address. It also established a pre-release program to allow persons in institutions such as mental hospitals and prisons to apply for food stamps and SSI benefits, in order to prevent their becoming homeless upon release. Also enacted in 1986 was the Homeless Housing Act, legislation creating two small "demonstration" programs to fund emergency shelter and transitional housing and appropriating $15 million to fund them.

Following these successes, grassroots and legal advocates worked in tandem over the winter of 1986–1987 on a major campaign to pass additional legislation. In the spring of 1987, the bill was passed with large, bipartisan majorities,[24] and in July, the bill was signed in to law by President Reagan, with an official statement of "reluctance."[25] Nonetheless, the Stewart B. McKinney Homeless Assistance Act (McKinney Act), named in honor of its chief Republican sponsor who died shortly after its passage, recognized homelessness as "an immediate and unprecedented crisis" requiring a federal response "to meet the critically urgent needs of the homeless of the Nation."[26]

As enacted in 1987, the McKinney Act consisted of nine separate titles, with shelter and transitional housing as central elements. These included the establishment of the Interagency Council on the Homeless as an independent agency charged with reviewing, monitoring, and coordinating all federal programs to assist homeless people, recommending improvements, and disseminating information. The act established several shelter and transitional housing programs, along with a small permanent housing program; it also created a program for federal surplus properties to be made available for use by states, localities, and nonprofits to house programs for homeless people. The remaining titles established a health care program, limited job training, and adult literacy programs, and a program to ensure access by homeless children to public school education, also providing for a legal right to such access. They also included provisions to improve access to food stamps and surplus food programs.

The McKinney Act authorized funding at just over $1 billion over two years: $438 million for 1987 and $615 million for 1988. The amount actually appropriated—through a process separate from that in which legislation is written or authorized—was significantly less: $350 million for fiscal year 1987 and $362 million for 1988. The McKinney Act programs consisted primarily of Title I (mainly emergency relief) of the HPSA; Titles II and III (preventative and long-term relief), were not enacted. In carrying out their campaign for what became the McKinney Act, advocates made a strategic decision to press for this first title based on a calculation that this was a goal that, although very ambitious in the then-political climate, was potentially achievable. A winter campaign focusing on immediate crisis needs would have more political currency than a campaign for longer-term solutions. But this same calculation also risked perpetuating the notion that emergency relief—such as shelter—could serve as a solution to homelessness.

Advocates and congressional supporters attempted to guard against this result. During the congressional debate on the legislation, then-senator Al Gore, a Democrat from Tennessee and the chief Senate sponsor of the HPSA, speaking on the floor of the Senate, said that "no one in this body should believe that the legislation we begin considering today is anything more than a first step towards reversing the record increase in homelessness."[27] And in an effort to reflect the continuum between actual homelessness and extreme poverty, and to trace a path for further action to address it, the Act's definition of homeless persons includes those lacking an "adequate nighttime residence."[28]

At the same time that advocacy for national legislation was proceeding, advocates also pressed the federal agencies to take action, sometimes through litigation. Following passage of the McKinney Act, these strategies intensified. Advocates initiated monitoring efforts to determine whether the Act's programs were being properly implemented, and several quick, successful suits were filed to require the federal agencies to disburse funds according to the urgent timetable established by Congress.[29] Subsequently, more complex suits to implement the new law were filed. Such suits have included litigation to enforce compliance with Title V, the Federal Surplus Property Program, which resulted in a court order requiring five major federal agencies to make available free of charge vacant property to providers of services for homeless people, by deed or lease.[30]

The 1990s—Two Steps Forward, One Step Back?

During the 1990s, much national advocacy focused on improving, expanding, and enforcing the provisions of the 1987 McKinney Act. Appropriations grew, and significant amendments strengthened many of the law's provisions and focused the McKinney Act's programs more on preventing and ending homelessness, reflecting the success of advocacy in shifting national policy in that direction. At the same time, however, many local governments focused on cutting back homeless people's rights and benefits. Further, they increasingly enacted laws that punished homeless people living in public spaces. Local advocacy focused on court challenges to these cuts and to city efforts to "criminalize" homelessness.

Local Government: Retrenchment and Criminalization

The 1990s saw increasingly harsh, punitive policies towards poor persons, notably including the enactment in 1996 of federal welfare "reform" and the elimination of the entitlement to aid for needy families. Parallel to these federal-level trends, localities increasingly sought to limit shelter rights where they had been previously established. Often accompanied by the rhetoric of "personal responsibility" and the claim that homeless people were otherwise receiving undeserved or unearned largesse, these limitations took the form of work requirements, time limits on shelter stays, "fault" standards, and in some cases elimination of the right to shelter. Local advocates found themselves fighting against this backslide instead of pushing for further progress.

For example, in New York City, advocates filed repeated contempt motions in *Callahan v. Carey* as well as subsequent shelter rights cases, challenging the city's refusal to provide adequate emergency shelter for homeless individuals and families. In New Jersey, where court rulings had established a right to shelter, advocates fought efforts to impose a "fault" standard on that right, requiring families to demonstrate that they had not had more than thirty days' notice of their impending homelessness, and thus had not been able to prevent it, effectively assuming that personal resourcefulness—as opposed to external resources such as the availability of affordable housing—was the key to avoiding homelessness. In Washington, D.C., advocates filed suit to enforce the right to shelter, and the city was repeatedly held in contempt for failing to provide it (see, e.g., *Atchison v. Barry*).[31] City officials then sought changes in the law to undermine the basis for the right, and in 1994 the law establishing the right was repealed.[32]

At the same time that they restricted or eliminated shelter rights, cities also tried to address the negative impact of growing numbers of homeless people living in public places. Some cities enacted new laws imposing criminal sanctions for sleeping or begging in public places; some resurrected old vagrancy laws and began applying them selectively to "sweep" homeless people out of particular city sections, sometimes before major city events.[33] In response, advocates challenged this trend in court, before city councils and in the media. Several important court rulings upheld challenges to such city laws and practices under the U.S. Constitution. But not all challenges were successful, and some cities responded by rewriting their laws to avoid challenge while still accomplishing their punitive goals. Increasingly, battles over the "criminalization" of homelessness replaced right-to-shelter advocacy as the dominant issue at the local advocacy level.

In a related trend, zoning laws increasingly excluded housing and services for homeless persons from certain areas. Just as with criminalization, some cities enacted new laws or more stringently enforced existing laws so as to exclude or severely limit housing or service providers. A particularly striking example occurred in November 1995 when the city of Hartford, Connecticut, imposed a moratorium on the creation and expansion of all social service facilities in the city.[34] Although litigation challenging such laws is somewhat constrained because federal antidiscrimination laws do not protect homeless people specifically, the prevalence of protected characteristics, such as disabilities, among the homeless population has been successfully cited to invoke the protection of federal fair housing laws barring discrimination on this basis.[35]

Both the retrenchment of shelter rights and the rise in punitive and exclusionary laws have been cited as evidence of declining public "sympathy" for homeless people; however, polls indicate otherwise. Several surveys of public opinion majorities have indicated that people are sympathetic, believe additional low-cost housing is needed, and would be willing to pay tax dollars to support it.[36] What may instead explain these harsh policies is the pressure placed on city officials by business groups concerned about homeless people's impact on their interests, and city officials' own concern about the impact on tourism. Despite the poll numbers, the business groups are likely in a stronger position to influence city policy.

Furthermore, the availability of even limited emergency shelter may give the appearance that solutions are in place. Studies—including studies by cities—regularly find that there is insufficient emergency shelter, by far, to accommodate the need.[37] Moreover, a shelter does not constitute a permanent home; even where it is available it often leaves its recipients unwashed, bedraggled, without a place to store their belongings, and without a place to go during the day. But the availability of even some shelter presents the appearance that some aid is available, making it possible to blame homeless people for "choosing" to be homeless despite the availability of these perceived "solutions."[38] Punitive and exclusionary measures then become easier to justify, and legislation to enact them can more readily proceed with public support or at least without public opposition.

National Advocacy: Moving beyond the McKinney Act

Advocacy efforts for additional, longer-term federal aid began shortly after passage of the McKinney Act, with proposed legislation for permanent housing as a long-term solution to homelessness. But with the infusion of new federal funds through the McKinney Act to communities, grassroots momentum stalled, and providers focused on obtaining funding and implementing programs.[39]

In 1992, an effort to move "beyond McKinney" was initiated, and a coalition of national and local level groups worked to define a comprehensive agenda for long-term solutions, focusing on the need for housing, adequate incomes, and social services. Meanwhile, amendments to the McKinney Act succeeded in moving its programs in the direction of longer-term solutions, with increased emphasis on homelessness prevention, housing assistance to disabled homeless people, and strengthened protections for homeless children's education rights.

The Clinton administration, endorsing the need for longer-term solutions, also put in place programmatic changes through the administrative process,[40] initiating the "Continuum of Care" process. This process brings together local government and nonprofit providers to identify gaps in services for homeless people and devise a plan to bridge those gaps, as part of the application process for McKinney shelter and housing funds. In addition to encouraging planning and coordination, this process also prioritizes funding for programs that include efforts to increase access to mainstream programs. During the 1990s, funding for the McKinney programs increased significantly, peaking at $1.49 billion in the 1995 fiscal year.

In addition to these changes, in 1994 Congress amended Title V of the McKinney Act, which grants a right of first refusal to federal surplus property to providers of services to homeless people, to exempt vacant military bases from its provisions. Many military bases were then being closed for conversion to civilian use, and this exemption threatened a serious loss of resources. However, also in 1994, advocates succeeded in obtaining a requirement in defense department legislation that the needs of homeless people be addressed in the process of converting military bases to civilian use. Thus bases were preserved as a resource, and numerous former bases and other federal and nonfederal properties are now being used for transitional and permanent housing for homeless people.[41]

Litigation to enforce Title VII of the McKinney Act, which requires state and local agencies to provide access to education for homeless children, was also filed. *Lampkin v. District of Columbia*, filed in the federal court, established important precedent holding that the McKinney Act education provisions are judicially enforceable. Following that ruling, a state court suit was successfully resolved, with a consent decree establishing detailed steps that the Chicago public school system would have to take to ensure homeless children's access to school. A more recent lawsuit, *NLCHP v. Suffolk County*, resulted in another federal court ruling upholding the enforceability of the law and a detailed consent decree covering the county and New York State.

RECENT AND CURRENT TRENDS

A broad range of advocacy and government responses are currently underway, nationally and locally. A common thread is the adoption, or at least statement, of a goal to end homelessness. Furthermore, most responses have adopted the "Housing First" approach that aims to move homeless people as quickly as possible into permanent housing, and to provide any needed services in conjunction with the housing, in contrast to the model that attempted to move people through a "continuum" of emergency shelter to transitional housing to permanent housing. Recognition that mainstream programs must be engaged to meet the needs of homeless people also cuts across responses. However, specific approaches vary widely, as do the goals—ranging from narrow efforts to end "chronic" homelessness to ambitious efforts to end and prevent homelessness for all.

Several of these approaches cite significant recent research that illuminates the nature of homelessness, such as the 1999 national study commissioned by the Interagency Council on the Homeless (ICH) and carried out by Urban Institute researchers, Among other things, the study indicated that significant numbers of families and children are homeless; that large numbers of homeless people work full- or part-time; that large percentages do not receive mainstream federal benefits such as food stamps, disability benefits, and temporary assistance for needy families for which they are likely eligible and to which they are likely entitled; and that homelessness affects urban, suburban, and rural communities. The study also found that not being able to pay the rent and loss of a job were most frequently stated as precipitating causes of homelessness by homeless people; for women in particular, domestic violence was frequently cited. Other influential studies by researchers at the University of Pennsylvania indicated that the costs of not addressing homelessness—as measured by increased use of emergency rooms, police, and other resources—roughly equals the cost of providing permanent housing with supportive services. These studies also indicated that people with multiple problems, primarily mental or physical disabilities, use a disproportionately large percentage of shelter and service resources. The studies have been cited to support a range of different remedies.

At the federal level, the government response to homelessness has received increased visibility. In 2002, the Bush administration publicly expressed a goal to end "chronic homelessness" in ten years and proclaimed this a priority. This policy emphasis was accompanied by the revitalization of the ICH, which had lost its funding and lain dormant for years. The commitment marked a dramatic shift from the Reagan administration's position. It is, however, quite narrow in scope; the goal's limitation to "chronically" homeless people—defined to include single adults, usually with disabilities, substance abuse problems, or both, who experience repeated episodes of homelessness—excludes all homeless families and children. The definition of homelessness adopted by the administration is also extremely limited, including only those who are "literally" homeless, and excluding those who are doubled-up, and thus much of the rural homeless population.

The rationale cited for this narrow focus is research showing that people with multiple problems use a disproportionately large percentage of shelter and service resources. Thus, ending homelessness for this population through permanent supportive housing would free up resources for many more needing only short-term help.[42] However, despite the stated commitment to solutions that are based on research, this narrow approach does not account for findings indicating that family and rural homelessness are significant.

The commitment has also been largely rhetorical in practice. The administration initiated and supported successful efforts to increase funds for U.S. Department of Housing and Urban Development (HUD) McKinney programs by almost $200 million. But at the same time, the administration has taken actions and supported legislative proposals to cut low-income housing and other social programs, exacerbating the causes of homelessness. For example, between 2004 and 2006 funding for HUD programs declined by $3.3 billion in real dollars, an eight percent reduction. This translates into a loss of nearly 150,000 housing vouchers.[43]

At the same time that federal funding has declined, the ICH, the top federal agency specifically charged with addressing homelessness, has focused much of its efforts on urging states and localities to adopt plans to end homelessness, in collaboration with some advocates.[44] The plans vary widely in specificity and scope.[45] Some have been developed in active partnership with local advocates, but others have not. Many focus on moving disabled homeless people into permanent supportive housing, preventing homelessness through discharge planning, moving homeless people rapidly into permanent housing, and improving access to mainstream services.

Significantly, although some cities are adopting such plans, many also continue to adopt punitive measures aimed at homeless people; often, cities pursue both responses simultaneously. In a recent new twist on the trend, growing numbers of cities are not only criminalizing homelessness but also those trying to help them. Several cities have passed laws prohibiting or restricting sharing food with homeless people (but not with others) in public places. At least one such law has been successfully challenged as violation of the U.S. Constitution; other challenges are pending. Perhaps following the lead of official punitive responses to homelessness, crimes by private individuals that target homeless people are also on the increase. Recent advocacy has focused on state legislation to declare such attacks hate crimes, warranting enhanced penalties; federal legislation is also pending.

In a few cases, cities have adopted positive, as opposed to "criminalizing" approaches to street homelessness. For example, following the success of *Pottinger v. Miami*, the Dade county government (where Miami is located) imposed a half-cent meal tax to raise funds for housing, job training, and substance abuse treatment for homeless people. In Philadelphia, police work with outreach workers to offer services to unsheltered homeless people, and the city has backed up this outreach with some increased funds for services.[46] However, these approaches represent a small minority compared to the still prevalent, even growing, criminalizing measures. At the local level, much advocacy has focused on efforts to fight these punitive laws, through litigation, organizing, or both, and to prevent city councils from adopting them. Advocacy has also worked to persuade cities to adopt constructive approaches in lieu of punitive measures.

Federal-level advocacy has focused on a variety of approaches. Some recent advocacy has worked to remove barriers to the mainstream anti-poverty programs as a means of preventing as well as ending homelessness. Because most government systems assume that applicants and recipients have fixed addresses, homeless persons are often excluded from their aid; removal of the barriers can help people out of homelessness or prevent them from becoming homeless.[47] Crucial to these and other efforts is advocacy to address measures introduced in the wake of the September 11 terrorist attacks that create barriers to homeless people seeking identification cards. Advocacy efforts to address this issue at the federal level are currently underway.

Some efforts to increase access to mainstream programs are succeeding, in some cases building on the McKinney-Vento Act. For example, litigation to enforce the education provisions of the McKinney Act established homeless children's right to education—a major mainstream program. Amendments to those provisions of the Act steadily improved access to public school for homeless children, as well as to related benefits such as school meals. Legislative advocacy has also succeeded in requiring the mainstream education program that addresses the needs of all disadvantaged children to include provisions for homeless children. Similarly, the program to ensure equal access to education for disabled children now includes special provisions for disabled homeless children. Currently pending amendments would further those legislative inroads, with amendments to the federal laws governing early childhood programs and access to higher education.

Advocacy has also focused on disability benefits under the Social Security Act, for which many homeless persons are eligible but often do not receive because of the identification barriers as well as the difficulty of the application process. In 2002, Congress required the SSA to develop and implement a plan to remove barriers to benefits for homeless people, and in 2003, following the issuance of the plan, Congress appropriated funds for "demonstration" programs for outreach and expedited application procedures for homeless people. More legislative proposals aimed at removing barriers from and opening access to a range of programs are currently in the works.

Some recent advocacy has focused on amending larger mainstream programs in order to prevent homelessness. In a major victory, the Violence Against Women Act, reauthorized by Congress in 2007, included new provisions to protect victims of domestic violence from losing their housing. Domestic violence is a major cause of homelessness for women, and advocates for homeless people worked with domestic violence advocates to secure these new protections.

Some federal level advocacy has focused on changes to the McKinney-Vento Act. Some advocates have worked to increase funding for permanent supportive housing by shifting HUD McKinney shelter and housing resources away from services—which could instead be funded by the mainstream programs—and towards funding permanent supportive housing. Beginning in 1998, Congress imposed a thirty percent maximum on the use of emergency shelter grants for services, and in 2000 required that thirty percent of McKinney shelter and housing funds be used to provide permanent supportive housing for homeless persons. These changes have been made through the appropriations process; the HUD McKinney-Vento programs have not been reauthorized since 1992.

Currently, however, legislation to reauthorize these programs is pending in both the House and Senate. In the House, the Homeless Emergency Assistance and Rapid Transition to Housing (HEARTH) Act also calls for increasing funding authority by $2.5 billion; it would also expand the definition of homelessness applicable to those programs to conform to that applicable to the Act's education section. That definition includes people who are doubled-up with others. The current HUD definition includes only those who are living in places "not fit for human habitation" in shelters or transitional housing programs for homeless people. That narrow definition is not required by statute but was adopted by HUD as a matter of policy. The HEARTH Act would also discourage localities from policies that criminalize homelessness. In the Senate, the Partnership to End Homelessness Act retains the narrow HUD definition but expands eligible activities to include prevention of homelessness for people. It calls for $1.8 billion in funding.

Despite the growing momentum for solutions, the changes now underway are by themselves unlikely to provide true solutions. The mainstream programs, although helpful, cannot end homelessness alone; the assistance they provide is not sufficient relative to housing costs. Moreover, the federal programs that fund low-income housing have been drastically cut back, and private efforts to make up the gap—such as nonprofit housing programs—have been inadequate. Recognizing this reality, some advocacy efforts aim to increase housing and other resources in order to end and prevent homelessness.

Currently planned for re-introduction in Congress is ambitious omnibus legislation, the Bringing America Home Act (BAHA), which would significantly increase such resources. Cast as a "message" bill, the legislation incorporates other ambitious proposals, including a bill that would establish a National Housing Trust Fund. It also includes measures that call for adoption of a living wage. But the bill also contains targeted provisions that would remove barriers to mainstream programs, discourage criminalization, and advocates plan a campaign for passage of these sections of the larger bill.

BAHA also contains provisions expressly acknowledging the U.S. government's obligation to implement the human right to housing and other economic and social rights under international human rights law. This language reflects another recent trend in advocacy: efforts by some advocates to incorporate human rights strategies in advocacy to end and prevent homelessness in the United States. Focusing primarily (but not exclusively) on the human right to housing, this effort aims to bring new tools and venues for advocacy to bear, to complement existing strategies. It also seeks to reframe the issues, to focus on justice, not charity, and on universal principles that apply to all. In so doing, it seeks also to create a framework for building a larger coalition to support measures to end and prevent homelessness.

Interest in this approach derives from the inclusion of economic and social rights, including the right to housing, within international human rights law, in contrast to purely domestic U.S. law. Although the International Covenant on Economic, Social, and Cultural Rights, the treaty most relevant to the right to housing, has not been ratified by the United States, courts have looked to human rights law and international standards in reaching decisions.

In 2003, advocates organized the first national forum on the human right to housing. Extremely well received, this initial event resulted in the formation of an informal coalition of organizations that continued to work together on this approach. More such events followed, and in 2005 advocates began organizing a series of local and regional training events in communities across the country. These events have drawn increasing numbers of participants, including lawyers, advocates, government officials, and poor and homeless people. Each forum and training event was organized to include a focus on practical ways to use human rights law and strategies to address issues affecting homeless and poor people, and each resulted in follow-up activities to implement these strategies locally.

These efforts, supported by the two advocacy groups organizing the events, National Law Center on Homelessness and Poverty (NLCHP) and the Centre for Housing Rights and Evictions (COHRE), an international housing rights group, have had some concrete results. For example, following training in Chicago, advocates there worked to secure passage of a county resolution recognizing the right to housing and successfully calling for additional state funding for low-income housing assistance. In Los

Angeles, advocates successfully pushed for inclusion of the human right to housing as one of seven major strategies adopted in that city's ten-year plan to end homelessness; they are currently working on a city council resolution recognizing not only housing but other economic and social rights. In Florida, advocates are incorporating human rights strategies in advocacy against the criminalization of homelessness.

Furthermore, advocates are beginning to take the issue of U.S. homelessness to international and regional forums. In 2005, NLCHP, COHRE, and a coalition of Chicago Public Housing tenants threatened with eviction testified before the Inter-American Commission on Human Rights at its first-ever hearing on the right to housing. In 2006, NLCHP, as part of a broader coalition of advocates on a range of domestic U.S. issues, presented testimony before and submitted a report to the U.N. Human Rights Commission, which was then reviewing U.S. compliance with the International Covenant on Civil and Political Rights (ICCPR), a treaty that the United States has ratified. The Committee questioned the United States on homelessness, and in its formal report specifically noted the extreme racial disparity in the incidence of homelessness and requested corrective action, which has not been forthcoming.

In another important recent development, in 2007, national organizations working on homelessness and related issues came together to begin developing a consensus position on how to work together to move national policy on homelessness forward. Convened at the start of the McKinney Act's twentieth-anniversary year, the groups developed a "consensus" statement on "five fundamentals" of needed policy change. These fundamentals cover reauthorizing the McKinney-Vento housing programs; significantly increasing low-income housing assistance; ensuring incomes (public benefits and wages) are sufficient to meet basic needs; providing health care, education, and social services; and protecting the civil rights of homeless people. Significantly, the statement also refers to basic human rights in issuing a call for a renewed national commitment to ending homelessness.

The coalition of national groups built on the five fundamentals by using the occasion of the twentieth anniversary of the McKinney Act to issue a call to Congress to fulfill its original promise to move beyond that act to longer-term solutions to end and prevent homelessness. The groups called on Congress to adopt ten steps that would help end homelessness—including increasing funds for the McKinney programs, increasing funding for low-income housing, health care, education for homeless children and youth, removing access barriers to public benefits, discouraging cities from criminalizing homelessness, and requiring the administration to develop a federal plan to end homelessness. Supportive members of Congress passed a resolution in the House to support the call for additional Congressional action to fulfill the original promise.

FUTURE DIRECTIONS: INCORPORATING HUMAN RIGHTS APPROACHES

To end homelessness, the severe lack of housing affordable to low-income people must be addressed and remedied. There is consensus among many advocates and government officials working on this issue that a major barrier to implementing true solutions is the lack of political will to do so. Homelessness can be ended, but homeless and poor people lack the political power to exert the influence needed to muster the resources to do so. Although they have achieved significant successes, advocates working with homeless and poor people have also not been able to exert sufficient pressure to end homelessness. Indeed, although advocacy groups have proliferated, they are often fragmented in their approaches. To exert the pressure and mobilize the support needed to enact more ambitious calls for increased housing and other resources, advocates need a much stronger and united voice.

Global trends provide some useful lessons and potentially some reason for optimism. In 2003, Scotland enacted legislation to establish the right to housing for all homeless people within ten years and adopted an incremental approach towards this end. In early 2007, following months of widely publicized protests by activists with strong public support, France began considering national legislation establishing a right to housing. The Scottish law makes explicit that although this may cost more in the short term, a high percentage of homeless persons had previously presented themselves to homeless agencies for assistance and were returning, so by providing the help they need the first time around, there would be efficiency savings in not having to reprocess these returning individuals. Significantly, according to at least one advocate for passage of the law, consensus among and collaboration by advocates was crucial to the success of advocates in Scotland in winning enactment of the law.

Equally important is public opinion. According to a 2007 poll, ninety percent of New York City residents believe that everyone has a basic right to shelter; seventy-two percent believe that as long as homelessness persists, the United States is not living up to its values; eighty-five percent approve of their tax dollars being spent on housing for homeless people; and sixty-two percent believe the city should increase spending on programs for homeless people.[48] A March 2007 national poll found that nine of ten Americans believe that providing affordable housing in their communities is important, and fewer than half believe that current national housing policy is on the right track.[49]

Judges, policy-makers, and advocates are increasingly in touch with their counterparts around the world; this trend seems virtually certain to continue to grow dramatically. The U.S. Supreme Court has recently looked to both human rights standards and trends in other legal systems to inform its interpretation of U.S. law (*Roper v. Simmons 2004*). Global developments in countries that are in many ways similar to the United States can serve as powerful policy models, as well as indications that similar efforts in the United States are feasible. Moreover, advocates can build on early national policy statements in the 1949 Housing Act, which envisioned in its preamble a "decent home and suitable living arrangement" for all Americans. Although adopting a human rights framework in the United States would signify a major shift in current policy, historically the United States has been a leader in developing these standards, and a shift in that direction would not be altogether foreign to U.S. policy.

CONCLUSION

The past three decades have witnessed a striking shift in rhetoric and stated policy. Although the Reagan administration publicly adopted the view that homelessness is a "lifestyle choice," and not a national policy concern, the current Bush administration has not only stated that homelessness is a national policy concern, but has also made a commitment to ending chronic homelessness in the next decade. Some policy shifts have accompanied the changed rhetoric, most notably during the 1990s, as funding for homelessness, housing, and other social programs increased and homelessness programs shifted away from crisis response and towards longer-term aid.

Currently, however, despite their stated commitment, the reality is that federal efforts have focused on attempts to spur local responses without a meaningful commitment of federal resources and with cuts in needed housing and other resources. Local-level policy over the same two decades has shifted from at least some recognition of the right to shelter to the adoption and promotion of punitive and criminalizing policies. Although some are now again moving in more positive directions, this shift is limited and the punitive trend continues.

Many factors are at play and may explain these movements in law and policy, including political trends much larger than and distinct from advocacy on homelessness. The initial focus by advocates and government on emergency shelter as a solution to homelessness may have facilitated the acceptance and institutionalization of homelessness, perhaps providing a justification for punitive measures and slowing momentum for long-term solutions to end and prevent homelessness. The current effort to focus instead on housing and other elements of more permanent solutions may help rectify this trend and move advocacy and policy towards solutions to end homelessness in the United States. However, without larger changes that extend beyond homelessness to create additional resources and affordable housing for low-income people, these efforts are unlikely to succeed. Unifying advocacy efforts in support of longer-range goals, if successful, could help move such goals forward. At the same time, efforts to implement the human right to housing aim to shift current policy paradigms and to support efforts to secure those resources.

ACKNOWLEDGMENT

I am grateful to Lucy Martin for her assistance with this chapter.

NOTES

1. M. Burt, L. Aron, E. Lee, and J. Valente, *Helping America's Homeless: Emergency Shelter or Affordable Housing?* (Washington, DC: Urban Institute Press, 2001).
2. B. Link, J. Phelan, M. Bresnahan, A. Stueve, R. Moore, and E. Susser, "Lifetime and Five-Year Prevalence of Homelessness in the United States: New Evidence on an Old Debate," *American Journal of Orthopsychiatry* 65 (1995): 347–54.
3. Interagency Council on the Homeless, *Homelessness: Programs and the People They Serve* (Washington, DC: U.S. Dept. of Housing and Urban Development, 1999), 18.
4. Ibid., 14.
5. Ibid., 29.
6. Ibid.
7. Burt, *Helping America's Homeless,* 2001; U.S. Conference of Mayors, *Hunger and Homelessness Survey: A Status Report on Hunger and Homelessness in America's Cities* (Washington, DC: U.S. Conference of Mayors, 2006), 63.
8. M. Stegman, R. Quercia, and G. McCarthy, *Housing America's Working Families* (Washington, DC: Center for Housing Policy, 2001).
9. National Low Income Housing Coalition, "Out Of Reach 2006," http://www.nlihc.org/oor/oor2006/?CFID=15818662&CFTOKEN=75808142.
10. U.S. Conference of Mayors, *Hunger and Homelessness Survey,* 2006.
11. Ibid.
12. M. Foscarinis and P. Julianelle, "Responding to the School Mobility of Children and Youth Experiencing Homelessness: The McKinney-Vento Act and Beyond," *The Journal of Negro Education* 72, no. 1 (2003): 39–55.
13. Ibid; Better Homes Fund, *Homeless Children: America's New Outcasts* (Newton, MA: Better Homes Fund, 1999).
14. M. Burt, *Over the Edge: The Growth of Homelessness in the 1980s* (New York: Russell Sage Foundation Publications, 1992); U.S. Conference of Mayors, *Hunger and Homelessness Survey,* 2006.
15. *Callahan v. Carey,* 13 Misc.3d 1241(A) (N.Y. App. Div. 1979), reprinted in *New York Law Journal* (December 1979), 10.
16. *Eldredge v. Koch,* 469 N.Y.S.2d 744 (N.Y. App. Div. 1983); *McCain v. Koch,* 523 N.Y.S.2d 112 (N.Y. App. Div. 1988).
17. *Koster v. Webb,* 598 F.Supp. 1134 (E.D.N.Y. 1983).
18. *Maticka v. City of Atlantic City,* 524 A.2d 416 (N.J. Super. Ct. App. Div. 1987); *Hodge v. West Virginia,* 305 S.E.2d 278 (1983); and *Hansen v. Department of Social Services,* 193 Cal.App.3d 283 (Cal. Ct. App. 1987)
19. The Committee to Save Initiative 17, "The History," 2004, http://prop1.org/history/1984/84i17.htm; F. Roisman, "Establishing a Right to Housing: A General Guide," *Clearinghouse Review* 25 (1991).

20. General Accounting Office, *Homelessness: A Complex Problem and the Federal Response* (Gaithersburg, MD: General Accounting Office, 1985); K. Hopper and J. Hamberg, "The Making of the New Homeless: From Skid Row to New Poor, 1945–1984," in R. Bratt and C. Hartmann, eds., *Critical Perspectives on Housing* (Philadelphia: Temple University Press, 1986).

21. B. Taylor, "Some Choose to be Homeless, President Says," *Boston Globe*, February 1, 1984.

22. M. Foscarinis, "Beyond Homelessness: Ethics, Advocacy and Strategy," *Saint Louis University Public Law Review* 12 (1993): 37–67.

23. Ibid.

24. *Congressional Record* A, B (1987).

25. R. Pear, "President Signs $1 Billion," *New York Times,* July 23, 1987.

26. *Stewart B McKinney Homeless Assistance Act*, 42 USC § 11301-04 (1987).

27. *Congressional Record* C (1987).

28. *Stewart B McKinney Homeless Assistance Act*, 42 USC § 11301(a).

29. *National Coalition for the Homeless v. Pierce*, No 87-2640 (DDC filed Sept 28, 1987); *National Coalition for the Homeless v Bennett*, No 87-3512 (DDC filed Dec 28, 1987).

30. *National Law Center on Homelessness and Poverty v. U.S. Veterans Administration*, 736 F Supp 1148 (D.D.C. 1990).

31. See, for example, *Atchison v. Barry*, Case No. 88-11976 (D.C. 1989).

32. District of Columbia Code Ann § 3-601 (1998) (repealed 1994).

33. National Law Center on Homelessness and Poverty (NLCHP), *Go Directly to Jail* (Washington, DC: NLCHP, 1991); NLCHP, *Right to Remain Nowhere* (Washington, DC: NLCHP, 1993); NLCHP, *No Homeless People Allowed* (Washington, DC: NLCHP, 1994); NLCHP, *Mean Sweeps* (Washington, DC: NLCHP, 1996); NLCHP, *Out of Sight, Out of Mind?* (Washington, DC: NLCHP, 1999); NLCHP and National Coalition for the Homeless, *Illegal to Be Homeless: The Criminalization of Homelessness in the United States* (Washington, DC: NLCHP and NCH, 2002); NLCHP, *Punishing Poverty: The Criminalization of Homelessness, Litigation, and Recommendations for Solutions* (Washington, DC: NLCHP, 2003).

34. NLCHP, *Mean Sweeps,* 1996.

35. *Turning Point v Caldwell*, 74 F.3d 941 (9th Cir. 1996).

36. A. M. Arumi and A. L. Yarrow, *Compassion, Concern and Conflicted Feelings: New Yorkers on Homelessness and Housing* (Washington, DC: Public Agenda, 2007); National Association of Realtors, "Americans Cite Affordable Housing As High Priority, NAR Joins Coalition To Kick Off National Campaign," http://www.realtor.org/press_room/news_releases/2007/realtors_and_housing_coalition_unite.html.

37. U.S. Conference of Mayors, *Hunger and Homelessness Survey,* 2006.

38. See also, K. Hopper and J. Baumohl, "Held in Abeyance: Rethinking Homelessness and Advocacy," *American Behavioral Scientist* 37, no. 4 (1994): 522–52.

39. Foscarinis, "Beyond Homelessness," 1993.

40. Interagency Council on the Homeless, *Priority Home!* (Washington, DC: U.S. Dept. of Housing and Urban Development, 1995).

41. M. Foscarinis, "Converting Military Bases and Other Vacant Federal Property to Aid Homeless People," *Clearinghouse Review* 28 (1995): 1365–74; L. Weir, "Update on Using Military Base Closures to Aid Homeless People," *Clearinghouse Review* 29 (1995): 771; L. Hallinan and C. Bishop, "Military Base Closure and Reuse Planning," *Clearinghouse Review* 28 (1995): 1339–69.

42. S. Metraux, S. C. Marcus, and D. P. Culhane, "The New York-New York Housing Initiative and Use of Public Shelters by Persons With Severe Mental Illness," *Psychiatric Services* 54 (2003): 67–71.

43. National Low Income Housing Coalition, "Out Of Reach," 2006, http://www.nlihc.org/oor/oor_current/.

44. National Alliance to End Homelessness, "A Plan, Not a Dream: How to End Homelessness in Ten Years," 2000, http://www.naeh.org/content/article/detail/585.

45. National Law Center on Homelessness and Poverty, "Adding Legal Teeth to Plans to End Homelessness," 2006.

46. National Law Center on Homelessness and Poverty and National Coalition for the Homeless, *Illegal to Be Homeless: The Criminalization of Homelessness in the United States* (Washington, DC: NLCHP, 2002).

47. General Accounting Office, *Homelessness: Barriers to Using Mainstream Services* (Washington, DC: GAO, 2000).

48. Arumi and Yarrow, *Compassion, Concern and Conflicted Feelings,* 2007.

49. National Association of Realtors, "Americans Cite Affordable Housing," 2007.

Chapter Nine

LAW AND ORDER? A REALITY FOR THE HOMELESS: THE LEGAL RAMIFICATIONS OF COURT DECISIONS ON THE TREATMENT OF HOMELESS PERSONS

Amy Presley Hauser

THE REALITY OF INATTENTION

The nation recently had an opportunity to get a closer glimpse of a homeless individual in the movie *The Pursuit of Happyness* starring Will Smith.[1] The movie is based on the true story of Chris Gardner, who goes from the streets, with his son at his side, to a Wall Street legend.[2] Most people probably left the movie with a sense of satisfaction and feeling "happy." To the average eye, this was a movie about success and a new version of the American dream. The movie depicted the thriving problem of homelessness through several scenes. The scenes included a man and his son trying to find a place to live after they had stayed a restless night in a men's bathroom in the subway. Smith asked a social worker for a place to sleep with his young son, but they were turned away because the shelter did not allow men. After spending one night in another shelter, Smith had to carry his suitcase and all of his belongings with him to work every day. When questioned, Smith told people that he was headed out of town for work.

The movie made several depictions of homeless individuals. There were images of men and women playing instruments to try to earn money. In one scene, a man slept in the middle of the sidewalk. Then there was the usual depiction of the homeless man who was mentally ill, thinking a bone density scanner is a time machine. The movie clearly presented the problem of living check to check, if you had one, and what it was like when there was not even a check coming in.[3]

Of course the movie did not show the night faced by those turned away from the shelters or if anything happened to the man sleeping on the sidewalk. Depending on the laws where they lived, those turned away from the shelter could have been cited or arrested because they did not get in line early enough. They could have a criminal record as a result of sitting or sleeping outside. These everyday activities have resulted in fines, jail time, and eventually warrants for their arrest.

According to the laws addressed in this chapter, homelessness is still a "problem" that individuals and cities try to push elsewhere off their streets. Laws are how our society deals with the problems facing us. We depend on them to provide a civil place to live and to create resolutions. Laws provide order and guidance to societal action and response; an interesting thought since many of these laws are inhumane and unreasonable. This chapter provides an evaluation of current laws and proposed laws that have affected or could impact the homeless. The laws, or the lack thereof, are telling of the priority of this problem. Some laws attempt to make the homeless invisible and some laws just have that effect. This chapter will also examine several court decisions brought by homeless individuals to challenge the punitive laws and ordinances that have been passed to make the homeless visible. The decisions reflect policy as to homelessness and an effort to protect the homeless from many of these punitive laws.

HOMELESSNESS MEETS THE LAW

The First Step: Stewart B. McKinney Act

Many homeless advocates saw 1987 as a bright year.[4] The Stewart B. McKinney Homeless Assistance Act, Public Law 100-77, was the first legislation passed evaluating and addressing the needs of the homeless population in America.[5] It is unfortunate that this is also the last "landmark" federal legislation for the homeless.[6] The legislation was intended to be a first step towards addressing homelessness.[7] Instead, it has been an insufficient attempt to address growing needs and issues.

The legislation covered a wide spectrum of issues and gave a first impression of who was homeless and what the country perceived the problem to be in the 1980s. The definition of homeless was as follows:

> (1) an individual who lacks a fixed, regular, and adequate nighttime residence; and (2) an individual who has primary nighttime residence that is (A) a supervised publicly or privately operated shelter designated to provide temporary living accommodations (including welfare hotels, congregate shelters, and transitional housing for the mentally ill); (B) an institution that provides a temporary residence for individuals intended to be institutionalized; or (C) a public or private place not designed for, or ordinarily used as, a regular sleeping accommodation for human beings.[8]

The Stewart B. McKinney Act has nine titles that range from establishing an Interagency Council on the Homeless[9] to authorizing the Emergency Food and Shelter Program and emergency shelter and transitional housing programs.[10] Since being amended four times, the Act has seen expanded programs and increased funding at times.[11] However, evaluation of the Act now reflects problems for the various programs. Funding has been an issue along with restructuring or even cutting some programs.[12]

Although criticized by some, the Act has aided many individuals through its programs, even to the point of helping many "regain independence and permanent housing and at reasonable costs."[13] However, the inevitable conclusion is that nothing has been done since 1994, and homelessness is not decreasing. The McKinney Act does not address all issues facing the homeless and does not mention criminalization of conduct. The old equation of supply and demand also applies to this legislation. The number of individuals needing assistance under the Act is increasing, but the funding is not meeting that need. Additionally, because the Act was intended to address emergency measures, the causes of homelessness have not been tackled through the Act.[14] The Act was renamed the McKinney-Vento Homeless Assistance Act by President Clinton in 2000.[15] As the Act itself stated, "[t]here is no single, simple solution to the problem of homelessness."[16] The legislation makes it clear that an emergency fix to such a long-term problem is not a solution. The National Coalition for the Homeless proposes that the only solution to bring homelessness to an end is to address the causes of homelessness.[17] Although there is no denying that a simple solution does not exist, what has been happening in city council meetings and legislatures across the country only contributes to the problem.

Other legislation addressing homelessness that could be "landmark" is discussed later in this chapter although it was just considered, not passed into law. What the McKinney Act started many years ago, particularly an effort at assisting the homeless, must be revived and continued. However, instead of assisting, the efforts have been towards ignoring or pushing the homeless out of sight.

The Courthouse: An Evaluation of Case Law

Although federal legislation has affected the homeless nationwide, how issues such as criminalization of homelessness affect the homeless may depend on where the individual lives. Similar to the McKinney Act, measures taken by cities that have been challenged in the cases mentioned herein also do not address the underlying causes of homelessness.[18] Although challenges have spanned across the recent years, a majority of cases have been considered on appeal in the past two decades. One of the earliest cases was *Callahan v. Carey*.[19] This suit was brought on behalf of homeless men against city and state agencies that were a part of the shelter system in New York City. The court, finding in favor of the plaintiffs, ordered the city to provide emergency lodging to all "needy, indigent men." Through the proceedings, the right to shelter was affirmed and minimal standards of decency were set.[20] As this one does, most other cases address the basic needs of the homeless.

Many of these cases involve the constitutional rights of the homeless. These rights that are constantly at risk include the First,[21] Fourth,[22] Eighth,[23] and Fourteenth Amendments.[24] The Fifth Amendment is also an issue.[25] The use of ordinances and laws to target everyday activities that a homeless person must carry out in public because he is without a private place to do so have been termed "criminalization of homelessness."[26] Often, city ordinances or local laws call for this sort of action against homeless persons, but these kinds of laws are not new. As one author states, "[t]hroughout American history, such policies [toward the homeless] have been based on the assumption that the homeless are lazy and irresponsible—a deviant group, perhaps incorrigible, but in any case outside the boundaries of mainstream society."[27]

Out of Sight, Out of Mind

Some court opinions serve to assist the homeless, and some assist in keeping the homeless invisible. Some courts contribute to the stereotypes of the homeless or describe or infer the homeless as a nuisance population. This was revealed in a decision by the U.S. Supreme Court. In 1988, the Supreme Court addressed the warrantless search and seizure of garbage left for collection outside of the curtilage of a defendant's home.[28] In this case, which did not involve a homeless party, the court observed that it is "common knowledge" that plastic garbage bags left on the street are "readily accessible to animals, children, scavengers, snoops, and other members of the public." The footnote to the word scavengers provided, "It is not only the homeless of the Nation's cities who make use of others' refuse."[29] Other preconceived notions are evident in the opinions examined herein. In *Cordova v. City of Reno*, a homeless alcoholic challenged the city ordinance that imposed criminal liability on anyone "engag[ing] upon a public street, highway, alley or premises to which the public has access or other public places within the city in conduct having a tendency to annoy, insult or disturb offensively any person passing or being therein."[30] The court found that the Reno ordinance was unconstitutional and noted selective enforcement was a risk against people "whose behavior is 'annoying' because their ideas, their lifestyle, or their physical appearance is resented by the majority of their fellow citizens.' "[31]

In *Johnson v. Board of Police Commissioners*,[32] a case about the visibility of homelessness in St. Louis, Missouri, the judge provided an interesting opinion filled with his views about homelessness. He stated,

> In a society that prizes beauty, youth, vigor, and success that is measured by accumulation of precious things; the disheveled, the aged, the weary; those whose

> accumulated wealth is carried in a tattered blanket, present themselves in some quarters as a distraction to a desired representation of how the 'best of times' should appear. They are extremely bright; they suffer from mental illnesses. They are capable of causing serious physical injury or death; their gentleness permits them to share their meager substance with birds that find a safe harbor at their feet. In making their claim to the American Dream, they participate in publicly sponsored, government-supported celebrations from distant bridges, rather than penthouses, knowing that their rights that Thomas Jefferson proclaimed inviolate, being life, liberty and the pursuit of happiness, are no less guaranteed to them than to those not so vulnerable because they carry evidence of their station in life in their wallets rather than in a bag or worn blanket. The homeless present many diverse faces. Gaining a better understanding of the daily life issues they face is necessary to judge whether relief is indicated in this case, considering at the same time the requirements law enforcement officials face in performing their lawful duties.[33]

Interestingly, the court expressed a better understanding about the daily struggles of the homeless under the facts of this case. The court also commented on the conduct of the plaintiffs, homeless individuals, in the courtroom, stating that they were "respectful" of the judge, attorneys, and court personnel.[34] Although an aside to the decision and consideration of the issues by the court, this is noteworthy to show several things about the homeless and the law. First, that educated individuals have mistaken understanding or prejudged conceptions of the homeless and their plight, if any knowledge at all. Second, that the individuals deciding these cases are most likely unable to relate to or potentially understand the situations presented to them by a homeless individual. Third, the expectations of people as to the homeless are low. It is uncommon to read an opinion that discusses how the court personnel were treated by a party.

In *Johnson*, several homeless individuals filed suit against the city police for mistreatment, particularly alleging that the police violated their constitutional rights by intimidating them and discouraging them from being in public areas.[35] All of this, the plaintiffs alleged, was in furtherance of an effort to "clean up" the downtown. Under their civil rights complaint, the plaintiffs requested relief in the form of injunctive and declaratory relief and damages. The evidence presented on behalf of the homeless plaintiffs was quite disturbing.[36] One man testified about a series of events involving police conduct on July 4, 2004. For instance, a car pulled up to where a group of homeless people was gathered and firecrackers came flying from the car in the direction of the group. Some of these individuals were then arrested. Another plaintiff said the car pulled up to where he was talking to a friend, and the officer suggested that they leave. Then another firecracker was thrown at the two of them, landing only a foot away. After identifying the offender who threw the firecracker, the man was arrested. Others who testified informed the court that they were arrested with plastic cuffs.[37] One lady testified about how she was treated about one month later when the event, Straussenfest, was going on in the downtown area. Sitting in front of the library on that day, a police officer approached her and several other homeless people and told them to leave by saying that with the activities downtown, "it doesn't really look prospective for the people to see homeless residing in the park."[38]

The court found that this conduct was unacceptable, stating that the plaintiffs made a sufficient showing of irreparable harm, and this conduct had resulted in a threat to their constitutional rights.[39] The court noted, "A poor person has the same expectation of constitutional protection as a rich person."[40] Granting relief under a temporary restraining order, the court ordered the St. Louis Board of Commissioners to cease directing or permitting their officers to clear homeless people from public areas "solely to sanitize public places where the homeless have a right to be because of the perception that homeless people present an appearance that detracts from an aesthetically pleasing environment that promotes commerce."[41] Injunctive relief was also granted to the plaintiffs against the City of St. Louis to preclude judicial imposition of punishment for violating a municipal ordinance before an accused individual is determined guilty under the ordinance.[42] On the basis of this, the city had been treating the homeless rudely and violently and violating their rights through issuing penalty before determining guilt. This violates everyone's expectations of being treated with decency and maintaining their constitutional rights.

In *Betancourt v. Bloomberg*, decided by the Second Circuit Court of Appeals in 2006, the case had its origination in "quality of life" initiatives from 1994 in New York City.[43] The initiative aimed at reducing the number of homeless in public places.[44] Armed with a guide provided to the city's law enforcement officers, police officers targeted those acting in the prohibited manner such as panhandling and residing in public places. One City Administrative Code stated:

> [i]t shall be unlawful for any person, such person's agent or employee to leave, or to suffer or permit to be left, any box, barrel, bale of merchandise or other movable property whether or not owned by such person, upon any marginal or public street or any public place, or to erect or cause to be erected thereon any shed, building or other obstruction.[45]

Laws such as this one are not discrete in their intent and target. Instead, these laws suggest an attempt to accomplish "out of sight, out of mind."

Supreme Court decisions have addressed vagrancy laws, begging, and stop and identify statutes.[46] The Fifth Amendment prevents a police officer from requiring someone to identify himself if the officer stops the individual for less than probable cause.[47] In *Hiibel*, a report was made to the police about an assault by a man on a woman in a particular vehicle. The investigating officer found Mr. Hiibel at the scene and requested identification eleven times from Mr. Hiibel who refused to produce it, eventually leading to his arrest.[48] Homeless advocates, in an amicus brief, informed the court of the right of a homeless person to be free from unreasonable seizures, particularly since the homeless have trouble obtaining identification.[49] It was also pointed out that there is a "growing phenomenon of criminalizing homelessness and its use as a tool for police to subject homeless people more frequently to unjustified investigations."[50] The court determined that Mr. Hiibel's Fourth and Fifth Amendment rights were not violated.[51]

The Supreme Court considered various stop and identify statutes. In *Papachristou v. Jacksonville*, a traditional vagrancy law was determined unacceptable due to vagueness because of its broad scope and imprecise terms.[52] The Court again did not uphold a stop and identify statute in Texas because it violated Fourth Amendment rights.[53] The requirement to show "credible and reliable identification" was invalidated based on a California statute.[54]

In 1980, the U.S. Supreme Court found that pursuant to the First Amendment, charitable solicitations are protected.[55] The case did not involve homeless individuals, but has had an impact on them, as the finding is cited in numerous cases related to anti-begging laws.

Some cases consider issues that are so basic that the rest of the population would not think a court needed to address the topics. In 2004, the Ninth Circuit Court of Appeals examined access of the homeless to their mail and to mailboxes. The National Law Center on Homelessness and Poverty got involved by filing an amicus brief in the lawsuit challenging the U.S. Postal Service's refusal to provide homeless persons with free PO boxes.[56] Under federal law, the postal service must provide free PO boxes to anyone who cannot receive carrier delivery service. The court dismissed the plaintiffs' claims for, among other reasons, the failure to state a claim finding there were no First Amendment or equal protection violations.[57] The court decided that requiring the homeless to travel to the main post office and failure to provide no fee boxes was reasonable and not discriminatory.[58] The dissenting judge saw it differently, finding that,

> The crux of the problem, as I see it, is that the U.S. Postal Service's current limitations on general delivery mail do not permit homeless persons to apply for general delivery at branch post offices under any condition whatsoever, even in cases of undue hardship. This unyielding policy unreasonably and substantially impairs the ability of some homeless persons to receive mail and to exercise their First Amendment rights. Nothing further can be declared in this case.[59]

As to the homeless, he observed, "That a segment of citizens of our great country are left by the struggles of life with no home is unfortunate, to say the very least, but the struggles of the homeless neither detract from their character nor limit their right to exercise freedoms guaranteed by the Constitution.[60] He argued that receiving mail is a fundamental part of the First Amendment freedom of speech. If a homeless person is unable to get mail at the main post office, then he or she will be "cut off from all communication" with everyone trying to reach him or her; of particular importance is the communication they may be awaiting regarding government services.[61] It is an unreasonable burden, and almost impossible for a disabled homeless individual, to expect a homeless person to take public transportation for hours to get his mail when most everyone else has the privilege of having it delivered to their home. The dissent explored the possibility that the individual could go to all the trouble to get to the post office and then have no mail or junk mail only.[62]

Criminalization of Homelessness

The criminalization of homelessness presents multiple obstacles for the homeless population in general. As to these laws, "[b]y penalizing people for innocent, necessary, life-sustaining conduct, cities are essentially punishing people for being homeless."[63] Although some cases may appear to be victories for the homeless, the number of similar ordinances nationwide and the news that such laws are still increasing predicts a different result.[64] Some cities have made a name for themselves in criminalizing activities such as sleeping, sitting, or eating in public.[65] There is also the issue of selective enforcement of general laws against homeless people. Obviously, these laws present additional barriers to an already challenged population. While being more aware of the problem of homelessness, it appears that cities are intentionally trying to make the homeless population disappear from sight through such laws. When the National Law Center surveyed forty-nine cities in 1999 and 2002, seventy percent of the cities had increased the number of laws that criminalize homelessness.[66] In a more recent survey of 224 cities, over twenty-five percent had a law prohibiting sitting or lying in particular public places.[67] Some cities have taken steps to remove the homeless from the heart of the city and have picked a location to push them towards.[68] The reality is that most cities have inadequate shelter for their homeless population.[69] This logically leads to the result that those without shelter space must sleep and sit someplace in public. Although creating laws that make such conduct a crime does not seem like the smartest solution, it is apparent that many cities think it is the easiest one. The problem is that by making certain conduct a crime, it means that the person can choose a different course of action if there is no place to go. This conclusion is contrary to the idea by many that homelessness is a choice. Plus, criminalizing basic conduct initiates a cycle that is not easily broken when a homeless person is caught violating the law.

Instead of creating alternative solutions, many cities have looked to the criminal justice system to deal with individuals living out in the open.[70] Criminalization of homelessness takes the form of legislation as to everyday activities, selective enforcement of laws, sweeps, and laws that prohibit begging.[71] Along the way, the constitutional and even international rights of homeless individuals are sacrificed.[72] Author Kathleen Arnold observed,

> With the shortage of emergency shelter and lack of affordable housing, arrest sweeps, prohibiting the homeless from sleeping in public parks, removing them

> from the city, burning possessions, and making begging difficult or criminal not only put the homeless in a double bind, but make their very existence questionable. In essence, homeless individuals are no longer considered citizens, as constitutional protections do not apply to them. They are treated as criminals although they have not committed any crimes; laws against vagrancy, for example, punish status rather than conduct.[73]

A sample of the more common laws will be examined as they have been presented in the court system.

"Spare Change?" Cases Involving Begging and Panhandling

Begging has been controlled one way or another for years.[74] While in the past most of these laws have not been challenged, the tide has turned as more cities revive these laws in an effort to keep the homeless out of the public eye.[75] In 1980, the U.S. Supreme Court found that charitable solicitations are protected.[76] According to the Court, whether on the street or door to door, these are protected under the First Amendment and the subject ordinance in *Schaumberg* violated free speech rights.[77] The ordinance enacted by a suburban community outside of Chicago required those who were going to solicit to obtain a permit and prove that a minimum of seventy-five percent of the receipts were going to charitable purposes of the organization. After being challenged by a nonprofit organization, the Supreme Court determined that the community could use a less intrusive means than direct prohibition on solicitation, and therefore the ordinance was unconstitutionally overbroad.[78] Although the facts of this case did not mention the homeless, this case has had an impact on interpretation of rights of the homeless in regards to begging and panhandling.

Cases evaluating laws that pertain to begging have been challenged on a variety of bases.[79] Some courts have held such laws were legitimate despite being opposed as a violation of freedom of speech.[80] In *Blair*, the statute provided that "anyone accosting another in any public place or in any place open to the public for the purpose or begging or soliciting alms" is guilty of a misdemeanor.[81] The opinion stated the subject statute was found by the district court to be facially unconstitutional under the First and Fourteenth Amendments.[82]

On review, the Ninth Circuit Court noted that when he sued, the plaintiff was not begging anymore because he had found steady employment.[83] The court ruled that under Article III, the plaintiff no longer had a personal stake in the declaratory judgment cause of action, thereby leaving the court unable to review the district court's order that classified this section as unconstitutional.[84] In essence, this finding punished the plaintiff for finding a steady job, and he could not proceed to challenge the statute.

In *Young v. New York City Transit Authority*, the statute forbids begging or panhandling in the subway system.[85] The court determined that the regulation passed scrutiny because governmental interests that were content-neutral and unrelated to the suppression of free expression were in existence and did not violate the First Amendment.[86] Both pre- and post-*Young* commentators have taken issue with the approach adopted by the Second Circuit Court in *Young*, particularly, that begging might be considered at most only expressive conduct and not fully-protected speech.[87] The case provided the history of anti-begging statutes with their roots in Elizabethan England.[88] The Supreme Court has acknowledged that "much of the rationale behind the creation of the Elizabethan poor laws is inapplicable to our present conditions, yet their 'archaic classifications remain.'"[89] In *Papachristou*, eight defendants challenged their convictions under a vagrancy law.[90] The Supreme Court struck down the ordinance because it did not give fair notice to anyone with normal intelligence of the conduct that was forbidden and further it encouraged arbitrary arrests and convictions.[91]

The Seventh Circuit Court upheld an ordinance that forbade panhandling of cash at night and near public transportation facilities or vehicles, even if parked or stopped; sidewalk cafés; or banks.[92] This court determined this was an ordinance benefiting the citizens on public streets and allowed feasible alternatives to reach downtown crowds.

However, other courts have distinguished similar laws as a violation of constitutional rights.[93] For example, in *People v. Griswold*, the court found that begging constituted speech. The defendant was picked up for standing silently on a sidewalk panhandling with a sign he wrote.[94] The city was unable to prove the panhandling ordinance was no broader than it needed to be to achieve its legitimate interest in protecting pedestrians and motorists from aggravation and intimidation that was unwelcome.[95]

In 1991, a New York State Penal Law stated that one is guilty of loitering if he "loiters, remains or wanders about in a public place for the purpose of begging."[96] The plaintiffs, two "regulars" in the East village section of Manhattan, claimed a violation of the First, Eighth, and Fourteenth Amendments of the U.S. Constitution and New York Constitution.[97] The court noted that at the time anti-begging laws were present in twenty-seven states.[98] Despite the city's arguments, the court noted that the city did not provide evidence on several important factual issues relating to implementation of this law. So, questions remained to the court as to the nature and effect of begging and enforcement of this law.[99]

The city tried to assert that its police power is at issue because it has an interest in banning this kind of conduct from its streets and public parks. As evidence, the city presented an affidavit of George Kelling, a Northeastern University professor in the College of Criminal Justice and a fellow at Harvard University's Kennedy School of Government. Mr. Kelling presented what the court considered to be expert testimony on a theory he deemed the "broken windows theory." This theory asserted that disorderly behavior when left unattended leads to more serious crime, similar to broken windows that are left unattended are signs of neglect and lead to more serious destruction and vandalism.[100]

The court declared that this theory was not supported by any facts nor did the city provide facts on the effect of begging if the law was enforced. After this examination, the court determined that unresolved factual issues as to the historical treatment of begging, the rationale behind and the enforcement of the penal law, and the nature of the city's police power and fraud interests prevented the city's motion for summary judgment from being granted.[101]

Other sources of challenge to laws addressing begging have been vagueness, equal protection, and unreasonable exercise of police power. Vagueness is a question of whether the ordinance or statute puts a reasonable person on notice as to the actions or conduct that is forbidden.[102]

Arguments as to both unreasonable exercise of police power and equal protection were presented in *Seattle v. Webster*.[103] In *Webster*, the "pedestrian interference ordinance" was at issue.[104] The ordinance was violated if one obstructed pedestrian or vehicular traffic or begged in an aggressive manner. The penalties were a fine, imprisonment, or both. Under the equal protection argument, the ordinance or statute was challenged as disparately affecting the homeless as a class.[105] In *Webster*, it was argued by the plaintiff that the homeless should be recognized as a protected class because "they are relegated to such a position of political powerlessness as to command extraordinary protection."[106] In addition, any such ordinance, similar to one as to begging, disparately affected the homeless as a class, in violation of their equal protection rights. The Supreme Court disagreed with this reasoning. This defendant was arrested and charged with pedestrian interference for asking passersby for extra change. The Municipal Court judge had previously granted the defendant's motion to dismiss because of the nature of the law, as she observed:

> [A] person could be charged with this, under this ordinance, and be doing something that no one in the world would think was unlawful conduct, including on a very nice hot sunny day being age sixteen sitting on a sidewalk watching cars go by, which of course I think that all of us have done; being a Santa Claus at Christmas time and standing ringing a bell at a front door of a department store; walking from the side of the store out to the street to see if your bus has come yet and making people walk around you. I just could imagine many, many, many circumstances under which it would be based on the discretion of police authority as to whether you should be charged or not based on conduct, that if you were an attractive looking person who probably was a person of some means [you] wouldn't be arrested, and if you were a scrubby looking individual looking like you didn't have the where with all [sic] for the next cup of coffee, you would be charged, or [sic] I find that unconstitutional.[107]

On review, the Supreme Court of Washington did not find that the homeless were deserving of the status of a protected class, instead finding that there had been no cases where the homeless were declared by a court as a protected class under the Fourteenth Amendment, and this case would not be the first.[108] Before reaching this conclusion, the court commented,

> Homelessness is a real national concern, particularly in metropolitan areas such as Seattle. We share compassion for those among us who suffer privation in the midst of plenty. However, the Seattle pedestrian interference ordinance with which we are here concerned is facially neutral. On the limited record before us there is no indication that Mr. Webster is indigent or homeless. His address in the police report merely indicated "transient." We cannot conclude from the limited information presented that homelessness is relevant to this case.[109]

Although the opinion does not expand on this, it is curious what "transient" actually means to these judges. This is a weak justification for their decision. The court finished with its effort to appear neutral by saying, "we recognize society's valid concern for the plight of the homeless." In reality, the court ignored its professed sympathy and found that the pedestrian interference statute applied equally to all persons and was constitutional.[110]

The First Amendment has also provided basis for constitutional challenge to panhandling ordinances. In *Henry v. City of Cincinnati*, the homeless plaintiffs were affected by a local code provision that limited the time, place, and manner to solicit vocally and required a registration from the police department in order to engage in requesting money at all.[111] The court initially noted that panhandling is not mere commercial speech but consists of more.[112] The code provision prohibited solicitations in certain places including any public transportation vehicle or any bus stop, within twenty feet of an ATM or bank entrance, from anyone driving or riding in a motor vehicle or getting into or out of a vehicle, and within twenty feet of any crosswalk.[113] The individual must also not solicit in a way that is aggressive, which is detailed in the provision.[114] These are all requirements after one has complied with the registration requirement. The court found that the very detailed code provision would have to be examined further and did not grant the defendant's motion to dismiss, therefore not really addressing the ordinance.[115]

This Cincinnati ordinance raises a question that applies to every one of these cases: how is a homeless person to know of these laws? Under this particular code provision, someone could ask for money twenty-one feet from an ATM but not a foot closer. Perhaps this person would learn about all these particulars after he knew to obtain a registration before getting started on requesting spare change. Cities have gone to lengths to detail the means to consent to the homeless begging, and many have succeeded.

You Can't Come In: Monitoring Public Places

Even if shelter space was unlimited, the homeless must still have someplace to be during the day. Some public places have enacted rules or guidelines restricting access or entrance to their establishment by the homeless.[116] Places to go during the day include restaurants, parks, and libraries. A public library rule requiring patrons to leave the building unless he reads, studies, or uses library materials; and prohibiting patrons from harassing or annoying others through noisy or boisterous activities, staring or following another with the intent to annoy, or behaving in a manner that reasonably could be expected to disturb other patrons, was not unconstitutionally overbroad or vague according to one court. In *Kreimer v. Bureau of Police for the Town of Morristown*, the Third Circuit Court of Appeals examined rules at the Joint Free Public Library that resulted in the plaintiff, a homeless man, being ejected from the library.[117] Rules of the library addressed patron conduct including prohibition of behavior that interfered with another patron's reasonable use of library facilities or the work of anyone on the library staff.[118]

The library staff declared that the plaintiff was disruptive while in the facility by staring at others and even following them, talking to himself and to others loudly, and having an offensive odor.[119] In 1987, the library began keeping a logbook of disciplinary problems and then in 1989 the library adopted written rules prohibiting certain conduct and directing expulsion of those breaking the rules. The purpose of the rules was to allow everyone in the town to use its facilities to the maximum. On the basis of the court's examination, the word "everyone" must have a unique definition.[120] An examination of the rules that match the alleged conduct of the plaintiff caused an inquiry as to which came first.

The plaintiff's appointed counsel filed a complaint against the Morristown Bureau of Police, the library, the Board of Directors, the library director, three library employees, and four police officers for violating the plaintiff's First and Fourteenth Amendment rights (due process and equal protection), and the New Jersey Constitution.[121] In response to the complaint, defendants counterclaimed for an order restraining and enjoining the plaintiff from entering the library and harassing patrons and employees, including those on the sidewalks near the library.[122]

After reviewing Supreme Court decisions, the court noted that the First Amendment encompassed the positive right of public access to information and ideas.[123] The court determined the library constituted a limited public forum to exercise First Amendment rights, disagreeing with the district court's findings.[124] The court also found that because it was a reasonable means to achieve the end to require its patrons to make use of the facilities in order to stay there, the first rule regarding activities while in the library was reasonable and valid.[125] The fifth rule, regarding being heard in the library, was also found to be reasonable because it provides a clear and direct way to achieve maximum use of the library.[126] While the court took longer to reach a decision, the ninth rule, addressing personal hygiene, was also declared as a rule promoting the library's interests. Additionally, since it allowed for the re-entry of a patron back into the library once he complied with the rule, then it was not a permanent bar to the facility.[127] The court did finally agree with the district court on one point—that the "rule may disproportionately affect the homeless who have limited access to bathing facilities", but "would not justify permitting a would-be patron, with hygiene so offensive that it constitutes a nuisance, to force other patrons to leave the Library, or to inhibit Library employees from performing their duties."[128] The court continued in favor of the library rules and found no violation as to the equal protection or due process under the Fourteenth Amendment nor that the rules were vague or overbroad.[129] The court found a lack of discriminatory intent in the library's actions, and instead only could identify that this was a fair manner to remove a disruptive patron from the library.[130] Since "a violation of the rules would disrupt the smooth functioning of the Library,"[131] the court permitted what was arguably a violation of plaintiff's rights.

However, the U.S. District Court in the District of Columbia disagreed with a similar provision set forth by the local library.[132] In *Armstrong*, the court evaluated an appearance regulation enforced by the D.C. Public Library.[133] The plaintiff claimed violations of the D.C. Human Rights Act, his civil rights, and the First and Fifth Amendment of the U.S. Constitution.[134] The challenged regulation was a part of written Guidelines for Handling Security Matters and told library personnel to deny access to the library to anyone who had an "objectionable appearance." Investigation into the background of the policy written in 1979 made it clear that the regulation was created to deal with the "proliferation of more street people and more homeless."[135]

The plaintiff claimed that he went to the Martin Luther King library on Sunday, February 14, 1993, where he was refused entrance after being told to "clean up."[136] At the time, the plaintiff was living in a shelter and wanted to read and take notes at a library table. Because of the cold winter month, he was dressed in a shirt, shoes, pants, several sweaters, and two winter jackets. After initially filing a complaint with the D.C. Department of Human Rights and Minority Business Development, the plaintiff withdrew his complaint and filed a lawsuit.[137] After dismissing the defendants in their individual capacities, the court addressed whether the plaintiff's case must be dismissed for failure to exhaust administrative remedies.[138] Although under the D.C. Human Rights Act discrimination is prohibited because of "personal appearance," this claim of the plaintiff's was dismissed because he did not follow the required procedures.[139]

Citing *Kreimer v. Bureau of Police for the Town of Morristown*, the court then evaluated the First Amendment issues. It determined that unlike in *Kreimer*, this regulation was a hygiene rule, not a conduct rule.[140] To support this, the defendants admitted that the regulation was triggered by the plaintiff's failure to be "clean[ed] up" and not his anticipated use of the library. Using a narrowly tailored standard of review, the court compared the case to the court's decision in *Kreimer.* It was found that there was not a precise method of preventing access to the library and instead that the library guards, employees, supervisors, and outside police officers had unlimited determination of enforcing the rule.[141] The court determined that this rule does not meet the objective standard needed to survive a vagueness challenge.[142] For example, there was no cognizable legal definition to determine what appearances or degree of odor were intended to be prohibited.[143] Under the regulation, the daily application was subjective, and basically without a standard.[144]

In conclusion, the court found in favor of the plaintiff on his First Amendment claim by holding that the appearance regulation was overbroad and vague.[145] The court went on to hold that the regulation also violated the Fifth Amendment under the due process clause. The reasoning was the unpredictable nature of the appearance standard as applied day to day. Because the outcome of exercising the resolution depended on how a staff member interpreted the regulation, the enforcement was arbitrary.[146] In addition, the regulation did not give fair notice to patrons.[147] Describing the regulation as "amorphous," the court decided that the regulation denied access to a public library, which is at the "core of our First Amendment values."[148] A running theme for many cities, as reflected in these decisions, and its reasoning is to hide the homeless, not to help them.

No Shelter: Sleeping in Public

Sleeping in public is a natural consequence of inadequate shelter, shelter rules that prohibit men to sleep with their families, and the environment of shelters. This attempt at criminalizing homelessness perhaps paints the clearest picture of the problem and the intent of cities across America. Obviously, sleeping on the streets poses a safety risk to the homeless anyway, though not often cited by lawmakers when they draft these ordinances. There have been reports over the years of a homeless person dying in severe weather conditions. In addition, there is the risk of being beaten as the joke of some teenagers, which can also result in death.[149]

Many of these laws have been found invalid. In *Fifth Avenue Presbyterian Church v. the City of New York,* a church had designated places on its property for the homeless to sleep at night.[150] After the city told the church it would not allow the homeless to sleep on the property and had conducted three sweeps to remove sleepers, the court held that the city's actions were an unconstitutional burden on the church's free speech right.[151] The court went further to permanently enjoin the city from entering onto the church's property for removing or arresting anyone lawfully sleeping.[152]

On the other side, a Texas court found that an ordinance criminalizing the removal of waste from receptacles does not impermissibly punish homeless persons for the mere status of homeless, rather for conduct.[153] In *Johnson,* the court examined ordinances that plaintiffs alleged were enacted to remove the homeless from sight.[154] The ordinance provided

> (a) A person commits an offense if he: (1) sleeps or dozes in a street, alley, park, or other public place; or (2) sleeps or dozes in a vacant lot adjoining a public street or highway. (b) It is a defense to prosecution under Subparagraph (2) of this section if the person owns the vacant lot or has the consent of the owner to sleep or doze on the vacant lot.[155]

According to the court, this ordinance did not violate the Eighth Amendment.[156]

A recent case that gives a great background and current look at criminalizing homelessness is *Jones v. City of Los Angeles.*[157] Although its decision was favorable to the homeless bringing the suit, it is very limited in its benefit. The ordinance that prohibited sitting, lying, or sleeping on public streets within city limits any time of day was challenged by six individuals who had been either cited or arrested for violating the ordinance.[158] The subject ordinance, Los Angeles Municipal Code section 41.18(d), provided:

> No person shall sit, lie or sleep in or upon any street, sidewalk or other public way. The provisions of this subsection shall not apply to persons sitting on the curb portion of any sidewalk or street while attending or viewing any parade permitted under the provisions of Section 103.111 of Article 2, Chapter X of this Code; nor shall the provisions of this subsection supply [sic] to persons sitting upon benches or other seating facilities provided for such purpose by municipal authority by this Code. A violation of section 41.18 (d) is punishable by a fine of up to $1,000 and/ or imprisonment of up to six months.[159]

The Ninth Circuit narrowed the issues in its twenty-four-page opinion to whether this law adopted in 1968 can be enforced under the Eighth Amendment right to be free from cruel and unusual punishment. According to the court, the plaintiffs are six of over 80,000 homeless individuals in Los Angeles County on any given night.[160]

According to the court, this ordinance was one of the most restrictive, as to regulation of public spaces, in the country.[161] By its comment pointing to the clear criminalization of homelessness under this statute, the court noted that many ordinances in other cities "avoid criminalizing the status of homelessness by making an element of the crime some conduct in combination with sitting, lying, or sleeping in a state of homelessness."[162]

Plaintiffs Purrie, Barger, Jones, and Vinson were sleeping on the sidewalk and plaintiff Cash was resting on a tree stump, all in violation of the subject section.[163] In their suit, the plaintiffs requested a permanent injunction against the city and Los Angeles Police Department officers preventing them from enforcing this section between the hours of 9:00 P.M. and 6:30 A.M.[164] The plaintiffs argued the section, if enforced any time of day or night, violated their Eighth and Fourteenth Amendment rights by criminalizing the status of homelessness. They had no place else to sit, sleep, or lie down because they were homeless. The court granted their request with conditions attached and surprisingly the decision has not been overturned, probably because of the limited nature.[165]

The district court, in finding that the section did not violate the Eighth Amendment, had relied on *Joyce v. City and County of San Francisco*, of which the Ninth Circuit disapproved of its analysis on the issues.[166] In *Joyce*, the court found that homelessness was not a status that could be protected under the Eighth Amendment, instead classifying homelessness as a "constitutionally noncognizable 'condition.'"[167] Contrary to the findings in *Joyce*, the court declared that Los Angeles would be expressly criminalizing the status of homelessness by making it a crime to be homeless and also by criminalizing acts fundamental to the status. The reason for this violation of this constitutional right in Los Angeles was due to the clear evidence that there were more homeless than available beds at all times.[168] The court concluded that homeless persons, including plaintiffs, are in a chronic state that may have been acquired innocently or involuntarily and sitting, lying, and sleeping are "universal and unavoidable consequences of being human" and biological requirements.[169] Therefore, those in skid row who are homeless can only do such acts in public because they lack any private space. Of course, this is true in many places outside of skid row.

At its basic level, the court cleverly remarked that plaintiffs cannot "avoid sitting, lying, and sleeping for days, weeks, or months at a time to comply with the city's ordinance as if human beings could remain in perpetual motion."[170] The subject ordinance does not recognize that it is impossible to do this, as the city suggested should be the case, and therefore making such conduct criminal is clearly criminalizing the status of homelessness.[171]

The court based its decision on several facts about the homeless population. First, a person can become homeless due to circumstances beyond his immediate control.[172] Second, the homeless are worthy of protecting even though they have shelter some nights and could eventually have it. Third, the plaintiffs could not be housed on the nights they were cited or arrested, proven again by statistics.

The court gave repeated reminders that its decision was limited. The limited nature was brought out by the request that the ordinance only be enforceable during certain hours. The decision does not address the situation in which there is shelter available.[173] These plaintiffs did not bring a facial challenge to the statute. Instead, the plaintiffs requested limited enforcement. The court only decided that the Eighth Amendment does not allow the city to "punish involuntarily sitting, lying, or sleeping on public sidewalks that is an unavoidable consequence of being human and homeless without shelter" in Los Angeles.[174] The court clarified that it is not into policy-making because that is for the legislature, mayor, and city council to do.[175] The court will only go so far to state that as long as there are more homeless than beds in Los Angeles, this section cannot be enforced anytime or anywhere when sitting, lying, and sleeping in public occurs without choice. Because of this, the city is narrowly enjoined from enforcing this section of the ordinance at specific times and places.[176]

The dissent disagreed with the majority opinion in numerous ways,[177] particularly that the ordinance criminalized homelessness, instead arguing that it merely punished conduct.[178] In support of his position, the dissent provided that proof did not exist that plaintiff Jones was in an involuntary condition that he could not change or avoid, or that there was no room for plaintiff Purrie in a shelter and he was turned away.[179] This implies some strange procedural requirement should exist in which homeless individuals who are turned away get a written receipt that they tried to enter a shelter and were denied access. That way they would have it just in case they needed to show a court about their efforts on a particular night. This clearly is not a realistic request or valid point. The dissent also disagreed that homelessness is an involuntary or innocent state, instead claiming that "some people fall into it, others opt into it"[180] and one can escape completely from homelessness.[181]

The *Jones* case is well known in the fight against criminalization.[182] Of course, it must be used with caution. The court brought many things to light, including the reality of this kind of law. The court recognized the contradiction of penalizing homeless individuals for sleeping, which we all must do, outside when the city has not provided them with somewhere inside to sleep. Such action does not achieve any goal and is counterproductive, leading to other problems. These seem like reasonable conclusions after only slight examination.

All My Belongings with Me: Personal Property

Another practical result of sleeping on the streets and even sitting on the streets is location and the protection of personal property. When a homeless person cannot take everything they own with them, they take the risk of it being stolen, picked up, or thrown away. In California, an ordinance banning camping and the storage of personal property in designated public areas is not unconstitutionally overbroad.[183] The alleged purpose behind the statute was to keep the public streets and areas clean and accessible.[184] The plaintiffs challenging the statute produced evidence that the ordinance was an effort to clear the city of the homeless population.[185] Denying the ordinance was invalid for its indirect impact on a person's right to travel, the Supreme Court of California held that the ordinance did not have a discriminatory purpose.[186] The court overturned the Court of Appeals' finding that the ordinance permitted punishment for the status of homeless or indigency.[187] The court added that the ordinance was not vague or overbroad because it gave sufficient notice of prohibited conduct.[188] What is unclear is to whom such an ordinance would apply.

Other homeless plaintiffs have fared better in such a challenge, although were not actually able to have their items returned. After their personal property was taken and destroyed without notice, the plaintiffs in *Cash v. Hamilton County Dept. of Adult Probation* brought claims of Fifth and Fourteenth Amendment violations.[189] Clean-up crews, with direction to clean up under the bridges, removed plaintiffs' property in their living space and would not return it when requested. After being unable to find their property, plaintiffs brought suit on the basis of the destruction of property without notice and a hearing.[190] The court remanded the case for consideration by the lower court as to whether adequate notice was given to the plaintiffs prior to taking their property and whether the city had a custom of destroying the property of homeless persons without notice and the right to reclaim what was taken.[191]

Many of these cases have been distinguished by other courts, reminding us that the findings are often particular to specific situations. If these cases and court decisions have not stirred some questions about the goals of cities as they affect their homeless, this final topic of the laws will clearly provide an answer. The National Law Center on Homelessness and Poverty reported that several cities have enacted ordinances that restrict or even prohibit charitable organizations and individuals from sharing food with homeless people in public places.[192] The cities include Dallas,[193] Las Vegas, and Orlando, where individuals or organizations would be fined and/or cited criminally for such philanthropic conduct.[194] These cities have decided that charities cannot assist this population without restriction, but the cities are unwilling to help them. This is a shocking move and presents the obvious question of who is going to help them.

The theme running throughout many of these cases is that the homeless are often forced to do things in public. In crafting ordinances prohibiting some behaviors, whether it is sleeping, sitting, or asking for change, legislators and city councilmen have forgotten to provide an answer as to where and when the homeless can do these everyday things.

HOMELESS COURT

A major effort to assist the homeless in undoing some of what has been done against them takes them to the courtroom, which is the last place most would like to be. Dealing with the aftermath of criminalization and other everyday events, courts have been designed specifically to assist the homeless population with their needs.[195] The Homeless Court started in San Diego County, an outgrowth of an event held since 1988 for Vietnam War veterans, was aimed to resolve minor misdemeanor matters.[196] After informal proceedings were begun by criminal justice agencies with this purpose, the San Diego County Public Defender's Office received funding[197] for a monthly "homeless court." The court's sessions are held in the homeless shelters with attorneys and a judge. Because the court is actually brought to them at the shelters, a lot of issues are erased and the problems can be dealt with. The evaluation of the program has revealed not only a positive impact on participants, but also a positive impact on the efficiency of the court system.[198]

The program allows participants, who "typically ha[ve] no means for making reparations to the criminal justice system for criminal conduct," to resolve outstanding criminal cases through exchanging fines, community service, and custody for participation in treatment programs. This is helpful to participants who have overlooked misdemeanor citations and infractions that lead to more fines and warrants. Under the procedure of the homeless courts, the individuals surrender themselves to the court without full knowledge of the pending charges or if any exist at all.[199]

Many of the participants have already completed some of their sentence by the time they participate in the homeless court. The court focuses on "what the defendant has accomplished on the road to recovery rather than penalizing him/her for mistakes made in the past." The courts have been even more successful than expected by resolving a large number of cases, improving access to the courts, reducing fear of law enforcement, and creating high collaboration among court personnel and participants.[200]

Interestingly, two-thirds of the participants in the homeless court have had at least one case whose subject was the failure to buy a valid pass or ticket to ride the trolley.[201] One can only imagine how something simple like this can transform into a big problem. For example, a homeless person who receives an illegal lodging citation from the San Diego Police Department starts to dig a hole for himself immediately.[202] This citation comes with a fine of $135 and then if the fine is not paid, the individual could receive six months in jail and/or an additional fine up to $500. A warrant is the likely result for a homeless individual who cannot afford to pay.[203] Additionally, a homeless person has to risk losing his belongings by entering a courthouse.[204] With such success, the homeless courts have already expanded to other cities within California, other states, and other programs.[205]

Homeless court appears to have been successful in case resolution, finding that many participants say they would have otherwise waited until arrested to address their case in court.[206] This certainly helps them deal with, and hopefully reduce, any intimidation of attorneys, judges, and the court system with a positive result. This is definitely a positive step to addressing the effects of criminalization, but the problems are still compounding before the homeless can experience relief.

LEGISLATING THE HOMELESS PROBLEM

From the Capitol

Legislators in capitol buildings across states and in Washington, D.C., certainly have not been busying themselves with concern over the needs of the homeless population. As previously mentioned, the Stewart B. McKinney Act was the last major legislative effort that materialized. Some laws are helping the homeless, but only if they know about them.[207] This section reviews other legislative attempts that have fallen short, reflecting the absence of a united effort to address homelessness in America.

A search of legislation introduced in 2007 revealed a small number of bills addressing the subject of the homeless by the 110th Congress.[208] There was a Senate Resolution entitled "Recognizing the Month of November as 'National Homeless Youth Awareness Month.'" Some big-named senators, including presidential candidate Barack Obama, introduced this as Senate Resolution 226 on June 7, 2007. The language of the resolution stated that between 1.3 and 2.8 million children and teens are homeless each year in America, many of whom sleep on the streets or stay in emergency shelters.

With the increasing number of families with children in the homeless population, the resolution noted that homeless teens have difficulty obtaining basic needs, much less receiving adequate medical or mental health care.[209] Although the resolution makes strong points about the plight of homeless teens, whose numbers are increasing daily; it is just that—a resolution. By passing this measure, it merely states researched facts. It does not pass any law that actually assists homeless teens. By passing the resolution, the Senate states they support the efforts of those meeting the needs of homeless children and teens, employ the time and resources to increase awareness of the problem, and recognize November as "National Homeless Youth Awareness Month." This is the substance of this resolution and all it does for the "tragedy of youth homelessness."

The hot topic involving homelessness for the past several years is Iraq veterans. With the history of a large number of homeless veterans, attention certainly is required.[210] For instance, the Homeless Veterans Housing at Sepulveda Ambulatory Care Center Promotion Act was introduced in the House of Representatives, along with Supporting Our Troops when They Come Home and the Wounded Warrior Assistance Act of 2007.[211] Other efforts do much of the same.[212] Another issue affecting the number of homeless is individuals released from prison. A recent bill introduced in the Senate to address this, known as the Recidivism Reduction and Second Chance Act, intends to promote programs that assist recently released inmates in finding safe, adequate, and affordable housing. Surprisingly, fifteen to twenty-seven percent of former prisoners "expect to go to homeless shelters" after release.[213] Yet another group facing homelessness is former foster care children who age out of the system. Legislation has also been introduced to address this problem.[214]

The 109th Congress had greater vision in the bills introduced. One bill introduced attempted to establish a grant program for organizations that provided housing and services to those experiencing chronic homelessness and having health conditions that were disabling, such as mental illness.[215] Another bill entitled "Services for Ending Long-Term Homelessness Act" also addressed long-term homeless individuals.[216] Even the Bush administration got involved in introducing legislation affecting the homeless through the Homeless Assistance Consolidation Act of 2006, with the purpose of combating homelessness nationwide.[217] This would be achieved by combining three competitive homeless assistance programs into a single program.[218] None of these bills made it into law.

The 108th Congress had set a high bar the previous session with one bill in particular. The Bringing America Home Act (BAHA) was intended to bring a permanent end to homelessness in America.[219] The legislation was a product of a yearlong collaboration of academics, social service providers, congressmen, and homeless advocates.[220] The bill did not pass, but Congressman Carson reintroduced the legislation in November 2005 as HR 4347.[221] As stated on her Web site, the motivation for the bill is as follows, "In a country that has been blessed with wealth and resources, there are so many who wonder daily when the next paycheck will come, whether they will be able to feed their children, or where they will sleep that night. We cannot simply accept this sub-standard living for our citizens."

Proclaiming it as the "only legislation to date that addresses all the major issues associated with homelessness," the legislation speaks to housing, health, income, and civil rights.[222] There is a provision for a National Housing Trust Fund that would provide funds to build and preserve 1.5 million affordable homes within ten years.[223] If passed, the Act advances job training, vouchers for child-care and public transportation, and emergency funds for families facing eviction.[224] Although some cities passed resolution in support of the measure, and advocacy groups proclaimed their support, the legislation did not pass.[225]

The National Alliance to End Homelessness has also set forth a ten-year goal to address the problems of the homeless.[226] BAHA attempts to alter the definition of homeless and includes more specific details than that provided in the Stewart B. McKinney Act. In effect, the definition expands to include more individuals.[227] One portion of the BAHA would change the McKinney Act.[228] Title IV of BAHA calls for a consolidation of homeless assistance programs under the McKinney Act and for codification in federal law of the Continuum of Care planning process. BAHA would also reauthorize HUD McKinney-Vento programs for five years.[229] Big dreams are a great start to the movement to end homelessness, although there will be no real movement until there is change in the current laws.

Additional legislation during this time included a bill to reauthorize programs under the Runaway and Homeless Youth Act and the Missing Children's Assistance Act.[230] The Homeless Veterans Assistance Act of 2004 was also introduced.[231] At this point, the McKinney-Vento Act is just a band-aid on a deep wound. More is needed at the federal, state, and local levels.

The Legal Picture

Although it can be said that more attention in the law is necessary, it may be better to say too much attention is being given to the homeless on our streets. They are getting the kind of attention that leaves them with arrest records, fines to pay, and encouraging the usual cycle of homelessness. Plenty of ordinances have not been challenged in the legal system, so the laws continue, often in violation of this population's rights. Although solutions to the policy gaps will continue to be suggested, there must be progress. Some have suggested that one way to encourage progression toward ending homelessness is to get the homeless involved.[232] Some strategies to achieve this could include asking homeless individuals to serve on governing boards or having them testify at legislative hearings.[233] A comprehensive policy is needed with many parts, including state and local strategies for outreach, services, and supportive housing and awareness of benefits.[234]

Some cases discussed herein have attempted to put a face on the homeless, which is positive because the laws they are subject to are demoralizing. It can sometimes be seen as being treated as a criminal for who you are, not what you have done, because how can we say that they have done something "wrong"? An eye opening examination of criminalization of homeless has been stated as follows:

> When one can no longer inhabit public space, have one's possessions and shanty towns (home, by some definitions) burned or bulldozed, be arrested for one's status rather than a crime (hence signaling a loss of civil rights), and only exercise political power with extreme difficulty, one cannot be said to be a citizen. This is exacerbated by the disappearance of truly public space. Decisions are no longer the prerogative of the individual; rather, they are made for the homeless by communities in the form of NIMBY-ism (Not In My Back Yard), by the police in the form of sweeps, and by local officials in outlawing panhandling or busing the homeless to other towns, for example. Whether full citizens or politicians decide to help the homeless or not, their freedom to make choices exists in a very narrow manner. Moreover, the help received by the homeless can be authoritarian and punitive in nature. Homeless individuals are to believe that they have become so through their moral failing and every day are reminded of this. Many shelters and agencies go beyond simple admonitions, however, and issue ultimatums. Some are contradictory and put the homeless in a double bind. Indeed, the system that helps them can often be erratic, disorganized, and pathological.[235]

As the Supreme Court recognized, "[D]iscrimination against the homeless is likely to be a function of deep-seated prejudice."[236] Another court viewed the existence of lawsuits in which their rights are sought to be upheld as evidence of political power of the homeless.[237] The court decisions examined, along with many others, have served to protect the homeless from many of the punitive laws and ordinances that have been passed to make the homeless less visible but also have made them more vulnerable to criminalizing conduct by cities and their officials. Criminalization of homelessness is not a solution, especially to the causes of homelessness. Although laws can make a positive impact on their status, many laws exist, many unchallenged, which attempt to make a vulnerable population invisible.

NOTES

1. *The Pursuit of Happyness,* DVD, directed by Gabrielle Muccino (2006; Los Angeles, CA: Sony Home Video, 2007), http://www.sonypictures.com/homevideo/thepursuitofhappyness/.

2. Ibid.

3. Ibid. The landlord yelled at the renter that he needed his rent check. Then, he received a letter from the Internal Revenue Service stating that since he owed them, the government had taken the money directly out of his bank account, leaving him unexpectedly with twenty-one dollars and change in his account.

4. K. Hopper, *Reckoning with Homelessness* (Ithaca, NY: Cornell University Press, 2003), 181. The Community for Creative Nonviolence and the National Coalition for the Homeless, along with nine other groups, collaborated in 1986 to write a comprehensive relief bill. Title one of the "Homeless Persons' Survival Act" is what we know now as the Stewart B. McKinney Homeless Assistance Act.

5. *Stewart B. McKinney Homeless Assistance Act*, Public Law 100-77, 101 Stat 482 (July 22, 1987); *McKinney-Vento Act*, (U.S. Department of Housing and Urban Development), http://www.hud.gov/ofices/cpd/homeless/rulesandregs/laws/index.cfm. The McKinney Act was signed into law on July 22, 1987, by President Ronald Reagan.

6. National Coalition for the Homeless, "McKinney-Vento Act, NCH Fact Sheet #18," 2006, http://www.nationalhomeless.org/publications/facts/McKinney.pdf.

7. Ibid; *Congressional Record*, (March 23, 1978). Senator Al Gore, as a sponsor, made the following comment about the Act before it was passed, "(McKinney) is an essential first step towards establishing a national agenda for action to eradicate homelessness in America ... No one in this body should believe that the legislation we begin considering today is anything more than a first step towards reversing the record increase in homelessness."

8. *McKinney Act*, Section 103(a) (2000).

9. *McKinney Act*, Section 102(b) (2000). The purpose is to coordinate better public programs and resources, and deliver funds to programs assisting the homeless.

10. "McKinney-Vento Act, NCH Fact Sheet #18," 2006. Title I included a statement of six findings by Congress and set out the definition of homeless. Title II deals with the Interagency Council on the Homeless. Title III addresses the Emergency Food and Shelter Program. Title IV addresses the housing issues administered by HUD. Title V sets requirements for provisions of surplus federal property by federal agencies. Title VI deals with providing health care services to the homeless. Title VII authorizes programs for education and job opportunities. Title VIII includes the homeless in the Food Stamp program. Title IX extends the Veterans Job Training Act.

11. Ibid; The first changes to the Act were in 1988 and were fairly minor. Under the 1990 amendments, additional eligible activities were added to some already existing programs and several new programs were created;. Hopper, *Reckoning with the Homeless,* 2003, 181–2. The provisions included, among other programs, funding and protection of education for homeless children and programs for individuals with mental illness;. *McKinney-Vento Act*, NCH Fact Sheet, 2006. The 1992 amendments focused on Title IV of the Act as to housing and shelter. The Education of the Homeless Children and Youth program and the Surplus Property Program were amended in 1994.

12. "McKinney-Vento Act, NCH Fact Sheet #18," 2006. Funding was at its all-time high in 1995 at $1.49 billion, but in 1996, funding for the programs was cut by 27%.

13. Ibid. This was a conclusion based on a 1995 evaluation of the HUD McKinney-Vento programs.

14. Ibid.

15. Ibid. The original legislation was named after the late Representative Stewart B. McKinney of Connecticut, chief Republican sponsor of the legislation. The name was changed to McKinney-Vento in honor of Bruce Vento, representative and leading supporter of the legislation since 1987.

16. *McKinney Act*, Section102(a)(4) (2000).

17. "McKinney-Vento Act, NCH Fact Sheet #18," 2006.

18. National Coalition for the Homeless and the National Law Center on Homelessness and Poverty, *A Dream Denied: The Criminalization of Homelessness in U.S. Cities*, 2006, 11, http://www.nationalhomeless.org/publications/crimreport/index.html. Jail costs were two to three times the cost of supporting housing according to a survey of nine cities.

19. This was an unpublished decision. See Hopper, *Reckoning with Homelessness,* 2003, 180–1.

20. Ibid.

21. B. A. Grant ed., *Black's Law Dictionary,* 8th ed. (Los Angeles: Thomson West, 2004), 666. The First Amendment guarantees the freedoms of speech, religion, press, assembly, and petition.

22. Ibid., 683. The Fourth Amendment prohibits unreasonable searches and seizures and the issuance of warrants without probable cause.

23. Ibid., 555. The Eighth Amendment prohibits excessive bail, excessive fines, and cruel and unusual punishment.

24. National Law Center on Homelessness and Poverty, "Combating the Criminalization of Homelessness: A Guide to Understand and Prevent Legislation that Criminalizes Life-Sustaining Activities," 2002, http://www.nlchp.org/FA_CivilRights/CR_crim_booklet.pdf; *Black's Law Dictionary*, 682. The Fourteenth Amendment prohibits states from denying due process and equal protection, effectively applying the Bill of Rights to the states.

25. *Black's Law Dictionary*, 660. The Fifth Amendment provides that one cannot be (1) required to answer for a capital or otherwise infamous offense unless a grand jury issues an indictment or presentment, (2) subjected to double jeopardy, (3) compelled to engage in self-incrimination on a criminal matter, (4) deprived of life, liberty, or property without due process of law, or (5) deprived of private property for public use without just compensation.

26. National Law Center on Homelessness and Poverty, "Combating the Criminalization of Homelessness," 2002.

27. K. L. Kusmer, *Down and Out, On The Road: The Homeless in American History* (Oxford: University Press, 2002), Preface.

28. *California v. Greenwood*, 486 U.S. 35, 37 (1988); *Black's Law Dictionary*, 411. Curtilage is defined as the yard or land adjoining a house, which is often within an enclosure.

29. *California v. Greenwood*, 486 U.S. 41 (1988).

30. *Cordova v. City of Reno*, 920 F.Supp. 135, 137 (D.Ct. Nev. 1996) (citing Reno Municipal Ordinance. Section 8.22.040).

31. Ibid., 139.

32. *Johnson v. Board of Commissioners*, 351 F.Supp.2d 929 (E.D. Mo. 2004).

33. Ibid., 930.

34. Ibid., 931.

35. Ibid.

36. Ibid., 935.

37. Ibid., 937.

38. Ibid.

39. Ibid., 934.

40. Ibid., 935.

41. Ibid.

42. Ibid., 945, 952. Injunctive relief is granted as appropriate relief when the requesting party can show he has no adequate remedy at law. The relevant factors for proof are: "(1) the probability of success on the merits; (2) the threat of irreparable harm to the movant; (3) the balance between this harm and the injury that granting the injunction will inflict on the other interested parties; and (4) whether the issuance of an injunction is in the public interest."

43. *Betancourt v. Bloomberg*, 448 F.3d 547 (2nd Cir. 2006).

44. Ibid., 549.

45. Ibid; *NYC Admin. Code*, Section 16-122.

46. See *Schaumburg v. Citizens for Better Environment*, 444 U.S. 620 (1980); *Papachristou v. City of Jacksonville*, 405 U.S. 156, 162 (1971). Such statutes allow an officer to ask or require a suspect to disclose his or her identity. See *Hiibel v. Sixth Judicial District Court of Nevada*, 542 U.S. 177, 183 (2004). "Stop and identify statutes have their roots in early English vagrancy laws that required suspected vagrants to face arrest unless they gave 'a good account of themselves,' a power that itself reflected common-law rights of private persons to 'arrest any suspicious night-walker, and detain him till he give a good account of himself'" (citing English law from 1787). State stop and identify statutes often combine elements of traditional vagrancy laws with provisions intended to regulate police behavior in the course of investigatory stops. They vary from state to state, but all permit an officer to ask or require a suspect to disclose his identity.

47. *Hiibel v. Sixth Judicial District Court of Nevada*, 542 U.S. 190 (2004); see also National Law Center on Homelessness and Poverty, "Combating the Criminalization of Homelessness," 2002. On December 15, 2003, the National Law Center on Homelessness and Poverty, the National Coalition for the Homeless, Judge David L. Bazelon Center for Mental Health Law, National Alliance to End Homelessness, National Health Care for the Homeless Council, and National Coalition for Homeless Veterans, with substantial assistance from Sidley, Austin, Brown, and Wood, filed an amicus curiae ("friend of the court") brief in support of the petitioner in this case.

48. *Hiibel v. Sixth Judicial District Court of Nevada*, 542 U.S. 180-1 (2004); Nev. Rev. Stat. (NRS) § 199.280 (2003). Mr. Hiibel was charged with willfully resist[ing], delay[ing] or obstruct[ing] a public officer in his duties. The government reasoned that Hiibel had obstructed the officer in carrying out his duties under § 171.123, a Nevada statute

that defines the legal rights and duties of a police officer in the context of an investigative stop. Section 171.123 provided in relevant part:

> 1. "Any peace officer may detain any person whom the officer encounters under circumstances that reasonably indicate that the person has committed, is committing or is about to commit a crime.... 3. The officer may detain the person pursuant to this section only to ascertain his identity and the suspicious circumstances surrounding his presence abroad. Any person so detained shall identify himself, but may not be compelled to answer any other inquiry of any peace officer."

Hiibel did not allege that the Nevada statute was unconstitutionally vague.

49. National Law Center on Homelessness and Poverty, "*Hiibel v. Sixth Judicial District of Nevada*," 2004, http://www.nlchp.org/view_report.cfm?id=122.

50. Ibid.

51. *Hiibel v. Sixth Judicial District Court of Nevada*, 542 U.S. 177-8 (2004). Hiibel argued that the statute allowed an officer to arrest someone for "being suspicious," which circumvented the probable-cause requirement intended to minimize the risk of arbitrary police conduct.

52. *Papachristou v. City of Jacksonville,* 405 U.S. 167-71 (1971).

53. *Brown v. Texas*, 443 U.S. 47, 52 (1979).

54. *Kolender v. Lawson*, 461 U.S. 352 (1983).

55. See *Schaumburg v. Citizens for Better Environment,* 444 U.S. 620 (1980).

56. See *Currier v. Potter*, 379 F.3d 716 (9th Cir. 2004).

57. Ibid., 723–731. The case was also dismissed for lack of subject matter jurisdiction.

58. Ibid., 731–32.

59. Ibid., 733.

60. Ibid.

61. Ibid., 734. Of course, family and friends also may be cut off from communication.

62. Ibid., 737.

63. K. R. Arnold, *Homelessness, Citizenship, and Identity: The Uncanniness of Late Modernity* (Albany: State University of New York Press, 2004), 111.

64. National Coalition for the Homeless, *Illegal to be Homeless*, 2004; http://www.nationalhomeless.org/publications/crimreport/meanestcities.html; National Coalition for the Homeless and National Law Center on Homelessness and Poverty, *Dream Denied*, 2006. In its 2006 report, the National Coalition for the Homeless and National Law Center on Homelessness and Poverty found that since 2002, sixty-seven cities had a twelve percent increase in laws forbidding begging in certain places, a fourteen percent increase in laws forbidding sitting or lying in certain areas, and a three percent increase in loitering or vagrancy laws. This report presented a top five list of the meanest cities in 2005, including Sarasota, Florida; Lawrence, Kansas; Little Rock, Arkansas; Atlanta, Georgia; and Las Vegas, Nevada.

65. National Law Center on Homelessness and Poverty, "Solutions Through Alternative Remedies: Practical Models to Help End Homelessness," 2004, http://www.nlchp.org/content/pubs/Solutions%20Through%20Alternative%20Remedies1.pdf.

66. Ibid.

67. National Coalition for the Homeless and National Law Center on Homelessness and Poverty, *Dream Denied*, 2006. The report also showed twenty-eight percent prohibit camping; thirty-nine percent forbid loitering in certain areas; and forty-three percent

prohibit begging in certain places. Even stricter, of these numbers, sixteen percent had a citywide complete prohibition on camping and loitering while twenty-one percent had the same prohibition on begging.

68. Hopper, *Reckoning with Homelessness*, 2003. For example, a Los Angeles councilman has made several proposals to drive the homeless to a camp in the Santa Monica Mountains or transport to ferryboats anchored in the harbor.

69. National Law Center, "Solutions Through Alternative Remedies," 2004. In a 2002 nationwide survey of fifty-seven communities, there was inadequate shelter in every community.

70. National Coalition for the Homeless and National Law Center on Homelessness and Poverty, *Dream Denied*, 2006.

71. Ibid., 9.

72. Ibid., 11–12, 18–19.

73. Arnold, *Homelessness, Citizenship, and Identity*, 2004.

74. T. A. Bateman, "Law Regulating Begging, Panhandling, or Similar Activity by Poor or Homeless Persons," 7 *A.L.R.* 5th 455 (1992): Section 2.

75. Ibid.

76. See *Schaumburg v. Citizens for Better Environment,* 1980.

77. Ibid., 633.

78. Ibid., 625–6, 637.

79. Bateman, "Law Regulating Begging," 1992.

80. See for example *Young v. New York City Transit Authority,* 903 F.2d 146 (2nd Cir. 1990); *Blair v. Shanahan,* 775 F. Supp. 1315 (N.D.Ca. 1991) (upholding a misdemeanor citation for accosting someone else in a public place—overturned by *Blair v. Shanahan,* 38 F.3d 1514 (9th Cir. 1994)); *Gresham v. Peterson,* 225 F.3d 899 (7th Cir. 2000). *Young* has been distinguished by several other New York courts. Interestingly, the opinion mentions a study performed on reactions to begging and panhandling. Defendants used the study to argue to the court that because people are intimidated by beggars there should be a distinction in laws against begging in the subway and out on the streets because of the "captive nature" of the subway.

81. *Blair v. Shanahan,* 38 F.3d 1516 (9th Cir. 1994).

82. Ibid.

83. Ibid., 1517.

84. Ibid., 1520.

85. *Young v. New York City Transit Authority,* 903 F.2d 146 (2nd Cir. 1990).

86. Ibid.

87. *Loper v. New York City Police Department,* 766 F. Supp. 1280, n.3 (S.D. NY 1991); see Hershkoff and Coen, "Begging to Differ: The First Amendment and the Right to Beg," *Harvard Law Review* 104 (1991): 896; Ciampi, "A Buberion Approach to Constitutional Analysis: So That We May Be Able to Face Our Poorer Brethren Eye to Eye," *St. John's Law Review* 65 (1991): 325; and Note, A. Rose, "The Beggar's Free Speech Claim," *Indiana Law Journal* 65 (1989): 191–228.

88. Ciampi, "A Buberion Approach," 1991. The comment was made, "Though begging has been regulated, monitored, and at times prohibited throughout history, there is nothing to suggest that begging has been universally viewed with the rancor and enmity of, say, obscenity."

89. *Papachristou v. City of Jacksonville,* 405 U.S. 161–2 (1971). Vagrancy laws became "criminal aspects of the poor laws." For various reasons out of their control, many men and their families took to a life of vagrancy. Some other individuals never intended any

other kind of life and formed a "brotherhood of beggars" rampant in the 16th and 17th centuries. The vagrancy laws, often very harsh, were aimed at these individuals.

90. Ibid., 158. The language of the ordinance was as follows:

> Rogues and vagabonds, or dissolute persons who go about begging, common gamblers, persons who use juggling or unlawful games or plays, common drunkards, common night walkers, thieves, pilferers or pickpockets, traders in stolen property, lewd, wanton and lascivious persons, keepers of gambling places, common railers and brawlers, persons wandering or strolling around from place to place without any lawful purpose or object, habitual loafers, disorderly persons, persons neglecting all lawful business and habitually spending their time by frequenting houses of ill fame, gaming houses, or places where alcoholic beverages are sold or served, persons able to work but habitually living upon the earnings of their wives or minor children shall be deemed vagrants and, upon conviction in the Municipal Court, shall be punished as provided for Class D offenses.

91. Ibid., 162.

92. *Gresham v. Peterson*, 225 F.3d 901 (7th Cir. 2000); *Bateman*, "Law Regulating Begging," 1992.

93. See, for example, *Loper v. New York City Police Department,* 766 F. Supp. 1282, n.3 (S.D. NY 1991); *Perry v. Los Angeles Police Dept.*, 121 F.3d 1365 (9th Cir. 1997); and *Thompson v. City of Chicago*, 2002WL31115578 (N.D.Ill. 2002) (denying defendant's motion to dismiss as to plaintiffs' challenges to a panhandling ordinance).

94. *People v. Griswold*, 13 Misc.3d 560, 821 N.Y.S.2d 394 (City Ct. 2006).

95. Ibid.

96. New York State Penal Law section 240.35(1); *Loper v. New York City Police Department,* 766 F. Supp. 1282, n.3 (S.D. NY 1991).

97. *Loper v. New York City Police Department,* 766 F. Supp. 1282, n.3 (S.D. NY 1991).

98. Ibid., 1287.

99. Ibid., 1288.

100. Ibid., 1289.

101. Ibid., 1290.

102. See *Chad v. City of Ft. Lauderdale*, 66 F.Supp.2d 1242 (N.D.Fla. 1998).

103. See *Seattle v. Webster*, 115 Wash 2d 635, 802 P.2d 1333 (1990).

104. The ordinance, SMC 12A.12.015 (1987), stated as follows:

> A. The following definitions apply in this section: 1. "Aggressively beg" means to beg with intent to intimidate another person into giving money or goods. … 3. "Obstruct pedestrian or vehicular traffic" means to walk, stand, sit, lie, or place an object in such a manner as to block passage by another person or a vehicle, or to require another person or a driver of a vehicle to take evasive action to avoid physical contact. Acts authorized as an exercise of one's constitutional right to picket or to legally protest … shall not constitute obstruction of pedestrian or vehicular traffic. … B. A person is guilty of pedestrian interference if … [that person] intentionally: 1. Obstructs pedestrian or vehicular traffic; or 2. Aggressively begs. C. Pedestrian interference may be punished by a fine not to exceed Five Hundred Dollars ($500.00) or by imprisonment in jail for a term not to exceed ninety (90) days or by both such fine and imprisonment.

This $500 in 1987 is a hefty fine for many individuals much less someone who is homeless.

105. Bateman, "Law Regulating Begging," 1992.

106. See *Seattle v. Webster*, 115 Wash 2d 646 (1990).

107. Ibid., 638.

108. Ibid., 656. The dissent commented on the issue of the homeless as a suspect class and agreed that there are no cases finding that the homeless are a suspect class. He added, "… by stating that no case law supports the argument, the majority unnecessarily intimates the view that the argument has no merit. I suggest we address the question of whether concepts of equal protection law justify identifying the homeless as a suspect class in a case squarely raising the issue."

109. Ibid., 647.

110. Ibid.

111. *Henry v. City of Cincinnati*, 2005 WL 1198814 (S.D.Ohio 2005).

112. Ibid., 6–7.

113. Section 910-12(b). The solicitor could also not do so after sunset or before sunrise. See Section 910-12(c).

114. Ibid., 2.

115. Ibid., 9.

116. See *Armstrong v. District of Columbia Public Library*, 154 F.Supp.2d 67 (D.C. 2001).

117. *Kreimer v. Bureau of Police for the Town of Morristown*, 958 F.2d 1242 (3rd Cir. 1992).

118. Ibid., 1246. The plaintiff had been ejected five different times for his conduct.

119. Ibid., 1246–7.

120. Ibid. The rules provided:

> 1. Patrons shall be engaged in normal activities associated with the use of a public library while in the building. Patrons not engaged in reading, studying, or using library materials may be asked to leave the building. Loitering will not be tolerated.… 5. Patrons shall respect the rights of other patrons and shall not annoy others through noisy or boisterous activities, by unnecessary staring, by following another person through the building, by playing walkmans or other audio equipment or that others can hear it, by singing or talking to oneself or by other behavior which may reasonably result in the disturbance of others persons.… 9. Patron dress and personal hygiene shall conform to the standard of the community for public places. This shall include the repair or cleanliness of garments. Any patron not abiding by these or other rules and regulations of the Library, may be asked to leave the Library premises. Library employees shall contact the Morristown Police if deemed advisable. Any patron who violated the Library rules and regulations may be denied the privilege of access to the Library by the Library Board of Trustees, on recommendation of the Library Director.

121. Ibid., 1248–9. The plaintiff had initially brought his own pro se complaint against the Morristown Bureau of Police, the library, the Board of Directors, Rice, three library employees, and four police officers for damages for pain and suffering, emotional distress, humiliation, negligence, and violation of civil rights, first amendment rights, harassment, defamation of character, and discrimination due to his homeless status.

122. Ibid.

123. Ibid., 1255–6.
124. Ibid.
125. Ibid., 1262.
126. Ibid., 1263.
127. Ibid., 1264.
128. Ibid.
129. Ibid., 1265–9.
130. Ibid. As to the final challenge by plaintiff, the court held that the Supreme Court of New Jersey would agree that the rules were constitutional under the state Constitution.
131. Ibid., 1270.
132. See *Armstrong v. District of Columbia Public Library*, 154 F.Supp.2d 67 (D.C. 2001).
133. Ibid., 69.
134. Ibid.
135. After amendments, the 1984 regulation, under Minor Offenses stated,

> Minor offenses are to be dealt with at the unit level first, using the following guidelines to determine the type and extent of action to be taken: A. Conduct or personal condition objectionable to other persons using the Library's facilities or which interfere with the orderly provision of library services. 3. Objectionable appearance (barefooted, bare-chested, body odor, filthy clothing, etc.) ACTION a. Martin Luther King Memorial Library department or division staff shall warn the person. b. If this fails, the Martin Luther King Memorial Library staff shall call the Library security office at once to ask the person to leave the building.... c.... If the patron fails to comply, the Metropolitan Police are to be called at once by the Librarian in charge, then the Library Police Office notified without delay. A written report should follow. Guidelines for Handling Security matters, Section II (December 7, 1984).

136. Ibid., 70.
137. Ibid., 70–1.
138. Ibid., 72.
139. Ibid., 74.
140. Ibid., 77.
141. Ibid., 78. The library's chief of security testified in his deposition that the library guards often are challenged in determining whether someone should be denied access under the rule. There was also no training or written guidance on application of the rule. If the chief of security was going to decide, then he would personally have to see the potential patron in order to make a decision under the rule.
142. Ibid.
143. Going even further, do the terms of the rule include a painter's overalls or a mechanic's shirt?
144. Ibid., 79.
145. Ibid.
146. Ibid., 81.
147. Ibid., 82.
148. Ibid.
149. In an article (*Las Cruces Sun-News*, February 1, 2007), reports indicated a "Homeless Man Was Stabbed and Beaten to Death" in Las Cruces, New Mexico.

150. *Fifth Ave. Presbyterian Church v. City of New York,* 2004WL2471406, 1 (S.D.N.Y. 2004). The church had designated the landings on the tops of the staircases that led into the church and along a wall of one side of the outside property as sleeping areas.

151. Ibid., 1, 6, 11. The city took drastic measures to carry out the removal of those sleeping. They brought twenty-two police officers to the church property "'bearing nightsticks and large clusters of handcuffs,' threatening arrest and accompanied by 'three police vans, two squad cars, and a paddy wagon.'"

152. Ibid., 12.

153. *Johnson v. City of Dallas*, 860 F. Supp. 344 (N.D. Tex. 1994), reviewed in part, vacated in part on other grounds, 61 F.3d 442 (5th Cir. 1995).

154. Ibid., 347, 355–6. The court examined whether homeless should be a quasi-suspect class.

155. Ibid., 350, FN 4.

156. Ibid., 350–1.

157. *Jones v. City of Los Angeles*, 444 F.3d 1118 (9th Cir. 2006).

158. Ibid., 1120.

159. Ibid; L.A., CA, Mun. Code, Section 41.18(d) (2005); L.A. Mun. Code, Section 11.00(m). Again, the fine is hefty. Those that this section affects will not be able to pay this amount, leading to other problems such as warrants.

160. Ibid (referring to L.A. Homeless Servs. Auth., Los Angeles Continuum of Care, Exhibit 1 Narrative, at 2–17 (2001)); P. Burns, D. Flaming, B. Haydamack, *Homeless in LA: A Working Paper for the 10-Year Plan to End Homelessness in Los Angeles County*" (Los Angeles: United Way, 2003).

161. The court provided numerous examples of other laws that achieve this. In Las Vegas, in Mun. Code § 10.47.020 (2005), one is guilty for standing or lying in a public way only if it obstructs pedestrian or vehicular traffic. Portland law prohibits "camping" on public property. Portland, OR., Mun. Code, Sections 14A.50.020, .030 (2006). In Seattle, Washington, sitting or lying on a public sidewalk is not allowed during the hours of 7:00 A.M. and 9:00 P.M.. Mun. Code, Section 15.48.040 (2005). Other cities have similar laws but with different times such conduct is prohibited. *Jones v. City of Los Angeles*, 444 F.3d 1123 (9th Cir. 2006).

162. *Jones v. City of Los Angeles*, 444 F.3d 1123 (9th Cir. 2006). See Tucson, AZ, Mun. Code, Section 11-36.2(a) (2005); Houston, TX, Mun. Code, Section 40-352 (a) (2006).

163. *Jones v. City of Los Angeles*, 444 F.3d 1124-5 (9th Cir. 2006). The plaintiffs' history was detailed in the opinion.

164. Ibid., 1125.

165. Ibid., 1137–38.

166. Ibid., 1132; *Joyce v. City and County of San Francisco*, 846 F. Supp. 843 (N.D.Cal. 1994).

167. *Jones v. City of Los Angeles*, 444 F.3d 1129 (9th Cir. 2006).

168. Ibid., 1136. Emphasis added. After examining two factors relevant to the cruel and unusual punishment clause's limits on the state's power to criminalize, there was a distinction between 1) pure status (state of being) and pure conduct (act of doing); and 2) the ability to distinguish an involuntary and voluntary act or condition.

169. Ibid., 1136–7.

170. Ibid.

171. Ibid., 1137.

172. Ibid. The court adds, especially considering who is homeless: mental illness, addicts, domestic victims, unemployed, and the unemployable.

173. This situation has been addressed by the Eleventh Circuit. See *Joel v. City of Orlando*, 232 F.3d 1353 (11th Cir. 2000).

174. *Jones v. City of Los Angeles*, 444 F.3d 1138 (9th Cir. 2006). The court clarified what it is not doing through its decision which includes: criminalizing conduct not unavoidable to the homeless such as panhandling or obstructing paths; telling Los Angeles to adopt a certain social policy, plan, or law to help the homeless; or telling the City of Los Angeles to provide sufficient shelter or let the homeless sit, lie, or sleep on its streets anytime, anyplace in the city.

175. Ibid. Obviously showing there is a "homeless problem."

176. Ibid., 1138.

177. Ibid., 1148. One reason he rejected the majority's decision is the necessity-due-to-homelessness defense available in California.

178. Ibid., 1139. As to the status of being homeless, the dissenting justice adds, "We do not and should not—immunize from criminal liability those who commit an act as a result of a condition that the government's failure to provide a benefit has left them in."

179. Ibid., 1139–40.

180. Ibid., 1146. I've always found this assertion interesting. To me "opting into homelessness" is defined as waking up one day and saying that homelessness is a life to be pursued. This is quite a conclusion to be drawn from a judge, whom I doubt has ever been homeless or done much research on the issue.

181. Ibid., (citing U.S. Conf. of Mayors, "A Status Report on Hunger and Homelessness in America's Cities," 2002, p. 312). His conclusion is based on this report, which noted people remain homeless in the cities considered for six months on average.

182. L.A. homeless situation in the wake of the key 9th Federal Circuit Court Jones decision last April, overturning the L.A. Sleeping Ban with significant implications for Santa Cruz and cities in nine other Western states. Gregory Afghani, author of *Guilty of Being Homeless in America—Sleepless on Skid Row*, will analyze the ACLU's current success or failure in its lawsuit against the LAPD, current LAPD policy using new tools to repress the homeless, and how mainstream media is distorting the issue.

183. See *Tobe v. City of Santa Ana*, 9 Cal. 4th 1069 (Cal. 1995).

184. Ibid., 1080–1.

185. Ibid., 1082. The city had also conducted a sweep of the homeless.

186. Ibid., 1102.

187. Ibid., 1106.

188. Ibid., 1108.

189. *Cash v. Hamilton County Dept. of Adult Probation*, 388 F.3d 539, 540 (6th Cir. 2004).

190. Ibid., 541.

191. Ibid., 544. The city claimed it published notice in the newspaper.

192. National Law Center on Homelessness and Poverty, "Food-Sharing Bans Shock U.N. High Commissioner," http://www.nlchp.org/news.cfm?id=4.

193. Ordinance No. 26023 (2005); National Law Center on Homelessness and Poverty, *Dream Denied*, 2006. This Dallas provision penalizes charities, churches, and other organizations with a fine of up to $2,000 if they serve food outside of certain areas.

194. Ibid. The NLCHP informed the U.N. High Commissioner and U.N. delegation of these ordinances and after hearing countless human rights abuses; the High Commissioner was "visibly shocked" when told about this conduct. These "Food-Sharing Bans"

are not only human rights violations, but cause specific concern for disabled homeless individuals who cannot reach centralized food distribution places. The NLCHP has already gotten involved in any litigation filed against these ordinances.

195. N. Kerry and S. Pennell, *San Diego Homeless Court Program: A Process and Impact Evaluation* (San Diego: San Diego Association of Governments, 2001).

196. Ibid., Abstract and iii.

197. Ibid. Funding was provided in 1999 by the Bureau of Justice Assistance.

198. Ibid., 52, 54–5.

199. Ibid., 3. Procedurally, the participants sign up in advance of the hearing so personnel can research criminal histories and case files. If constructive, attorneys negotiate a case and then the court order is satisfied by the alternative sentence.

200. Ibid., 3–4.

201. Ibid., 5.

202. Ibid., 12. San Diego Police Department issued 1,129 such citations in 2000.

203. Ibid.

204. B. Shirk, "San Diego's Homeless Court Taking It to the Shelter," September-October 2004, http://www.courtinfo.ca.gov/programs/collab/documents/TakingittotheShelter.pdf.

205. L.A. County Department of Public Social Services, "Homeless Court," http://www.ladpss.org/dpss/grow/homeless_court.cfm; Coalition for the Homeless of Houston/Harris County, Inc., "The City of Houston Municipal Court-Homeless Court," http://www.homelesshouston.org/hh/Homeless_Court_EN.asp?SnID=2; Phoenix Municipal Court, "Regional Homeless Court," http://phoenix.gov/COURT/homeless.html; and Kerry and Pennell, *San Diego Homeless Court Program*, 2001. Other cities include Los Angeles, Houston, and Phoenix. The San Diego court also started an initiative called the Non-Custodial Parent Program, which assists those living in a homeless shelter to work out a manageable payment plan after participating in treatment services, contacting the Employment Development Department, and seeking full-time employment. The district attorney is in cooperation with this program on payments. This program is expected to bring more homeless individuals back into the working population through services and acceptance of financial responsibility.

206. ABC 7 News, Arlington, VA, "Homeless Court Works to Help Such People," http://www.wjla.com. One participant said, "If you really want to get your life back together, this helps you do it."

207. For example, the Earned Income Tax Credit assists working homeless individuals.

208. Current and past legislative information is available at Library of Congress, "Thomas," http://thomas.loc.gov/.

209. Ibid. The resolution also states that thirteen homeless youth die every day. The causes of death are physical assault, illness, and suicide. The resolution notes the problems posed to homeless teens by insufficient financial and housing resources for young people leaving juvenile corrections and foster care situations.

210. National Coalition for the Homeless, "Who is Homeless?" NCH Fact Sheet #3, June 2006, http://www.nationalhomeless.org/publications/facts/Whois.pdf; National Coalition for the Homeless, "Homeless Veterans," NCH Fact Sheet #14, http://www.nationalhomeless.org/publications/facts/veterans.pdf. The National Coalition for the Homeless reports that approximately forty percent of homeless men served their country. This is compared to thirty-four percent of the general adult male population. In 2006, the National Coalition for Homeless Veterans estimated that 20,000 veterans are homeless each night.

211. Library of Congress, "Thomas." It was May 7, 2007, when the "Homeless Veterans Housing At Sepulveda Ambulatory Care Center Promotion Act" was introduced. "Supporting our Troops when They Come Home" was introduced in the House of Representatives on March 20, 2007. Representative Filner mentioned the strain on health services and the Veterans Administration from returning troops from Iraq and Afghanistan. In assessing the problem, he added, "how veterans are falling through the cracks. There was an incredible documentary on how Iraqi troops returning were homeless already." The *Wounded Warrior Assistance Act of 2007* was introduced in the House of Representatives on March 28, 2007.

212. Ibid. In the House of Representatives on January 17, 2007, H579 was introduced. Representative Drake stood to congratulate Norfolk, Virginia Beach, and Portsmouth, Virginia, for opening a new complex to house formerly homeless people. This complex was unique because it was the first in the nation that is financed and supported by more than one city. This complex will serve over sixty adults providing other comprehensive services such as job counseling, mental health, substance abuse, and drug-abuse treatment as well. Representative Drake encouraged other regions of the country to display the same teamwork showed by these cities.

213. Ibid. This was introduced in the Senate on April 12, 2007. Figures published by the Volunteers of America in 2004 indicated that two-thirds of former prisoners who lacked adequate housing had committed crimes within one year of their release, compared to only one-quarter of those who had housing. Another recent study released by the National Criminal Justice Reference Service showed that thirty to fifty percent of parolees in urban areas such as Los Angeles and San Francisco are homeless, which compounds the profound hardship that re-integration already places on urban communities. The *Second Chance Act* supports our communities and local law enforcement by supporting housing programs for ex-offenders, so that they can take the first steps towards getting back on their feet and rejoining the community.

214. Ibid. *Eliminating Poverty* was introduced in the House of Representatives on January 23, 2007. In the House of Representatives, on February 15, 2007, the *Foster Children Self Support Act* was introduced as an effort to "prevent abused and neglected children from being used as a funding stream for states that should be acting in the best interests of these extremely vulnerable children. Then, when children emancipate from care they are dependent on public assistance, become incarcerated or homeless, and are unemployed at rates higher than nearly any other group of Americans."

215. Ibid. The program would be administered by the Substance Abuse and Mental Health Services Administration.

> The Department of Health and Human Services currently operates grant programs for homeless individuals, but none of them are specifically focused on services such as mental health services, substance abuse treatment, health education, money management, parental skills training, and general health care, coordinated with permanent supportive housing. Chronically homeless individuals need more than housing. In order to truly help, the federal government needs to provide grants that will enable communities to coordinate and deliver health care-related services to these individuals. Without these services, it will continue to be very hard to end the root causes of chronic homelessness. The Department of Health and Human Services defines "chronically homeless" as an individual or family who is currently homeless, has been homeless continuously for at least one year, or has been homeless on at least four separate occasions in the last three years, and has a head of

household with a disabling condition. Applicants that target funds to individuals or families that are homeless for longer than one year, frequently use the ER, or interact regularly with law enforcement are given priority. The set requires initial grant awardees to provide $1 for every $3 of federal money. If renewing grants, awardees must provide $1 for every $1 of federal money. The representative gave a picture of homeless in his district. Chronic homelessness is a dreadful but solvable problem. In my district, the most recent one-day survey (February 27, 2004) in Santa Clara County identified over 7,000 homeless individuals, with over 1,000 defined as chronic. In San Mateo County, over 1,730 individuals are homeless, with approximately 650 defined as chronic. Chronic homelessness is very costly to emergency rooms, psychiatric hospitals, VA hospitals, and the criminal justice system. This legislation will provide more resources to reduce these costly expenditures, while simultaneously permitting individuals with complex health needs to be housed and begin their journey to a productive life.

216. Ibid. On July 31, 2006, Senator Mike DeWine introduced the bill as follows:

It establishes a grant program, run by the Substance Abuse and Mental Health Services Administration, SAMHSA, for services to end chronic homelessness. They usually have one or more disabilities, and often cycle between homeless shelters, the streets, mental health facilities, emergency rooms, hospitals, and jails. The public cost for their continued care is extremely high, and their medical outcomes are generally very poor. Based on several estimates, including an estimate published in the President's New Freedom Commission on Mental Health Report, it will take approximately 150,000 units of supportive housing and over 10 years to end long-term homelessness. S. 709 would authorize funding for a flexible array of services in permanent supportive housing, focused on helping people move toward recovery and self sufficiency. Although I support the bill and its intent, I am very concerned about its cost. S. 709 provides accountability, has mechanisms for controlling costs, and mechanisms for maximizing cost savings. For example, the bill prioritizes accountability and cost control through a required competitive process. In an effort to save on overall public spending, the bill gives priority to applicants who serve individuals who have proven to be more expensive to the public health system and to law enforcement. Additionally, S. 709 requires that the grantee match the federal funds received, and the match requirement increases over time. It is important to note that the amount of funding an applicant receives cannot rise above the rate of inflation. Finally, the bill ensures accountability by requiring grantees to report on their performance. This effort is to ensure that chronic homelessness is being reduced, thus reducing costly mental health and substance abuse problems, and increasing education and employment.

217. Library of Congress, "The Homeless Assistance Consolidation Act of 2006,"
218. Ibid. Comment (source unknown) on the bill was as follows:

The Homeless Assistance Consolidation Act of 2006 would consolidate three competitive homeless assistance programs within the Department of Housing and Urban Development—Supportive Housing, Shelter Plus Care, and Section 8 Single Room Occupancy—into a single program aimed at alleviating homelessness in this country. Consolidation of these programs would provide more flexibility to localities, fund prevention of homelessness, and dramatically reduce the time required to distribute grant funds to groups combating homelessness. The legislation would streamline the three programs into one competitive program with a single set of eligibility requirements and would provide incentives for communities to carry out permanent housing activities with supportive services for the homeless. In the past, Congress has provided HUD significant funding over the years to distribute to groups to fight homelessness. Millions of individuals and families are, or have in the past, faced homelessness. They deserve our help, and I am committed to fighting on behalf of the homeless, and I am hopeful that this legislation will further this most important effort.

219. Library of Congress, "Thomas," http://thomas.loc.gov/. The bill was introduced by Congressman Julia Carson and multiple cosponsors and coined the Bringing America Home Act. HR 2897.

220. U.S. House of Representatives, "Congresswoman Julia Carson Introduces Comprehensive Legislation to Address Homelessness in America," July 25, 2003, http://www.bringingamericahome.org.

221. U.S. House of Representatives, "The Bringing Home America Act," http://www.bringingamericahome.org.

222. Ibid.

223. In an article about an attempt to reduce homelessness, (*Los Angeles Times*, September 19, 2006), Richard Winton describes "Plan would End Homeless Tent Cities."

224. National Coalition for the Homeless, "Bringing America Home Act," http://www.bringingamericahome.org.

225. Bringing America Home, The Campaign, "Supporters of the Bringing America Home Act," http://www.bringingamericahome.org/endorse.html.The U.S. Conference of Mayors, the Corporation for Supportive Housing, and the National Housing Trust Fund Campaign are among those groups supporting the legislation.

226. National Alliance to End Homelessness, "A Plan, Not a Dream: How to End Homelessness in Ten Years," http://www.endhomelessness.org/ content/article/detail/585.

227. Section 402 provided the change to the definition of a homeless individuals as follows:

Section 103 of the McKinney-Vento Homeless Assistance Act (42 U.S.C. 11302) is amended—

(1) by striking subsection (a) and inserting the following new subsection:
  (a) IN GENERAL—For purposes of this Act, the terms "homeless," "homeless individual," and "homeless person"—
    (1) mean an individual who lacks a fixed, regular, and adequate nighttime residence; and
    (2) include—
      (A) an individual who—
        (i) is sharing the housing of other persons due to loss of housing, economic hardship, or a similar reason;
        (ii) is living in a motel, hotel, trailer park, or camping ground due to the lack of alternative adequate accommodations;
        (iii) is living in an emergency or transitional shelter;
        (iv) is abandoned in a hospital; or
        (v) is awaiting foster care placement;

(B) an individual who has a primary nighttime residence that is a public or private place not designed for or ordinarily used as a regular sleeping accommodation for human beings;
(C) an individual who is living in a car, park, public space, abandoned building, substandard housing, bus or train station, or similar setting; and
(D) migratory children (as such term is defined in section 1309 of the Elementary and Secondary Education Act of 1965) who qualify as homeless for the purposes of this Act because the children are living in circumstances described in any of subparagraphs (A) through (C); and

(3) in subsection (c)—
(A) by striking "or otherwise detained"; and
(B) by inserting after the period at the end the following: "Such term includes individuals who have been released from prison on parole."

228. Ibid., Section 401.

229. National Coalition for the Homeless, "Bringing America Home Act," http://www.bringingamericahome.org.

230. "Thomas," Library of Congress, http://thomas.loc.gov/.

231. Homeless Veterans Assistance Act of 2004; Transitional Housing Program for Homeless Veterans; Homeless Veterans Assistance Reauthorization Act of 2004; Thomas, Library of Congress, http://thomas.loc.gov/; and National Law Center on Homelessness and Poverty, *Dream Denied*, 2006.

232. S. Yeich, *The Politics of Ending Homelessness* (Lanham, MD: University Press of America, 1994), 71–2.

233. Ibid., 72.

234. National Law Center, "Solutions Through Alternative Remedies," 2004.

235. Arnold, *Homelessness, Citizenship, and Identity*, 2004.

236. *Papachristou v. City of Jacksonville,* 405 U.S. 161-2 (1971). Reports that expand on this notion include: H. Simon, "Towns Without Pity: A Constitutional and Historical Analysis of Official Efforts to Drive Homeless Persons from American Cities," Tulane Law Review 66 (1992) 631, 635–45 (tracing the history of "official attempts to punish and control the displaced poor," noting that between the seventh and beginning of the twentieth century, more than two-hundred statutes against vagrancy existed in England) and R. Teir, "Maintaining Safety And Civility In Public Spaces: A Constitutional Approach To Aggressive Begging," Louisiana Law Review 54 (1993): 292–300 (chronicling antivagrancy and like laws from classical Athens to modern times).

237. *Johnson v. Board of Commissioners*, 356 F.Supp.2d 929 (E.D. Mo. 2004). Such regional and national organizations like the National Law Center on Homelessness and Poverty, Food Not Bombs, the Coalition on Homelessness, and Independent Housing Services account for the homeless in the political arena.

Chapter Ten

THE HISTORY AND FUTURE OF HOMELESS MANAGEMENT INFORMATION SYSTEMS

Stephen R. Poulin, Stephen Metraux, and Dennis P. Culhane

A major transformation has occurred in the way organizations manage their data since the advent of affordable computing. Most of the transactions conducted by businesses, government agencies, and nonprofit organizations are "paperless," meaning that they are recorded electronically. Business transactions are recorded at electronic cash registers or via online purchases, and the services provided by government and nonprofit organizations are often entered directly into a computer at the point of contact with the client. The transformation of data from paper to computers has made it possible to manage and analyze data in ways that were never before possible.

CONGRESSIONAL INITIATIVES

This transformation has occurred in programs serving persons experiencing homelessness, in large part due to Congressional legislation and the U.S. Department of Housing and Urban Development (HUD). Beginning with the fiscal year 1999 HUD Appropriations Act, Congress required HUD to take the lead in the development of Homeless Management Information Systems (HMIS). The rationale and objectives of this directive was stated in House Report 105-610:

> HUD is directed to work with a representative sample of jurisdictions to collect, at a minimum, the following data: the unduplicated count of clients served; client characteristics such as age, race, sex, disability status; units (days) and type of housing received (shelter, transitional, permanent) and services rendered. Outcome information such as housing stability, income and health status should be collected as well. Armed with information like this, HUD's ability to assess the success of

homeless programs and grantees will be vastly improved. If funds are necessary to implement this directive with new tracking systems, HUD may use the funds requested for technical assistance.[1]

Congress went further in its push for HMIS by authorizing the use of Supportive Housing Program funds for the development of such systems, and ambitiously establishing a deadline that client-level data should be available from an HMIS within three years. This initiative was articulated in the fiscal year 2001 Senate Report 106-410:

> The Committee believes that HUD must collect data on the extent of homelessness in America as well as the effectiveness of the McKinney homeless assistance programs in addressing this condition. These programs have been in existence for some fifteen years and there has never been an overall review or comprehensive analysis on the extent of homelessness or how to address it. The Committee believes that it is essential to develop an unduplicated count of homeless people, and an analysis of their patterns of use of assistance (HUD McKinney homeless assistance as well as other assistance both targeted and not targeted to homeless people), including how they enter and exit the homeless assistance system and the effectiveness of assistance. The Committee recognizes that this is a long-term effort involving many partners. However, HUD is directed to take the lead in approaching this goal by requiring client level reporting at the jurisdiction level within three years.[2]

In 2006, Congress once again urged HUD to develop HMIS nationwide, and to produce Annual Homeless Assessment Reports from HMIS data. The intent of Congress was expressed in Senate Report 109-109, which stated:

> In order to improve efforts in addressing homelessness, it is critical for providers and government officials to have reliable data. To address this matter, the Committee began an effort in 2001 that charged the Department to collect homeless data through the implementation of a new Homeless Management Information System (HMIS). The implementation of this new system would allow the Department to obtain meaningful data on the Nation's homeless population and develop annual reports through an Annual Homeless Assessment Report (AHAR).[3]

EARLY EFFORTS TO DEVELOP HMIS

Not all of the impetus for HMIS was federal. In 1986, New York City implemented an HMIS on its own initiative, and in 1993 the City of Philadelphia developed an HMIS to the track the "purchase of service" orders submitted by local shelters to the city. New York City and the City of Philadelphia were also among the few cities that provided funding to homeless shelters; according to HUD's 1988 Survey of Homeless Shelters, almost ninety percent of all emergency and transitional shelters were private nonprofit organizations.[4] Public funding of shelters provided these cities with an important advantage in creating an HMIS—it enabled them to mandate shelter participation in the system.

By the late 1990s, although New York City and Philadelphia had the most advanced HMIS, they were by no means the only jurisdictions that were interested in creating an administrative database on shelter users and the provision of homeless services. Numerous jurisdictions recognized the potential benefits of such systems, and independently set out to establish a system that sought to collect a uniform set of data elements from a majority of the persons and families receiving homeless services. Such local initiatives were, however, largely ad hoc undertakings in that they set out to fulfill local needs for data and they used a variety of different software platforms for collecting this data. Where Philadelphia and New York City had the advantage of having almost all homeless services providers funded through a municipal entity that oversaw shelter services, in other jurisdictions agencies that provided shelter and other homeless services were considerably more independent and it was more difficult to get these providers to collect data on their services.

In 1999, under the joint sponsorship of HUD and the U.S. Department of Health and Human Services (HHS), approximately twenty jurisdictions met as the Homeless Services Data Systems User Group to discuss these issues and to explore different ways to coordinate and standardize data collection efforts. As a result of this meeting, nine jurisdictions—six cities, two counties, and one state—with the most advanced HMIS collaborated on a report that acted as the prototype for establishing an ongoing measure of the parameters of the services using homeless population and for tracking related trends on the use of homeless services over time.[5] The establishment of a standardized reporting format allowed a comparison of different jurisdictions on the basis of their HMIS, as well as the basic numbers and rates of the local homeless populations. This served as a precursor for the HUD-sponsored data reports based on HMIS that will be discussed in the next section.

In 1997, HUD initiated an exhaustive review of all existing HMIS in the United States to produce a national report on homelessness. The study revealed that in 1999 only twelve jurisdictions appeared to have a sufficient proportion of shelters represented (known as "coverage"). The study recommended the development of standard data elements for all HMIS and the use of HMIS data for cross-jurisdictional homelessness research.[6]

HUD and the Annual Homeless Assessment Report

HUD has maintained its support of HMIS by creating a series of technical assistance publications and offering direct assistance to jurisdictions that were implementing an HMIS. The technical assistance publications have addressed such topics as the selection of HMIS software, implementation of an HMIS, enhancing HMIS data quality, producing unduplicated counts of homeless clients, integrating HMIS data with other services data, and using HMIS data for improving local homeless services. HUD has sponsored several conferences and workshops to disseminate HMIS development strategies. In addition to the Congressional authorization to use Supportive Housing Program (SHP) funds for HMIS, HUD has also awarded additional "points" to the competitive applications for SHP funding that include HMIS development.[7]

In July of 2002, HUD issued a contract to produce the first Annual Homeless Assessment Report (AHAR). The first task of the project was to convene an "Expert Panel" to develop the National HMIS Data Standards, as recommended in its 1999 national report on HMIS. After an extensive review process, the Standards recommended by the Expert Panel in 2002 were finally promulgated in July of 2004. Meanwhile, the project created a nationally representative sample of eighty jurisdictions to contribute aggregated HMIS data for the AHAR. The sample was constructed from eighteen large cities selected from four geographic strata with certainty, and sixty-two cities selected randomly from sixteen geographic strata. Because many HMIS were still in an incipient stage, the data were collected for only a three-month period, from February 1, 2005 to April 30, 2005. In February of 2007, HUD finally released the first AHAR, with a national estimate of the prevalence of homelessness in the United States and a profile of the persons sheltered.[8]

Although some growth of HMIS was inevitable, it is likely that HUD's efforts greatly accelerated this growth, and HUD's data standards helped ensure that HMIS were developed consistently. HUD has closely monitored the status of HMIS implementation since 2001 and found that in 2005 seventy-two percent of all jurisdictions receiving HUD funding for homeless services were in the process of implementing an HMIS, whereas in 2001 only sixteen percent of these jurisdictions were doing so. Only twenty percent were still in the planning stages, and seven percent had not yet considered implementation of an HMIS.[9]

The Current and Future Role of HMIS in Homelessness Research and Policy

The challenges of generating HMIS data that can be used for homelessness policy decisions became clear during the process of producing the first AHAR. Although a majority of jurisdictions have implemented HMIS, many of them struggled to enlist a majority of shelters within their jurisdiction to participate in the HMIS. As is the case with missing data in any research, low bed coverage compromises the representativeness of HMIS data.[10]

Another challenge to the quality of HMIS data is the omission of homeless clients from the HMIS. Low client coverage obviously results in an undercount and underestimates the prevalence of homelessness in a community. Higher omission rates among types of homeless clients will also bias the profile of persons served.[11]

An unexpected problem encountered during the production of the first AHAR was the frequency of missing exit dates. In addition to overestimating the average length of stay, this problem makes it appear in the data that some clients have never left a shelter, resulting in occupancy rates that exceed 100 percent.[12]

Despite the data quality issues found nationwide, an increasing number of jurisdictions have successfully resolved them, and many others are in the process of improving their data quality. HUD's push for HMIS has brought the data quality issues to the forefront, and technical assistance has been developed to address them. HUD's conferences and workshops have also enabled jurisdictions to learn from the successful efforts of others. The HMIS data standards have helped ensure that all shelters are collecting the same information, which will facilitate cross-jurisdictional analysis. Although the first AHAR was more useful for revealing the strengths and weaknesses of HMIS data than it was for influencing national homelessness policies, the promise of data-driven homelessness policies can be realized on a local level.

One of the most important advantages of HMIS is that it produces longitudinal data. Every shelter record is in effect a survey of a person experiencing homelessness. Until the advent of HMIS, most homelessness research was conducted with cross-sectional data. This means that the data was collected with a point-in-time survey, using a sample of homeless persons who were either residing in a shelter or found living "on the street" (i.e. places not intended for habitation). Although all survey data is prone to sampling bias, cross-sectional samples of homeless persons are also more likely to include persons who are experiencing long episodes of homelessness. Research by Culhane and Kuhn indicates that more frequent users of shelter are more likely to manifest health, mental health, and substance abuse problems.[13] To the extent that persons experiencing longer episodes of homelessness differ from the persons with shorter episodes, homelessness research using cross-sectional data will be biased.

As a relatively new source of data for homelessness research, new avenues of inquiry are now possible. One of the earliest demonstrations of the potential of HMIS for homelessness research was the period prevalence estimates made by Culhane et al., using HMIS data from New York City and Philadelphia.[14] Culhane et al. estimated that one percent of the populations in both cities had experienced homelessness over a one-year period, and three percent had experienced homelessness over a period of three years in Philadelphia and five years in New York City. These rates were three times the point-in-time estimates of homelessness made from cross-sectional data. This suggests that period prevalence estimates of homelessness provide policy-makers with a more accurate measure of the magnitude of homelessness in their community, which in turn serves to better evaluate the effectiveness of measures to reduce homelessness.

Since longitudinal data are more representative of the persons experiencing homelessness, it is better suited for comparing the prevalence of homelessness across demographic groups. Again using HMIS data from New York City and Philadelphia, Culhane and Metraux used prevalence estimates to calculate the relative risk of homelessness between the two cities and between groups defined by gender, age, and race.[15] The differences in relative risks can help policy-makers understand the causes of homelessness and to target their efforts to reduce homelessness.

Aggregating HMIS data to the total number of people served in a time period (e.g. daily, weekly, or monthly) makes it usable for time-series analysis. Time-series analysis can be used to make short-term forecasts of shelter caseloads based on the net of shelter admissions and exits. When shelter admissions exceed shelter exits during the same time period, the shelter caseload will increase, and when shelter exits exceed shelter admissions, the caseload will decrease. The caseload effects of changes to shelter admission and exit policies can be estimated based on the anticipated change in the number of admissions and exits after implementation of the new policies.

Time-series analysis can also be used to evaluate the relationship between presumably related trends and events. Culhane, Poulin, Hoyt, and Metraux used aggregated data from Philadelphia's HMIS to evaluate the effect of welfare reform on the admissions of homeless families. They used interrupted time-series analysis to evaluate whether the number of homeless family admissions changed significantly after the implementation of welfare reform in Pennsylvania (it did not, most likely because sanctions were rare), and the relationship between the shelter caseload trends, welfare caseload trends, and economic trends (a significant association was not found between shelter and caseload trends, but an extremely strong association was found between welfare caseloads and the unemployment rate).[16] Using New York City HMIS data, O'Flaherty and Wu found a strong effect of September 11, 2001, on the shelter caseload.[17]

The electronic nature of HMIS data makes it feasible for matching to other databases that include the records of persons who have either experienced homelessness or are at risk of it. The matching process requires common identifiers in each database, such as social security numbers (the HMIS Data Standards require shelter staff to request this information) or unique combinations of name, gender, and birth dates. This matching creates an integrated database that enables research about a homeless client's circumstances before entering a shelter and their experiences after leaving the shelter.

Culhane and his colleagues have already begun to use integrated databases to expand homelessness research. By matching Philadelphia HMIS data with a database of general assistance recipients, the rate of shelter admissions was determined for persons terminated as a result of new laws passed in Pennsylvania.[18] Merges of Philadelphia HMIS data and the Philadelphia AIDS Registry revealed the risk of AIDS among homeless persons and the risk of homelessness among persons with AIDS.[19] A merge of New York City permanent supportive housing records with HMIS data and other service utilization records demonstrated that placement into permanent supportive housing dramatically reduces the use of shelter and other services by persons with severe mental illness (mental illness was identified by matching the New York City HMIS data with records of psychiatric services obtained from the Medicaid office of the New York State Department of Health, the New York City Health and Hospitals Corporation, the New York State Office of Mental Health, and the U.S. Department of Veterans Affairs).[20] Matching New York City HMIS data with New York jail and prison data revealed the risk of incarceration among shelter users, and the shelter stay patterns of persons who have been incarcerated.[21]

The large number of cases in HMIS databases makes the data well suited for statistical analysis. The outcomes (i.e. dependent variables) that could be investigated with statistical techniques include first admission into a shelter, return to shelter, and the length of time in shelter. HMIS data are especially useful for evaluating the determinants of chronic homelessness because HUD has officially defined this as being disabled and having a continuous shelter stay of at least 365 days or four or more episodes of homelessness in three years.[22] The differential effects on exits to housing, the street, or to unknown destinations could also be evaluated if exit data are included in an HMIS. Matching HMIS data to other databases will provide more independent variables for better statistical modeling.

HMIS-based research will never be a substitute for homelessness research on the basis of customized surveys, nor will it offer the richness of interviews conducted with homeless persons selected by the researcher. HMIS data also do not include persons living on the street who have never entered a shelter, although it is likely that many people on the street use shelters as well. Nevertheless, the research that has already been conducted with New York City and Philadelphia HMIS data demonstrates its potential with the HMIS data becoming available in many other communities. Cross-jurisdictional research will enhance this potential by introducing differences in local policies and population composition as additional causal variables. The volume and quality of HMIS data will continue to grow in the foreseeable future, offering unprecedented opportunities for new homelessness research.

NOTES

1. House Report 105-610, 32-3.
2. 2001 Senate Report 106-410, 51-2.
3. Senate Report 109-109, 176.
4. U.S. Department of Housing and Urban Development, *The 1988 National Survey of Shelters for the Homeless* (Washington, DC: Office of Policy Development and Research, 1989).

5. S. Metraux, D. P. Culhane, S. Raphael, M. White, C. Pearson, E. Hirsch, P. Ferrell, S. Rice, B. Ritter, and J. S. Cleghorn, "Assessing Homeless Population Size through the Use of Emergency and Transitional Shelter Services in 1998: Results from the Analysis of Administrative Data in Nine U.S. Jurisdictions," *Public Health Reports* 116, no. 4 (2001): 344–52.

6. D. P. Culhane, S. Metraux, and S. R. Poulin, *The Prevalence of Homelessness in 1999: Rates of Unduplicated Service Users and Service Days for Selected U.S. Jurisdictions* (Washington, DC: U.S. Department of Housing and Urban Development, Office of Community Planning and Development, 2001).

7. U.S. Department of Housing and Urban Development, *Report to Congress: HUD's Strategy For Homeless Data Collection, Analysis and Reporting* (Washington, DC: Office of Community Planning and Development, 2001); U.S. Department of Housing and Urban Development, *Report to Congress: Progress on HUD's Strategy For Improving Homeless Data Collection, Reporting and Analysis* (Washington, DC: Office of Community Planning and Development, 2002); U.S. Department of Housing and Urban Development, *Report to Congress: Progress on HUD's Strategy For Improving Homeless Data Collection, Reporting and Analysis* (Washington, DC: Office of Community Planning and Development, 2003); U.S. Department of Housing and Urban Development, *Report to Congress: Third Progress Report on HUD's Strategy For Improving Homeless Data Collection, Reporting and Analysis* (Washington, DC: Office of Community Planning and Development, 2004); U.S. Department of Housing and Urban Development, *Report to Congress: Fourth Progress Report on HUD's Strategy For Improving Homeless Data Collection, Reporting and Analysis* (Washington, DC: Office of Community Planning and Development, 2005); U.S. Department of Housing and Urban Development, *Report to Congress: Fifth Progress Report on HUD's Strategy For Improving Homeless Data Collection, Reporting and Analysis* (Washington, DC: Office of Community Planning and Development, 2006).

8. U.S. Department of Housing and Urban Development, *The Annual Homeless Assessment Report to Congress* (Washington, DC: U.S. Department of Housing and Urban Development, Office of Community Planning and Development, 2007).

9. U.S. Department of Housing and Urban Development, *Report to Congress: Fifth Progress Report,* 2006.

10. U.S. Department of Housing and Urban Development, *The Annual Homeless Assessment,* 2007.

11. Ibid.

12. Ibid.

13. D. P. Culhane and R. Kuhn, "Applying Cluster Analysis to Test a Typology of Homelessness by Pattern of Shelter Utilization: Results from the Analysis of Administrative Data," *American Journal of Community Psychology* 26, no. 2 (1998): 207–32.

14. D. P. Culhane, E. F. Dejowski, J. Ibanez, E. Needham, and I. Macchia, "Public Shelter Admission Rates in Philadelphia and New York City: The Implications of Turnover for Sheltered Population Counts," *Housing Policy Debate* 5, no. 2 (1994): 107–40.

15. D. P. Culhane and S. Metraux, "One-Year Rates of Public Shelter Utilization by Race/Ethnicity, Age, Sex and Poverty Status for New York City (1990 and 1995) and Philadelphia (1995)," *Population Research and Policy Review* 18 (1999): 219–36.

16. D. P. Culhane, S. R. Poulin, L. M. Hoyt, and S. Metraux, *A Study of the Impacts of Welfare Reform in Philadelphia: Public Shelter Utilization, Demand for Public Housing Programs, and Public Housing Program Recipient Outcomes* (Washington: U.S. Department of Housing and Urban Development, Office of Policy Development and Research, 2002).

17. B. O'Flaherty and T. Wu, "Fewer Subsidized Exits and a Recession: How New York City's Family Homeless Shelter Population Became Immense," *Journal of Housing Economics* 15, no. 2 (2006): 99–125.

18. D. Culhane, M. Koppel, S. Metraux, and I. Wong, *Mitigating the Impact of State Welfare Cuts for Single Adults: The Implementation and Autilization of the Homelessness Prevention Pilot Project in the City of Philadelphia* (Philadelphia: University of Pennsylvania, School of Social Policy and Practice, 1997).

19. D. P. Culhane, E. Gollub, R. Kuhn and M. Shapner, "The Co-occurrence of AIDS and Homelessness: Results from the Integration of Administrative Data for AIDS Surveillance and Public Shelter Utilization in Philadelphia," *Journal of Epidemiology and Community Health* 55 (2001).

20. S. Metraux, S. C. Marcus, and D. P. Culhane, "Assessing the Impact of the New York/New York Supported Housing Initiative for Homeless Persons with Severe Mental Illness on Public Shelter Use in New York City," *Psychiatric Services* 54, no. 1 (2003).

21. S. Metraux and D. P. Culhane, "Recent Incarceration History Among a Sheltered Homeless Population," *Crime and Delinquency* 52, no. 3 (2006).

22. M. R. Burt, J. Hedderson, J. Zweig, M. J. Ortiz, L. Aron-Turnham, and S. M. Johnson, *Strategies for Reducing Chronic Street Homelessness* (Washington, DC: U.S. Department of Housing and Urban Development, Office of Community Planning and Development, 2004).

INDEX

ABOUT THE EDITOR AND CONTRIBUTORS

Robert Hartmann McNamara is currently a professor of Political Science and Criminal Justice at the Citadel. He is the author of several books including *Multiculturalism and the Criminal Justice System*; *The Times Square Hustler: Male Prostitution in New York City*; and *Social Gerontology*. Dr. McNamara has also served as a Senior Research Fellow for the National Strategy Information Center, the Policy Lab, the Police Executive Research Forum, in Washington, DC, and the Pacific Institute for Research and Evaluation in Baltimore, MD. Dr. McNamara has published numerous articles on a variety of topics and has been a consultant for state, federal, and private agencies on topics such as AIDS, drug abuse, urban redevelopment, homelessness, policing, gangs, and health care. He worked with the Regional Community Policing Institute at Eastern Kentucky University to study school safety in eight high schools across the state. He also worked with the Mexican government and the National Strategy Information Center to develop an anticorruption curriculum in their public schools. Dr. McNamara holds a Ph.D. in Sociology from Yale University.

Ronald G. Burns, Ph.D., is an associate professor and Director of the Criminal Justice Program at Texas Christian University. He is the author or editor of five books and over thirty-five journal articles and book chapters. His research interests include criminal case processing, corporate deviance, environmental crimes, and policing issues. Recent publications include articles in the *Journal of Criminal Justice Education*, the *Journal of Criminal Justice*, and *Crime and Delinquency*.

Michael Chesser, Th.D., is the Executive Director of the Carolina Upstate Homeless Coalition. He earned a Th.D. in from the University of South Africa.

Charles Crawford, Ph.D., is an associate professor of sociology at Western Michigan University. He has recently published in the areas of police use of excessive force, the criminalization of car stereo culture, and the influence of space and time on police use of force. His current research involves measuring police use of force, and the impact of time and space on police activities.

Dennis P. Culhane, Ph.D., is a professor of social welfare policy at the University of Pennsylvania's School of Social Policy and Practice, and is affiliated with the Center for Mental Health Policy and Services Research at the University of Pennsylvania. Dr. Culhane's primary areas of research are homelessness, housing policy, and policy analysis research methods. His current work includes studies of the impact of homelessness on the utilization of public health, corrections, and social services in New York City and Philadelphia. He is currently leading an effort to produce an annual report for Congress on the prevalence and dynamics of homelessness based on analyses of automated shelter records in a nationally representative sample of U.S. cities. He is also working with several jurisdictions to develop a typology of homelessness among families, and to test various interventions to prevent or reduce homeless spells among families.

Mary Cunningham is the Director of the Homelessness Research Institute. She is responsible for helping monitor and measure progress by the National Alliance to End Homelessness on the Ten Year Plan to End Homelessness and for building and disseminating knowledge about solutions to end homelessness. Prior to joining the Alliance, Ms. Cunningham managed and directed numerous quantitative and qualitative research studies at the Urban Institute, where her research focused on public housing, the Housing Choice Voucher Program, and family self-sufficiency programs. At the Urban Institute, her work included serving as deputy director of a research project that counted homeless people living in vacant public housing units and co-authoring "The Transformation of Public Housing and the Hard to House," a paper published in *Housing Policy Debate* that examines alternative housing models for public housing residents whose service needs go beyond housing. Mary earned a master's degree in public policy from Georgetown University.

Ralph da Costa Nunez, Ph.D., is President/CEO of Homes for the Homeless and the Institute for Children and Poverty and has served as an adjunct professor of public policy at Columbia University's School of International and Public Affairs since 1978. Prior to joining Homes for the Homeless, he was First Deputy Director of the Mayor's Office of Homelessness and SRO

Services among other executive-level government positions. He is the author of *Moving Out, Moving Up: Families Beyond Shelter* (2006), *A Shelter Is Not a Home … Or Is It?* (2004), *Beyond the Shelter Wall: Homeless Families Speak Out* (2004), and *The New Poverty: Homeless Families in America* (1996).

Amy M. Donley is a doctoral student in sociology at the University of Central Florida. Her research and teaching interests include homelessness, race, social welfare, and social policy. She currently serves as the project manager for the Institute of Social and Behavioral Sciences and is writing her Ph.D. dissertation on crime and homelessness. She has presented research papers at the annual meetings of the Southern Sociological Society, the Society for the Study of Social Problems, and the American Society of Criminology. Her first refereed journal article, "For Richer or for Poorer: The Impact of State Level Legislation on Marriage, Divorce and Other Outcomes" is forthcoming in *Sociological Spectrum.*

Maria Foscarinis is founder and executive director of the National Law Center on Homelessness and Poverty, a not-for-profit organization established in 1989 as the legal arm of the nationwide effort to end homelessness. Ms. Foscarinis has advocated for solutions to homelessness and poverty at the national level since 1985. She is a primary architect of the Stewart B. McKinney Homeless Assistance Act, the first major federal legislation addressing homelessness, and she has litigated to secure the legal rights of homeless and poor persons. Ms. Foscarinis writes regularly about legal and policy issues affecting homeless and poor persons, and her work has appeared in legal journals, general audience publications, and books. She is a frequent speaker at conferences and other events, and is frequently quoted in the media.

Amy Presley Hauser is an attorney who currently resides in Monroe, Louisiana. She received her B.A. from Furman University in Greenville, South Carolina, and her J.D. from the University of Kentucky College of Law. She was licensed to practice law in Kentucky in 2004 and New Mexico in 2005. While living in Las Cruces, New Mexico, she practiced law and also provided her services at a homeless legal clinic. She was a staff member on the *Kentucky Law Journal* and authored a published article for the journal, titled "Child Custody for Disabled Adults: What Kentucky Families Need." She coauthored the book *Boundary Dwellers: Homeless Women in Transitional Housing* with Dr. Robert Hartmann McNamara and Carrie Flagler and has written other published articles on homelessness and teenagers aging out of foster care.

Sharon McDonald, Ph.D., is a senior policy analyst with a focus on policy and program strategies to address family homelessness. Dr. McDonald joined the National Alliance to End Homelessness in 2001. Prior to joining the Alliance, she was a direct practitioner in a Richmond, Virginia, community-based service center for people who have been homeless for nearly seven years. She has experience providing service-enhanced housing in a subsidized housing development for low-income families with children and in housing for people living with HIV/AIDS. She served as a Social Work Congressional Fellow in Senator Paul D. Wellstone's office, where she focused on welfare and housing issues. Dr. McDonald has been a Licensed Clinical Social Worker since 1991 and holds a Ph.D. in Social Work and Social Policy from Virginia Commonwealth University.

Stephen Metraux, Ph.D., is an assistant professor in the Department of Health Policy and Public Health at the University of the Sciences in Philadelphia. Dr. Metraux obtained his Ph.D. in sociology at the University of Pennsylvania and is also affiliated with Penn's Center for Mental Health Policy and Services Research. His research interests center around urban health, especially in the context of issues such as homelessness and housing, community mental health, and incarceration and prisoner reentry. His current research includes examining services-use patterns by people diagnosed with mental illness following release from prison, using administrative data for evaluation of homeless services, and assessing residential segregation among persons with mental illness.

James Petrovich is a doctoral candidate at the University of Texas at Arlington School of Social Work. Involved in the helping professions since 1989, he has been a practicing social worker since 2001, holding a BSW degree from Mississippi College and an MSW from New York University. Mr. Petrovich's research interests include the social problem of homelessness, with a specific interest in the factors that influence the use of assistance services, the resiliency of people who are homeless, and nontraditional approaches to outreach.

Stephen R. Poulin, Ph.D., is a senior programmer analyst at the Center for Mental Health Policy and Services Research at the University of Pennsylvania. In that capacity, he has been involved in HUD-sponsored projects that have supported the development of Homelessness Management Information Systems (HMIS) nationwide. He is currently working as part of the current Annual Homeless Assessment Report (AHAR) project research team, which is collecting and analyzing HMIS data to produce the AHAR. Dr. Poulin has also served as the director of a shelter for homeless men, women, and children and developed an HMIS for the agency. His primary research interest is the analysis of HMIS data for policy research.

Emily Spence-Almaguer, MSW, Ph.D., is an assistant professor and Director of Community Development Services in the School of Social Work at the University of Texas at Arlington. She conducts needs assessment and evaluation research studies for nonprofit organizations and communities in north central Texas. Her substantive interests include poverty, intimate partner violence, homelessness, and stalking, as well as community and organizational social work practice.

Norm Suchar is a senior policy analyst with a focus on chronic homelessness. He joined the staff of the National Alliance to End Homelessness in 2002. Mr. Suchar promotes effective policies and practices related to supportive housing, mental health, substance abuse treatment, health care, and other services for homeless people as well as programs that facilitate rapid re-housing for families and individuals. His prior experience includes three years in the Budget Office at the U.S. Department of Housing and Urban Development, where he focused on homelessness and community development programs, and two years working in child welfare for the state of Utah.

James D. Wright, Ph.D., is an author, educator, and the Provost's Distinguished Research Professor in the Department of Sociology at the University of Central Florida (UCF). Wright also serves as the Director of the UCF Institute for Social and Behavioral Sciences and as editor-in-chief of the journal *Social Science Research*. He received his B.A. from Purdue University in 1969 and his Ph.D. from the University of Wisconsin in 1973. He has published eighteen books and more than 300 journal articles, book chapters, essays, reviews, and polemics on topics including poverty, homelessness, guns, NASCAR, and survey and evaluation research methods. He also serves on the Board of Directors of the Coalition for the Homeless of Central Florida and chairs the Board's Research and Evaluation Committee

DATE DUE

APR 2 8 2013	